The
Blood Tub

General Gough
and the
Battle of Bullecourt 1917

THE
BLOOD TUB

GENERAL GOUGH AND THE
BATTLE OF BULLECOURT 1917

by

Jonathan Walker

Foreword by Jonathan Nicholls

SPELLMOUNT
Staplehurst

British Library Cataloguing in Publication Data:
A catalogue record for this book is available
from the British Library

Copyright © Jonathan Walker 1998, 2000
Foreword copyright © Jonathan Nicholls 1998, 2000

ISBN 1-86227-087-2

First published by Spellmount in the UK in 1998

This paperback edition published in the UK in 2000 by
Spellmount Limited
The Old Rectory
Staplehurst
Kent TN12 0AZ

Tel: 01580 893730
Fax: 01580 893731
E-mail: enquiries@spellmount.com
Website: www.spellmount.com

1 3 5 7 9 8 6 4 2

Typeset in Palatino by MATS, Southend-on-Sea, Essex
Printed in Great Britain by
T.J. International Ltd, Padstow, Cornwall

Contents

'We all probably know of exceptions
but the broad fact remains that on the whole
it was the best and not the worst
who were killed.'

Rev. Ernest Crosse
Chaplain, 8th Devons
Bullecourt

For Gill,
Edward & Giles

List of Maps

List of Plates

Acknowledgements

A study of the combined operations at Bullecourt requires a thorough examination of archive material in both Britain and Australia. This can present logistical problems even in the age of the Internet. Without the help of Christine Gairey in Canberra, I could not have carried the project through and her work in searching out volumes of material, establishing contacts and interviewing veterans was most valuable.

While Bullecourt is a well established name in Australian military history, the battle is less well known in Britain. This applies to most of the actions and battles which made up the Arras Offensive in the Spring of 1917. In a field of study which has long been dominated by the battles of the Somme and Passchendaele, Jonathan Nicholls' *Cheerful Sacrifice* has done much to remind us of the even heavier sacrifices of the Arras battles. I am indebted to him for his help and encouragement throughout.

I am most grateful to Peter Fanshawe for his hospitality and for allowing me to consult and quote from the private papers of his grandfather, Lieutenant-General Sir Hew Fanshawe; my thanks also to Jane d'Arcy for allowing me to quote from the lively diaries of Major-General Sir John Gellibrand; Jean Letaille, Claud Durrand and many others in the Bullecourt locality offered me help and hospitality during my trips to the battlefield. Ross Bastiaan, the creator of numerous bronze plaques which highlight Australian battlefields all over the world, provided much initial inspiration and my thanks to Peter Sadler, the biographer of Major-General Sir John Gellibrand, for his support, knowledge and companionship.

I am grateful to the following for allowing me to examine or to quote from archive material within their collections: The Trustees of the Liddell Hart Centre for Military Archives, King's College, London; Peter Liddle and the Trustees of the Liddle Collection, Leeds; the Trustees of the Australian War Memorial, Canberra; the Trustees of the Imperial War Museum, London; Lady Derham for allowing access to the papers of her father, Sir Cyril Brudenell White and Lord Birdwood for the papers of his grandfather, Field-Marshal Lord Birdwood; the Trustees of the National Library of Scotland; Earl Haig; the National Library of Australia; Stuart Allan and the Trustees of the Gordon Highlanders Museum; the Trustees of the Devonshire Regiment Museum, Exeter; the Trustees of the Tank Museum, Bovington. The use of Crown copyright material in the Public Record Office is by permission of The Stationery Office. Every effort has been made to trace and obtain permission from copyright holders of material quoted or illustrations reproduced.

I also wish to acknowledge the help I have received from Paul Chandler of RMA Sandhurst Central Library. Similar help was forthcoming from Richard Bland and Derek Winterbottom who provided useful material from the Clifton College archives. My thanks to Michael Walker for locating regimental and battalion histories and Henry Thoennissen for translating German unit histories.

I am indebted to Major-General John Strawson and the late Major-General John Cubbon for their encouragement and advice; also to Brigadier 'Birdie' Smith and Colonels Dick Sidwell and Roy Maxwell for their guidance and support. David Fletcher, the Keeper of the Tank Museum, Bovington, was most kind in allowing me access to material on the tanks at Bullecourt and I am grateful for his help and the benefit of his vast knowledge. William Prout, Hugh and Bryan Davies, Michael Drakely, Garry Denison, Paul Jarvis, Beryl Metcalfe and Nick Yeomans all kindly provided details on the backgrounds of the early 'tankers', whilst veteran Edward Wakefield vividly recalled what it was like to actually drive and fight in the first tanks. In particular, Anne Davison was good enough to allow me to consult and quote from the letters of her uncle, Hugh Swears, which was invaluable. Further help in my research was forthcoming from BBC Radio and numerous newspapers who kindly published articles on the subject; likewise my thanks to Jasper Humphreys, John Terraine, Christian de Falbe, Ray Westlake, Terry Nixon and Mo Stokes, all of whom provided advice and encouragement.

For allowing permission for the reproduction of photographs, my thanks to Ian Carter and the Trustees of the Photograph Archive, Imperial War Museum; the Australian War Memorial; the Tank Museum, Bovington; the Bundesarchiv, Koblenz; Anne Davison; Jane d'Arcy; Melba Alexander; Robert Comb; King's College, Cambridge; St Paul's, Beckenham. I acknowledge permission to quote passages from the following; to Random House UK Ltd for *A Frenchman in Khaki* (William Heinemann) by Paul Maze, *On the Psychology of Military Incompetence* (Jonathan Cape) by Norman Dixon, *Storm of Steel* (Chatto & Windus) by Ernst Jünger and *The Girl at the Lion d'Or* (Hutchinson) by Sebastian Faulks; to Eric Dobby Publishing Ltd for *Allenby* (George Harrap) by Sir Archibald Wavell.

My appreciation also to Professor Ian Beckett for constructive advice and similarly my publisher Jamie Wilson. My gratitude to my wife Gill and my family for patiently supporting me on the long journey back to

1917; and finally my grateful thanks to the AIF veterans who actually travelled that road from Bullecourt, Roy Hankin (together with Melba Alexander) and the late Robert Comb and Clive McKenzie – the boys who really 'hopped the bags'.

Jonathan Walker
Sidmouth, Devon
1998

Foreword

Bullecourt. A sleepy village which lies in the midst of rich farm land in a country where farmers get richer. Most local people can tell you little or nothing of what happened here eighty years ago, even though there is a small museum. Few of them know. Few seem to care. To students of the Great War of 1914-18, the name Bullecourt is synonymous with Australia, yet Londoners and Yorkshiremen died here in their thousands. There are secrets under the corn. Here, hearts were broken and reputations destroyed in the space of a few weeks of intense fighting. Bullecourt saw the first breakthrough of the much vaunted Hindenburg Line. And it went horribly wrong.

Some years ago I was approached by Jonathan Walker, who was looking for information for a book he was planning to write on the Battles of Bullecourt, which come under the broad arm of the Battle of Arras 1917, a subject close to my own heart. Unfortunately, I was not able to offer him much help as I had only studied the operations at Bullecourt briefly. Back in the early 1980s, I made several journeys to this part of the old Western Front, searching for remains of the Hindenburg Line. I tramped round the pleasant fields and lanes but was disappointed at the lack of any immediate evidence of the savage fighting that had once taken place there. There is a dearth of British cemeteries on the actual battlefield and a study of the nearest cemetery registers revealed few graves of soldiers killed during April – May 1917. Most of the dead listed are those from the battles of 1918. What then, really happened at Bullecourt? Where are the graves of the men who fell in such vast numbers on that battlefield?

The best account I could find of the battle, at the time, was by Charles Bean in the *Australian Official History*. But there was no other definitive work on the subject. It was touched on lightly by Edward Spears in his excellent, *Prelude to Victory* and Hubert Gough, that much maligned instigator of the Bullecourt affair, makes a frugal comment in his autobiography, *Soldiering On*. He says, 'eventually the Fifth Army became involved in some bitter fighting round Bullecourt, in an endeavour to assist Allenby's right but there was insufficient cooperation between the two armies.' That was about the only information I had on my bookshelf.

The memory of Bean's harrowing description of the Australian infantry advancing across the snow-covered plain and their heroic efforts to struggle through the great belts of wire, which seemed to 'swarm with fireflies as the bullets struck the strands', has never left me. My vision was to be suitably widened over the following months by freshly written chapters sent to me by Jonathan Walker, in which he described, in accurate and chilling detail, the bloody events of the battle. This reinforced my belief that Bullecourt was, undoubtedly, the greatest horror story of the war. As one witness remembered – 'At Mory, three miles to the rear, the awful stench of the dead came down on the wind from the front.'

Much venom has been directed over the years at British strategy and tactics at Bullecourt. Spears himself wrote, 'a study of Bullecourt makes dismal reading to the professional soldier, trained to avoid the mistakes that were committed with such flagrant irresponsibility'. Yet many of those mistakes were made by Anzac Staff Officers, who had themselves devised a weak battle plan. Another cause of the disaster at Bullecourt was that seemingly unseen phenomenon that many British writers on the First World War choose to ignore – the presence of the enemy.

Not so in this account. The fine quality of the German infantry stationed at Bullecourt in 1917 reminds one of the battle-hardened SS Panzer Division which 'just happened to be at Arnhem for a refit', and led to another British defeat. It was bad luck that these excellent German soldiers were there in 1944. It was bad luck that their fathers admirably defended Bullecourt in 1917. This sturdy defence by the Württembergers was the cause of the worst Australian defeat during the Great War. It was easy for the Australian commanders to criticise the newly arrived British 62nd (West Riding) Division, 'never left their trenches', which incidentally lost a mere 191 officers and 4,042 men in this, their first real test in battle. But now the full story has been told. In this book, we can also follow the battle through the eyes of the young tank crewmen, as they lumbered forward into the unknown. They too were blamed by the Australians, but the sublime courage of the majority of those inexperienced boys in their primitive tanks in their hellish introduction to battle, has never been in doubt.

There was much in-fighting within the Australian Imperial Force and the thread of bickering and dissent wove its way far past 1918 and into the late 1930s. Australia's finest fighting soldier, Albert Jacka VC, one of the heroes of 1st Bullecourt, was a case in point. His brigade commander, C. H. Brand, reported (*Reveille* 1929) that he had recommended Jacka for a Bar to his VC, for his bravery at Bullecourt but it was not to be, because 'VCs are rarely awarded where enterprises fail'. The *real* reason however, was his outspoken criticism of Brand, which almost ended in blows at Polygon Wood later that year. Over dinner, at a farmhouse in Auchonvillers in the late summer of 1996, an Australian author, friend and historian of the 1914-18 War, proclaimed to a small audience, 'a film with warts and all, can never be made about Bert Jacka, because it would air too much dirty washing and would have to include the shameful squabbling and petty jealousy that was rife among AIF commanders in 1917. It is something that has been swept under the carpet.'

Jonathan Walker does not let this dark backdrop to the Bullecourt battles detract from the real heroes, or the real truth. Through all the fumbling and incompetence, the magnificent courage of the Australian, British and German infantry shines through. The defence of Bullecourt was undoubtedly the finest achievement of the 27th Württemberg Reserve Division, which their historian describes as 'more bitter than the Somme'. Indeed, they were the toughest opponents ever faced by the Australians. They stubbornly stood their ground and shot straight. Walker's description of the determined Australian assaults on the wire is sufficient to make one shudder. These were brave men indeed.

There has been a recent shower of new books on the Somme, with the promise of more to come. In this, the 80th Anniversary year of the Battle of Arras (doubtless soon to be swamped by Passchendaele celebrations) *The Blood Tub* will take pride of place. Jonathan Walker's first book will receive the acclaim it so deserves. It is a stunning read. It is also an unforgettable contribution to the literature of the Great War.

Jonathan Nicholls
1998

Introduction

On Armistice Day, 1993 the body of an 'unknown soldier' was buried with full military honours at the Australian War Memorial, Canberra. He was the first fallen member of the Australian Imperial Force to be repatriated since Major-General Bridges in 1915.[1]

As the coffin was lowered into its tomb in the Hall of Memory within the AWM, a twelve-man firing party loosed off three volleys. A veteran 'digger' stepped forward and sprinkled earth, taken from the Western Front, onto the lid of the coffin. Ninety-three-year-old Robert Comb then rejoined the thirteen other AIF veterans as the 'Last Post' sounded. They bowed their heads and remembered.

'Lucky Combsy' had come through the Great War without a scratch. Too young to catch the first big 'stunt' at Gallipoli, he was pitched into the horrors of the Western Front at the age of sixteen. Pozières was gruelling in 1916, but the following year saw him in the middle of an even more desperate battle at Bullecourt.

Bullecourt has survived in the memory of Robert Comb and other Australians as one of the great ordeals of the AIF. It sucked in all four of its young divisions, and there were few diggers in France in the Spring of 1917 who avoided the blood bath. Even the designer of the Hall of Memory, Napier Waller, had lost an arm at Bullecourt.

The two battles were immortalised by Charles Bean in his *Official History of Australia in the War*. It is not hard to see why. The story contains all the swashbuckling heroes of AIF lore. 'The Fighting Leanes', the family who dominated the 48th Battalion; Bert Jacka, the most decorated soldier in the AIF; Percy Black, the heroic gold prospector; and dominating the Anzac story were two celebrated brigadiers, John Gellibrand, probably the finest operational officer in the Corps and that supreme 'Antipodean Ajax', Pompey Elliott.[2] Independent, brave and spirited to a man, they all embodied the Australian ideal.

The course of the battles provided dramatic ebb and flow. At 1st Bullecourt in April 1917, new tank tactics were attempted for the first time but ended in disaster. Australia also suffered her greatest number of soldiers taken prisoner in one action, a calamity only surpassed at Singapore in 1942.[3] 2nd Bullecourt, fought for two weeks in May, saw not only Gellibrand's extraordinary capture of part of the Siegfried Line but also the worst Australian rout of the war.

Bean wrote his account of this turmoil from the viewpoint of an Anzac Corps History and therefore concerned himself with the Australian fighting man. But Bullecourt was a combined operation. The British role, tarnished over the years, has often been portrayed as only producing 'windy officers' in the field and reckless planners to the rear. However, the huge losses of the British 2nd line territorials together with those of the Honourable Artillery Company, Queen's Regiment and Royal Welsh Fusiliers tell another story, a story which Bean largely confined to private correspondence. Captain Cyril Falls, who wrote the British Official History for the first part of 1917, was fascinated by Bullecourt. But although he devoted over sixty pages to the operations in the History, they were inevitably overshadowed by Arras and Messines.[4]

The private papers of officers show both British and Australian Commands riven with factional strife while their field commanders wrestled with new technology that they were unable to handle. Letters and diaries confirm the terror felt by both officers and men, while eye-witness accounts tell of the vital supporting role of the medics and padres.

In a battlefield no bigger than Hyde Park, 1,000 casualties a day were being lost.

After 3 May, when the great Arras offensive petered out, Bullecourt surprisingly continued its bloody course for two further weeks. How did it maintain its momentum as the only major action on the Western Front during this crucial period?

One clue must lie with the Commander of the Operation, General Sir Hubert Gough.

NOTES

1   Bridges' charger Sandy was similarly the only AIF horse to come back to Australia. It followed its master's gun carriage at his funeral.

2   The role of these figures in Australian war literature is analysed in Robin Gerster's *Big-Noting: The Heroic Theme in Australian War Writing*, p. 68-72.

3   Australian PoWs captured at 1st Bullecourt accounted for 30% of her total PoWs for the Great War.

4   Cyril Falls to Charles Bean, 25 May 1937, Australian War Memorial, Canberra (hereafter AWM) 38 3DRL/7953 Item 30.

CHAPTER I
The Wicked Baron

The young German was totally unaware of his fate. He sat alone in the basement of the headquarters of the British 2nd Cavalry Division, situated on the corner of a wide pavé square dotted with poplar trees, in the village of Messines. The previous day, he had discarded his uniform as he crept across the lines and was caught by a British cavalry patrol in civilian clothes. It was Autumn 1914 and stories of German espionage were rife among the British troops near the Belgian border. Orders had come through from Cavalry Corps HQ that he should be shot as a spy. The execution was to be carried out immediately.

Paul Maze, a French interpreter with the Division, was given the task of informing the prisoner of his sentence. Maze knew the German was a deserter and had pleaded to that effect with his commanding officer, Major-General Hubert Gough, who refused to countermand the Corps order.

Maze stood face to face with the German, who silently handed over his personal possessions, as souvenirs for the guards, together with his last letters to his mother and girlfriend. Outside, the General's car was starting up for the morning's brigade visit, as the shooting party arrived to carry out the execution. Maze dashed out to confront a startled Gough and, putting his head through the car window, pleaded one more time for the German's life. Gough retorted, 'Well, do what you like with him.' [1]

Maze's account of this small incident in the early months of the war conveys much about the impulsive nature of Hubert Gough. As one of the most controversial generals of the Great War, it has always been this side of Gough's character that has been most easily recognised and most commonly damned. The problem in command was that his qualities of drive and verve were often unchecked. It is true that his chief, Sir Douglas Haig, did at times attempt to curb his excessive zeal, but Gough was a difficult man to restrain. In the plan to capture the Gheluvelt Plateau during Passchendaele in 1917, Haig attempted to restrain him, advising, 'you must have patience and not put in your infantry attack until two or three days of fine weather', but Gough did not accede.[2] Assigned tasks for siege warfare instead of the pursuit for which he was eminently suited, he was nevertheless often left to his own devices.[3] To be fair to Gough, this vacuum between GHQ and its Army Commanders sometimes meant that he could never be sure whether his brief was to 'bite and hold' enemy lines or to break through. Fast changing events, such as those of the Spring of 1917, further complicated that brief and posed many 'command and control' problems for him.[4] Control of his Army operations was not helped by his appointment as his Chief of Staff, of Neill Malcolm, who often failed to temper his excesses but, more importantly, cut him off from subordinate opinion.[5]

Gough was essentially a highly charged and spirited commander, a single-minded man and one who had little time for the more leisured and cautious attitudes of his contemporaries. Unfortunately, his earlier successes in the war were later eclipsed by the disasters of 1917 at Bullecourt and Passchendaele and ironically, when he exercised great generalship in the face of the 1918 German Spring Offensive, he fell foul of political intrigue.

Because he stamped his mark on every battle he directed, the story of Bullecourt is incomplete without a study of his character and career. His rise within the British Army was nothing short of meteoric, and this speed of promotion inevitably cut across many of his fellow officers. On his own admission, he was too quick to sack subordinates and this built up a cluster of disgruntled brigadiers and major-generals. It was wretched that at Bullecourt they should once more come together.

Hubert Gough was born in 1870, into an Irish family renowned for its military tradition. His ancestor, Lord Gough, had conquered the Punjab and no fewer than four members of his family won the Victoria Cross. It was a heady precedent and one which Hubert Gough took up with relish. After service in the Boer War, in 1904, he took up an appointment as lecturer at Staff College, Camberley, under Brigadier-General Henry Rawlinson. During the three years that Gough taught there, most of the future Great War commanders passed through its doors as instructors or students. Others on the directing staff included Richard Haking, Thompson Capper, Launcelot Kiggell and John Ducane, all of whom went on to make their mark, for better or worse, on the fortunes of the British Army.

The prevailing attitudes at Staff College were important, as they shaped the opinions of a generation of young officers whose conduct in battle would be critical. Many of the junior commanders who fought at Bullecourt had attended the College, while three senior Bullecourt commanders, Gough, Malcolm and Braithwaite had actually been on the lecturing staff.[6] The philosophy of the College was deeply instilled in many of these officers, who treated it as a creed, never to be broken. But when war broke out, some were tragically ill-equipped to grasp that tactics had to change with conditions: that new lessons had to be learnt quickly and that the new technology, which frightened many, would not go away. Few realised that this technology would accelerate so rapidly and produce a host of terrifying new weapons, which could spew out shells at an unbelievable rate. This new ordnance, however, created as many problems as it solved, and most officers were slow to realise that it had to be harmonised to be effective. To win battles, commanders would now not only have to employ superior tactics but also co-ordinate a bewildering array of new weapons. This was simply beyond the comprehension of many.

One obstacle to progress was that the teaching at Staff College reflected the attitudes and conventions of a British Army which was still clinging to Victorian ideas in an Edwardian age. The army carried itself on its reputation, because in reality it was hardly the army of a world power. While it was efficient for its role in colonial wars and the provision of small expeditionary forces for coalition wars in Europe, its officer corps was essentially amateur in nature, and advancement continued to have more to do with patronage, social position and wealth than military skills.[7] According to James Edmonds, who later became the Official British Historian, little was taught about Staff duties or Military Administration and the main problem was finding instructors who had enough military experience.[8] Consequently there was an overriding suspicion of anything intellectual and the students' military studies received little in the way of critical evaluation. This of course didn't worry the majority, who were happy to indulge in an abundance of hunting, polo or cricket.[9]

However, at the College there were exceptions to the rule, those who were not field sportsmen and were not content to grind through familiar but out-of-date theories. Captain John Gellibrand arrived as a junior student at Camberley in Gough's last year in 1906. The thirty-four-year-old Tasmanian was educated in England and passed through RMC Sandhurst with the top marks in his year. By the time he reached Staff College, he had already experienced command with a company of the South Lancs Regiment in the Boer War and was impatient to get on. Possessed of an extremely sharp and questioning mind, Gellibrand's diary gives interesting, if unflattering portraits of his fellow student officers:

Isacke (later Major-General):	Lecture by student Isacke on Abyssinia – very thin tosh and no idea of what a lecture is.
Buckley (later Brigadier-General):	Has teachers 'orders' and works according to rule of thumb.
Kendrick (later Brigadier-General.):	Believes what he has been taught (where?) and would never change his mind without a surgical operation.[10]

The only student who escaped Gellibrand's caustic pen was another Australian on an exchange scheme, Captain Brudenell White. They later became friends, but it was always a relationship that was dogged by competition as they both scaled the Australian staff ladder.[11] White was certainly competent, but Gellibrand would later complain that some of his own countrymen were also capable of hidebound thinking. And to be fair to the British officer caste, Gellibrand's year may have been a particularly poor one, for the previous year's intake had included Johnnie Gough, Hubert's younger brother, and five other VC holders. Johnnie had neither the sharp wit nor the boundless energy of Hubert, but he was a thorough administrator and tough advocate who went on to become Sir Douglas Haig's Brigadier-General, General Staff (BGGS). Haig may have paid great tribute to Johnnie but, according to Hubert, he remained jealous of him, and made little attempt to keep him.[12]

However, if the object of the Staff College was to turn out commanders, Gellibrand observed some fundamental flaws in the system;

Anything approaching independence is conspicuous, unpopular and to be avoided ... Considering this place as an Army University to qualify for command and General Staff, it seems to turn out either subservient minds of the birdcage type, good for an office or one-sided arrogance. In both cases, well pleased with themselves.[13]

Gellibrand reserved most of his criticism for the lecturers. After barely three months of study, he observed:

At this place, the essential should be originality of mind, strength of character and general knowledge, with power of application. DuCane and possibly Gough appear to fill this requirement but Banon [later Brigadier-General] perhaps never did an independent thing in his life. He compiles his lectures and illustrates them but criticism or construction is beyond him.

Braithwaite is to my mind worse. Imagination is as foreign to him as independence. To sum up, a good regimental officer, fair office man and Brigade Major but a mind like a waiter's and the independence of a tick. Besides, he appears over anxious to please those he thinks influential and this again betrays his waiter's mind.

Rawlinson, so far, seems replete with platitudes, well meaning and fills his looks with a certain air of satisfaction.[14]

Lieutenant-Colonel Walter Braithwaite, the subject of Gellibrand's ire, would later command the 62nd (West Riding) Division at Bullecourt. He had originally failed his entrance exam to Staff College but got in by nomination in 1898.[15] Subsequently, as a lecturer, he was said by

4

Gellibrand to epitomise a Staff College which 'lacks initiative, promotes timeservers and fails to offer its students any critical appraisal'.[16]

Gellibrand was not the only student to be appalled by the standards of the College. Edward Beddington, who became Gough's General Staff Officer 2 (GSO2) in the Fifth Army, noted: 'The training was poor, great insistence on drill, practically no tactics or leadership but a good deal of useless staff.'[17]

The main established sources used by the lecturers were Henderson's *The Science of War* and Hamley's *The Operations of War*, both of which were based on military theories evolved over more than one hundred years of warfare. The main problem was that the size of armies had increased dramatically and solutions that did not take into account the huge new logistical problems of supplies and communications were really no longer valid.[18]

A study of *The Operations of War*, however, says a lot about the limits in military thinking before 1914. While lessons of the Boer War were still being digested, it was still frequently seen as a 'one-off', where conditions and tactics had been on too small a scale to be relevant to a future war involving massed armies.[19] This was correct as far as casualties were concerned, but any lessons on the effect of the new fire-power were soon dismissed by an assumption that moral courage was still the prime weapon. Even the lessons of the 1905 Russo-Japanese War were muted by the feeling that the Japanese had really won by moral spirit, rather than fire-power.[20] Courage went hand in hand with an offensive spirit and a bold commander and it was no accident that these traditional martial qualities were found in a cavalry officer like Hubert Gough:

> Above all things, he must have energy, perseverance, and determination. He must have courage, moral and physical. Boldness is a valuable quality as he can spoil his offensive movements by hesitation.[21]

It is easy to see how a temperament like Gough's prospered in this prevailing military mood. However, one drawback of 'boldness' is that it often fosters impetuosity and it was widely known that, in the Boer War, Gough had carelessly careered into a trap at Scheeper's Nek with his small force of Mounted Infantry. The party suffered casualties and was captured by a Boer Commando.[22] Gough escaped shortly after and, on his return, received a letter written on behalf of Lord Kitchener, the Commander-in-Chief, reassuring him that he had done his best and should not worry. Despite its reassuring tone, Gough would remember in years ahead that the signature on the condescending letter was that of Kitchener's Secretary, Major William Birdwood. Birdwood went on to command I ANZAC Corps at Bullecourt and eventually took over the

Fifth Army from Gough when he was dismissed in 1918.

Analyses of past campaigns were also a prominent feature of the syllabus at Camberley. The study of Waterloo was always mandatory but Gough failed to absorb one of its significant lessons, 'do not commit the fundamental tactical error of attacking your enemy when he is formed up in a re-entrant' [the opposite of a salient]. The Frenchman d'Erlon did exactly this when he attacked the British and Prussian line at Waterloo. He found to his cost that it enabled the defenders to enclose his flanks, thereby restricting his attacking force to only firing directly ahead, for fear of hitting their own men. Fourteen years later, Gough was to find himself tempted into attacking two re-entrants either side of Bullecourt and unfortunately his 'energy and determination' would override his military education. [23]

It is worth looking at one other gospel that was to affect Gough's future career. Haig had learnt in his studies, also at Camberley, that the Commander-in-Chief should set strategy and then leave his Army Commanders to devise their own tactics for their offensives. This displayed 'singleness of purpose and the unanimity of GHQ', which was considered essential in preserving the authority of the Commander-in-Chief.[24] This idea was fine as long as the Army Commander knew how far to press his attacks. But in some campaigns, directives from GHQ were vague and, if one of the 'wicked barons' (as GHQ called the Army Commanders) was determined to 'get at the enemy' at all costs, there were few constraints on him. Gough recalled that, apart from a few visits, GHQ largely left him alone.[25]

Gough, at thirty-six, was the youngest Lieutenant-Colonel in the army and in December 1906 he was given command of the 16th Lancers at Aldershot. During this posting which lasted four years, he became Chief of Staff to Douglas Haig, the Inspector-General of Cavalry. Gough's name had become synonymous with 'soldiering and sport' and he had all the talents that were appreciated in this cavalry age. But most of all, he had the 'offensive spirit':

> Riding generates audacity, and he who does not relish taking risks will never be any good. To exercise 'l'esprit cavalier', one must ignore danger and never draw back in front of an obstacle.[26]

Progressing through the army did not depend solely on being a good cavalryman. Army and Corps Commanders came from all arms of the services and although both C in C's and three Army Commanders were from the cavalry, the vast majority of divisional commanders were infantrymen. But Sir John French and his successor Haig had both risen through the cavalry, appreciated the qualities of its officers and therefore pushed like-minded soldiers. Not surprisingly, Edmonds believed that for

French and Haig, 'their one dominant idea was to keep command in the hands of the cavalry'.[27] However, Gough had not only 'an eye for country' and an ability to make a quick decision but he also had a directness and clarity of purpose which was admired by Haig, a man who found conversation difficult.[28] Others who served under Gough were similarly impressed. Edward Beddington, who joined Gough's Regiment in 1907, recalled that soldiering with Gough as his CO was an 'inspiration'. 'His only failure was that though a good disciplinarian himself, he had no respect for those above him, unless they came up to his own standards, and he frequently announced what he thought of those senior officers who failed in that respect.'[29] Frederick Oliver, a businessman who knew the Gough brothers well, enthused about Hubert: 'What I like about him, and what makes him such a tremendous force among the younger men in the Army, is that he brings something in the nature of religious fervour into his profession'.[30] That fervour was evident in his testing of his subordinates and he would frequently push junior officers to see whether they had the nerve to speak up for themselves. Beddington realised that 'if you made a good quick verbal counter attack, all would be well'.[31] But Gough often showed a rather contrived attitude to military conventions, and he enjoyed playing the cavalier on parade as well as in the field:

> Good morning Gentlemen. I noticed No.1 Squadron on parade this morning, 5 minutes early. Please remember it is better to be late rather than early. The former shows a sturdy independence and no undue respect for higher authority. The latter merely shows a womanish excitement and nervousness. [32]

As Beddington observed, despite Gough's encouragement, no one dared to be late.

Continuing his advance, Gough was given command of the 3rd Cavalry Brigade in 1910. The unit was based at the Curragh, just west of Dublin, and became notorious as the base from which he challenged the army leadership over Home Rule. He believed that the onset of Home Rule in Ireland in early 1914 would bring with it the coercion of Ulster, which the army would be compelled to implement. He was violently against the use of British troops in this capacity and felt that he had the support of most Regimental and junior Staff Officers.[33] This opposition to the policy of the Secretary of State for War (Colonel Jack Seely) became known as the 'Curragh Incident', and had the sniff of mutiny surrounding it. It almost finished Gough's military career and that of his brother, Johnnie, who had joined him.

Their powerful adversaries were eventually forced to climb down and the Home Rule Bill was killed off. This saved the Gough brothers, but some Liberal politicians would never forget their humiliation and they would exact their revenge against Hubert in 1918. Even former friends turned against him after the Curragh Incident.

Among these new enemies was Sir John French. He had felt compelled to resign his post of Chief of Imperial General Staff over Gough's intransigence, so inevitably his bitterness ran deep. Gough had forced French (who was once well-disposed towards him) into a corner and French's other political and military opponents made the most of it.[34] Whenever French had the opportunity, he railed at Gough. General Allenby, who was a contemporary of Gough's at the Curragh, was left in no doubt about French's feelings:

> The CIGS [French] strode up and down the room, and every time he passed Allenby, who was standing by the fire, hit him in the chest and said, 'Damn that ***** '[referring to Gough]. In view of the respective sizes of Sir John and Allenby, the scene has a comic side.[35]

The Curragh Incident destroyed friendships and alliances right across the military and political spectrum. Apart from the enmity between French and the Gough brothers, the tricky Sir Henry Wilson, Director of Mititary Operations at the War Office, was drawn into the fray. Gough had made another dangerous enemy in Wilson, who became even more hostile when Gough subsequently censured him over his command of IV Corps. Wilson eventually retaliated by spreading stories that Gough was responsible for the Passchendaele carnage, and finally denounced him over the 1918 retreat.[36]

For ambitious career officers, it was imperative to be adopted by a patron. Haig had been an early protégé of both Major-General Sir Evelyn Wood (later Field-Marshal) and Sir John French. When Haig's career was underway, he ditched French after the Curragh Incident and became an outright opponent after French's performance at Loos in 1915. Although French's stock was falling, he remained a pivotal figure in this network system and most of his protégés subsequently became Corps and Army Commanders. Among those were two brothers from an already illustrious military family, Edward and Hew Fanshawe, whose careers and fortunes repeatedly crossed with Gough's.

Hew Fanshawe in particular was close to French. He was already well connected with the military establishment, having married Sir Evelyn Wood's daughter. As a cavalryman, he had come to French's notice during the Boer War, when he was mentioned twice in despatches.[37] By Christmas 1914, he was commanding the 1st Indian Cavalry Division on the Western Front and his appointment by French made him a close ally. That was enough to jeopardise his future as far as Haig and Gough were concerned.

Meanwhile, Haig was already lining up Gough for preferment and, from the time Haig became Commander-in-Chief, Gough had secured a powerful protector. Their friendship was well known in the army and some jealousy arose among other officers, especially when doors opened quickly for Gough. Contemporaries thought that 'Gough's promotion was always uppermost in Haig's mind' and that 'Haig was infatuated with Gough'. Although Haig would eventually tire of Gough and take on 'Bob' Greenly (Gough's former principal staff officer in the 2nd Cavalry Division) as his new protégé in 1918, he continued to support and protect Gough throughout 1916 and 1917, despite pressure to have him removed.[38]

This pattern of personal alliances was shown to be fragile by the Curragh Incident but it was still an important tool for advancement in the British Army. Although patronage existed in the German Army, she did not have a vast empire like Britain, which could allow power bases to build up without interruption. So within the British Empire, opposing interest groups developed, revolving around a patron.[39] A fall-out in the hierarchy could have reverberations down the scale, as patrons looked to their protégés for support. Consequently, at the outbreak of war in 1914, there was a long 'tailback' of old scores to be settled between many senior British Commanders. Hew Fanshawe was to find that the bitterness between Haig and French followed him to Bullecourt and beyond. Unfortunately this rivalry went beyond personalities and was seriously to affect operations in the field.[40]

In 1914 Gough was still very much under Haig's umbrella. In August, he took his 3rd Cavalry Brigade over to France, to serve under Allenby's Cavalry Division. This division was part of I Corps, which was commanded by Haig with Johnnie Gough as Chief of Staff. From the start, Hubert Gough was his own master. In the midst of the British fall back towards Le Cateau in late August, he sought advice from GHQ as to the deployment of his cavalry. 'As you are on the spot, do what you like, old boy,' replied Sir Henry Wilson.[41]

Gough thrived on this sort of independence and, by September 1914, he was commanding the 2nd Cavalry Division alongside Allenby's 1st Cavalry Division. Now, at forty-four, the Army's youngest temporary Major-General found himself in charge of three cavalry brigades at the 1st battle of Ypres.

During January 1915, the BEF was reorganised into two Armies. Haig took the First Army with Johnnie Gough as his BGGS, but this appointment did not last long. The following month, Johnnie was killed by a sniper at the front, near Hooge. The news of his death shattered all his contemporaries but Haig and Rawlinson felt it could have been avoided.[42]

Reconnaissance missions by senior Staff officers, like Johnnie Gough, were a controversial issue. If they stayed well back or never moved out of

HQ, they were criticised for being ignorant of conditions at the front. Many, including Hubert Gough, were damning of Haig's CGS, Sir Lancelot Kiggell, for never leaving his office, for had he gone up to the front, he would have understood the conditions and seen the terrain over which HQ plans would be carried out. Photographs of Kiggell in the open air are indeed rare and it was reputed that he never visited the front line until relieved of his post as CGS. To be seen out in front would be a morale booster, but the sacrifice of competent staff officers to this end, like Johnnie Gough, dislocated command and was clearly a waste.[43]

In April 1915, Thompson Capper, commander of the 7th Division, was wounded and Gough was chosen to replace him. Haig quickly warned Gough of the difficulties of divisional command, particularly when exercised in the vicinity of Major-General Henry Rawlinson:

Rawlinson had asked for Major-General Davies to be removed from command of 8th Divn. on account of his failure to carry out Corps orders ... on Davies putting forward a statement showing the orders received and those issued by him, R had written in to say that he accepted all the blame for the delay ... I gave Gough this information because Davies had told me privately that neither he, nor his staff, had full confidence in Rawlinson.[44]

It was unusual, to say the least, for an Army Commander to discuss a Corps commander with a more junior officer like Gough. It showed the confidence that Haig placed in his protégé and no doubt he was also aware of Rawlinson's feelings about Gough's new appointment.[45]

The first main challenge to the new commander of the 7th Division was the assault on Aubers Ridge on 9 May 1915. Rawlinson, commanding IV Corps, ordered Gough to relieve the 8th Division at night and assemble his division for an attack at first light. But the state of the trenches was appalling. Due to constant bombardment, they had collapsed and were filled with dead and wounded. Gough then made a startling decision. After consulting with his brigadiers, he countered Rawlinson's order and cancelled the attack. He believed he had no chance to assemble his troops because of the state of the trenches and any attack was bound to fail.[46]

Although Gough reported his lack of action to Corps HQ, it was an extraordinary decision for a commander who relished his reputation for the 'offensive spirit'. He would make similar decisions again and argue that they were the actions of a pragmatic commander, yet in the coming battles of 1916 and 1917, he would ruthlessly sack officers who were slow to attack or who challenged tasks assigned to them. The threat to a career officer of being sent home was very real. It was known variously as being 'degummed' (unstuck), 'stellenbosched' (when an officer was sent home to Stellenbosch in the South African war), or 'limoged' (a return to

Limoges for French officers). And understandably, the loss of dignity, not to mention a job, was enough to concentrate most minds on 'the offensive spirit'.

Oddly enough Rawlinson did not even rebuke Gough for his conduct. Perhaps he did not get the chance, as the following morning, the 7th Division were moved south. A week later, they were ready to attack at Festubert, in a combined British and French assault. As the French guns started their preliminary bombardment, Sir Henry Wilson, now the principal liaison officer, witnessed the crescendo:

> The Frenchmen began to fire at 6 am and fired till 10 am. The gunning was incessant. Appalling. Twelve hundred guns served by Frenchmen and lashing to their utmost. No living person has ever heard or seen such a thing. The shells passing over my head, made one steady hiss. I heard later that the French fired 176,000 rounds and in the last ten minutes, they were firing 46 shells a second. We fired 50,000 rounds.[47]

Artillery preparation on this scale was astonishing to everyone who saw it for the first time but like so many future fire-plans, it didn't fulfil its promise. Battalions of the 7th Division, including the Royal Welsh Fusiliers, Queen's and South Staffordshires assaulted the German positions, which were still largely intact despite the shelling. As wave after wave attacked, casualties in Gough's 7th Division mounted. Amazingly, the men remained steady, which was due in no small part to the work of the chaplains, who moved among the battalions waiting in their 'jumping off' trenches. The Rev. Hon. Maurice Peel who was chaplain to the 1st Royal Welsh Fusiliers (1/RWF), told the waiting men to pass along the words, 'remember this, God so loved the world that he gave his only begotten son'. Hard-bitten soldiers, fixing their bayonets, found themselves repeating it down the line. Peel then got permission from Gough, which was rare from a commander at this stage of the war, to go over the top with his men in order to comfort the wounded in no man's land. The fifty-year-old Peel, armed only with a walking stick and a Bible, went over with the first wave and was shot. He was badly wounded but subsequently recovered and went back to his old battalion with whom he would repeat his extraordinary bravery at Bullecourt.[48]

After Festubert, the 7th Division rested, but it was not long before Gough was on the move again. Thompson Capper had recovered from his wounds and took back his old division. Meanwhile, in the summer of 1915, Gough was promoted to command I Corps, serving under Haig's First Army.

Now Gough would discover for the first time the strictures placed on Corps and more senior commanders. Like his brother Johnnie, he had never hesitated to go up to the front line when the situation warranted it, to see the conditions or progress of a battle. A 2nd Division cavalry officer clearly remembered seeing 'Goughie hopping over the shell holes on his way to see his division, accompanied by a staff officer, broad daylight and lots of shelling going on'.[49] Gough didn't find it difficult to chat and banter with troops in the line, but there were many other senior officers who felt that it was not quite 'the done thing'. To be fair, there were many practical difficulties. Fronts held by units were often up to six miles wide and visibility was invariably limited to the next trench traverse. Consequently, if a General did go forward, he could hardly expect to direct more than a few brigades. Units and corps had grown to such a size, that there was certainly no question of him commanding his troops by his own voice.

The fundamental problem was that once troops had gone into the attack, control was largely lost. This resulted in ignorance of what was actually happening on the battlefield as wave after wave of attackers went over the top, to the same fate.[50] Walkie-talkie communication, taken for granted in World War II, did not exist at this time and the only way for a general to co-ordinate his infantry and artillery was at the end of a telephone line, back at his HQ.[51] Even if he was keen to go up to the front line, there was no quick, armoured transport to move generals around, and such was the turnover of units, that divisional troops could hardly be expected to recognise their Corps, let alone their Army Commander. Bernard Montgomery, the later famous Field-Marshal who served as Chief of Staff to 47th Division in the Great War, claimed that he never once saw his Commander-in-Chief and only twice saw an Army Commander. So the idea that spread later in the war, that ranks relished or conversely were horrified to serve under certain Army Commanders like Gough, is unrealistic. It was mostly senior staff officers or 'degummed' Brigadier-Generals who fanned Gough's fearsome reputation. Any grousing from the ranks tended to be directed towards GHQ in general.[52]

Gough now found that the image of the dapper chief, checking on a brigade here and chivvying a divisional staff there, was no longer appreciated. Capper naturally wanted to reassert his old authority and his fellow divisional commander, Major-General Horne, saw no value in visits to units by Corps Command.[53] So although he found himself tethered to the rear, he continued to exhort his subordinates to 'push, push, push', overriding reservations about the distance and obstacles to be covered. He always had in mind that maxim of the Field Service Regulations, 'The ultimate overthrow of the enemy demands offensive action.'

In the aftermath of Loos, the knives were out for French. Haig jockeyed for the position of Commander-in-Chief and helped engineer the removal of his old patron. The King, ever eager to seek a consensus despite his friendship with Haig, sought out Gough and Haking for their opinions.

They confirmed that everyone had lost confidence in French, as his deployment of the reserves at Loos had been a disaster. On 6 December 1915, Sir John French handed in his formal letter of resignation.[54]

Now that Haig was appointed the new Commander-in-Chief, he was keen to carry out an attack in Flanders without delay. It was an old plan, from the early days of the war, to strike at the Germans from this point and roll them back from the Channel ports. It was certainly preferable to the talk of a combined British and French offensive on the Somme. So advanced planning got underway to capture the Messines-Wytschaete ridge, a necessary vantage point, imperative to any attack on Ypres. Gough was warned that he would be going north and sent Paul Maze, who was an accomplished artist as well as interpreter, ahead to draw the battle fronts of the ridge for the forthcoming attack. While Maze was away, events changed dramatically.

Verdun put paid to the allies' plans. The French fortress was attacked by the Germans on 21 February 1916 and besieged in an attempt to grind down the French Army. General Joffre, the French Commander-in-Chief, warned Haig of the urgent need to relieve the pressure on Verdun, by a British-French operation on the Somme. Haig had already received instructions, upon his recent appointment, that the overall policy was to be one of a united army of the two countries. So there was now no other plan to be contemplated, especially as General Rawlinson's Fourth Army was already on the Somme. Haig put the Flanders offensive on hold. There was no doubt that he would return to it, should the new operation prove a failure.[55]

Haig wanted Gough to have a role in the forthcoming Somme offensive. It was not only Edmonds, the Official Historian, who observed the smoothing of Gough's path. Aylmer Haldane, then commanding the 3rd Division, observed that Haig was removing Corps commanders who were senior to Gough, in order to allow him a clear run for command of his own Army.[56] The battle for St Eloi Craters in the Spring of 1916 saw the removal of one obstacle in the shape of Lieutenant-General Hew Fanshawe, Commander of V Corps. As he was a French protégé, Haig and Gough were happy to see Fanshawe go, but the manner of his 'degumming' was unsavoury. Ironically, V Corps was now taken on by Hew Fanshawe's elder brother Edward, who had returned from Gallipoli.

Meanwhile plans were afoot for the 'big push' on the Somme. Rawlinson's Fourth Army was to capture the high ground above Albert and, once this German defensive line had been punctured on the right, a swift cavalry force would be required to sweep through to Bapaume. To this end, a Reserve Army, of three cavalry divisions, was formed on 23 May 1916.

Gough was the inevitable choice to command this force, for Haig hoped that his quick brain would soon exploit any gap. In any event, Rawlinson would not be able to control and direct his flanks once a breakout was achieved.[57] So Gough set about recruiting a small staff, based at Regnière Ecluse, near the old battlefield of Crécy. He asked for men he knew and trusted from the Cavalry, his old I Corps and even old school friends. On the Operations side, the first to arrive as GSO2 was Brevet Major Edward Beddington. He was soon joined by Colonel Richard Howard-Vyse (known as 'Wombat') who was responsible for Intelligence. Signals were directed by Colonel Sadlier-Jackson and Captain Maurice Arbuthnot became Gough's ADC. Gough chose as his Chief of Staff his old friend Major-General Neill Malcolm, who had recently seen action at Gallipoli. Malcolm had been a lecturer at Staff College, edited Henderson's *The Science of War* and was therefore very much a man imbued with 'offensive spirit' and moral courage. He was originally a GSO1 to the hapless General Hammersly of 11th Division and, more recently, had served under Hammersly's replacement, Major-General Edward Fanshawe. Other later arrivals on the Army Staff were Major-Generals Cyril MacMullen (GSO1), Richard Lee (Chief Engineer), Harry Sargent (QMG) and Herbert Uniacke (Artillery).

In preparation for the Somme offensive, Paul Maze had been drawing more panoramas, this time of the country and villages between the Ancre and the Somme that would come within the Reserve Army boundary. On 30 June, the eve of the great battle, preliminary bombardments had already begun. Maze surveyed the scene:

> With my field-glasses, I scanned the ground and made my drawings. Every house was obliterated by clouds of dirty yellowish smoke and brick-dust. Trônes Wood and Bernafay were barely discernible through the haze on the horizon-line. Bazentin, Contalmaison and Pozières, which were nearer objectives, stood out plainly, stern and for-bidding. Not a living soul could be seen on the whole of this expanse of ground, either on the German side or on ours. I made my last drawing from Bonté Redoubt. It was late in the evening; the sun had set, but the light still lingered on the baked battle-field. The guns had eased off their firing and a fictitious peace was creeping over that immense stretch of broken ground up by the maze of trenches that the Tommies were to storm at dawn. Nature at that moment was overpowering everything with its beauty, the only sound that now and again would disturb the serenity of the scene, being an occasional ticking noise as a bullet struck a tile on a roof in Carnois . . . I waited until the darkness had fallen to go home.[58]

At 7.30 the following morning the front erupted. Fourteen British divisions, totalling 120,000 men, surged forward. Among those first 'over the top' was twenty-year-old Lieutenant Valentine Braithwaite, leading his platoon from the 1st Battalion, Somerset Light Infantry. Recently back from Gallipoli, where he was ADC to his father, Major-General Walter Braithwaite, Valentine had been in line for a comfortable staff job prior to the Battle of the Somme. But Walter Braithwaite, to his credit, refused to allow this preference for his only son. Valentine never even got close to his objective at Beaumont Hamel. He and seventeen other officers from the battalion were immediately shot as they rose out of the trenches.

Whilst the terrible culling got underway, Gough quickly made his way to the Fourth Army HQ at Querrieu to follow events. He heard that virtually everywhere the attack had failed, except on the right. By 7 o'clock that evening, Rawlinson urged Haig to put Gough in command of his X and VIII Corps on the left, to reorganise the attack astride the river Ancre. Haig, judging by his diary entries at the time, was ignorant of the scale of the casualties on the first day. He was singularly unimpressed by the performance of VIII Corps, believing that few battalions had ever left their trenches.[59] He wanted Gough to put his cavalry back into their billets and push on these infantry units at dawn the next day. Unfortunately, had Gough been given the right wing, as originally planned, where some progress was made, he could have used his cavalry to create havoc behind the enemy lines.[60]

Instead, Gough soon realised from speaking to Lieutenant-General Hunter-Weston of VIII Corps and Lieutenant-General Morland of X Corps, that their shattered troops were in no position to repeat the assault. The VIII Corps, attacking between Beaumont Hamel and Serre, had suffered over 50 per cent casualties in four divisions and, between the two corps, 20,000 casualties were later confirmed. They were back where they had started. Detailed casualty figures were not known until 3 June, and so Fourth Army HQ were still unaware of the extent of the disaster on the first morning.[61] The order to repeat the attack still stood. It was too much even for Gough to contemplate and he cancelled the order. It was the second time in his recent career that he had cancelled one of Rawlinson's orders and, as at Aubers Ridge, he got away with it. But the same could not be said of Gough's subordinates.

On 3 July, after pressure from Rawlinson, Gough put in the 32nd Division (part of X Corps) to assist III Corps in the capture of Ovillers, near Thiepval. It failed, with terrible casualties. The GSOI of 32nd Division, Major Edward Wace, recalled Gough's reaction:

It was another of Gough's mad ideas. Gough was furious with our division and with Rycroft [GOC] and me in particular. He 'threw' the unfortunate Jenkins [Brigade Commander], but couldn't fix the blame on us. But Rycroft knew he'd 'got it in for us', and when at Bethune we got orders to go back to the Somme in October, he turned to me and said wryly that this would be his undoing unless we went to Rawly's Army . . . He was terrified of Gough. [62]

Major-General Sir William Rycroft and his division were subsequently moved back to Gough's Army in October. Rycroft's prediction was correct and Gough 'degummed' him, together with a number of brigadier-generals after the failure of an attack during the Battle of the Ancre in November 1916. However, Rycroft was not alone in his fear of Gough, as many cavalry officers had already been axed by him when he assumed command of the Reserve Army. The weeding out of unsuitable officers was of course part of a commander's brief, but Gough was rapidly attracting a reputation for too many summary dismissals.[63] As one contemporary observed:

> Gough was out to fight and get forward. He had no idea how to conduct the action Haig required and would not take advice. I heard him complain that the officers had 'no spirit of the offensive'.[64]

This climate of dread goes some way to explaining why so many officers (and their careers depended on it) carried out orders that were foolhardy or plain suicidal. There is a well-known story which Edmonds included in his unpublished memoirs, concerning Gough's attitude to faint hearts:

> I was having tea in the Staff Mess of the Fifth Army. He (Gough) burst into the room almost yelling 'I want to shoot an officer'. There was an awkward pause till the APM rose and said apologetically that there were no officers under sentence. To this end Gough rejoined that he knew that, but wanted to get hold of an officer, who he could shoot as an example to the others. (Gough complained of a lack of blood-lust among the troops) He did get hold of one who had momentarily failed and he was shot. It was said that Gough in a brass hat was a very different person to Gough in a billy-cock [bowler].[65]

Even allowing for Edmonds' customary embellishments, this account must refer to the unfortunate case of Sub-Lieutenant Edwin Dyett of the Royal Naval Division, who was shot for desertion on 5 January 1917. After his trial, his divisional commander recommended that the sentence be commuted but Gough, as Army commander, upheld it. Edmonds did later exaggerate the story to 'two officers shot' and no doubt Gough's personal involvement in the case was limited but, nevertheless, an 'example' was made.[66]

With pressure growing for results on the Somme, Fourth Army HQ now decided to try and breach the German second line of defence. Frontal attacks were ruled out, although if Gough's Reserve Army could attack the enemy flanks in the south, the Fourth Army stood some chance of advancing in the centre. Inroads or 'saps' would have to be made into a string of fortified villages along the ridges above the British lines. To deal with these strongholds, Gough's boundary was extended to take in the Albert-Bapaume road. Thiepval, the most impregnable fortress, lay to the left of this road. A frontal assault on this fortress was ruled out. But if the villages of Ovillers and Pozières, which lay on the road ahead, were captured, Gough could work up the German lines behind Thiepval. Ovillers, the first of these villages, was a tough nut to crack. It took until 16 July to fall.

Elsewhere on the front, the message from GHQ was the same, 'cut out the preliminaries and push on'. On 14 July, at 12.25 am, Major-General Maxse telephoned the 54th Brigade from his HQ at 18th Division. He ordered Brigadier-General Shoubridge (later to command the 7th Division at Bullecourt) to capture Trônes Wood. 'Can we wait until daylight to make a reconnaissance?' asked Shoubridge. 'None of my people have seen it.' Maxse said there was no time to spare. The attack went in at dawn the same day.[67]

In other Divisions, where there was the luxury of a recce., it did little to relieve the chaos and bloodshed once the whistles were blown. 2nd Lieutenant Harold Davies, 38th (Welsh) Division[68], recorded his battalion's action in his diary:

> Go out reconnoitring, take two new officers with me. New officers a nuisance, too risky taking duds with you. Terrible scrapping and shelling. We take Mametz Wood. But my God at what cost. 12 officers and 400 men.

Having survived Mametz, Davies would soon leave the 13th Battalion, Welsh Regiment, to join the newly formed Heavy Branch Machine Gun Corps. His next view of the enemy would be from the inside of a tank at the Battle of Bullecourt.

Meanwhile, the cost of biting into any of the enemy held woods or villages on the Somme was high. Mametz Wood held up the Allied push for three days whilst the Germans continued to consolidate their hold on the Ginchy-Pozières ridge. As the British Army entered the second phase of the Battle of the Somme, it did so without any single objective. From 15 July to 14 September it remorselessly attacked fortified positions on narrow fronts, and suffered casualties comparable to the first day.[69]

General von Falkenhayn, the German Commander, ordered that no positions were to be given up and that every yard of territory was to be contested. Against this, Haig prescribed the tactic of 'methodical progress'. A comfortable enough description but, when this tactic was put into practice, it meant repeatedly hammering the same enemy positions regardless of casualties.

After the 24th Division had failed to capture Pozières on 18 July, Haig gave the task to Gough. To achieve it, Gough was given 1st Australian Division with the proviso from Haig that they were only to be given a simple operation. Haig was well aware that it was their first involvement in a major offensive.[70]

From this time, the Australian divisions of I ANZAC Corps began their association with Gough and the Fifth Army. It was an uneasy and sometimes bitter relationship that reached its nadir at Bullecourt in 1917. But for the moment the Australians had to prepare for a bloody apprenticeship at Pozières.

NOTES

1   Paul Maze, *A Frenchman in Khaki*, p.78-79.
2   Robin Prior & Trevor Wilson, *Passchendaele – The Untold Story*, p.100-101.
3   T.H.E. Travers, *How The War Was Won: Command and Technology in the British Army on the Western Front 1917-1918*, p.177 ; 'A Particular Style of Command: Haig and GHQ 1916-18', p. 365, *The Journal of Strategic Studies*, Vol 10 # 3 (Sept. 1987).
4   Dominick Graham & Shelford Bidwell, *Coalitions, Politicians and Generals: Some Aspects of Command in Two World Wars*, p. 29-30.
5   Liddell Hart had illuminating meetings with Gough in the 1930's. For notes on a *rapprochement* dinner between Gough and Lloyd George, see 11/1935/72 & 11/1936/31, Liddell Hart Papers, King's College London (hereafter KCL).
6   For a history of the Staff College, see Brian Bond, *The Victorian Army and the Staff College 1854-1914*.
7   For an assessment of the capabilities of the British Army, its Command and General Staff see Graham & Bidwell, *Coalitions, Politicians and Generals: Some Aspects of Command in Two World Wars*, p.9-23.
8   *Army Quarterly*, Vol LXV, p.42; T.H.E. Travers, 'The British Officer Corps 1900-18', *Journal of Contemporary History*, Vol 17, 1982.
9   E & J. Gellibrand Diary, Feb/March 1906, Jane d'Arcy; Edward Spiers, 'The Regular Army' *p.43* in Dr Ian Beckett (ed), *A Nation in Arms*.
10   E. & J. Gellibrand Diary, 23 & 24 Feb. 1916.
11   Correspondence with Peter Sadler, biographer of Sir John Gellibrand.
12   Notes on meeting with Lloyd George and Hubert Gough, 27 Jan. 1936, LH11/1936/31, Liddell Hart Papers, KCL.
13   E. & J. Gellibrand Diary, 3 March 1906.
14   E. & J. Gellibrand Diary, 10 March 1906.
15   *The Times* Obituary,10/9/1945.
16   Brudenell White was more charitable in his assessment of Braithwaite, White Diary, 23 Jan. 1906, Lady Derham.
17   Edward Beddington, 'My Life', p.6. Beddington Papers, KCL ; 'Four Generations of Staff College' (1896), Brigadier-General Sir James Edmonds, *Army Quarterly* Vol. LXV, No.1 (Oct. 1952).
18   *Army Quarterly*, April 1923, p.120; E. & J. G. Diary, Nov. 1906.
19   *Report of Committee of Education and Training*. P.P. Vol X p.101.
20   T.H.E. Travers, 'The Offensive and the Problem of Innovation in British

Military Thought 1870-1915,' p.546, *Journal of Contemporary History*, Vol. 13, 1978.

21 Sir Edward Hamley, *The Operations of War*, p.406-407. See also Kiggell's preface to the later 1909 edition.

22 Sir Archibald Wavell, *Allenby*, p.109.

23 Hamley, *The Operations of War*, p. 414-415. It was not only Gough who failed to absorb such tactics. Edmonds refers to French's total inability to grasp the contents of the book, 'Memoirs' (ch. XXIII), Edmonds Papers, KCL.

24 T.H.E. Travers, 'A Particular Style of Command: Haig and GHQ, 1916-18,' p. 365, *The Journal of Strategic Studies*, Vol 10 # 3 (Sept. 1987). See also T.H.E. Travers, 'The Army and the Challenge of War', p.218-219, in David Chandler and Dr Ian Beckett (ed), *The Oxford Illustrated History of the British Army*.

25 Liddell Hart Papers, LH/1936/31, KCL; T.H.E. Travers, *The Killing Ground*, p.215-216; Shelford Bidwell, *Gunners at War*, p.37.

26 *Revue des deux Mondes*. Quoted in *Army Quarterly*, Vol XXIII, p.149.

27 Edmonds to Swinton, 21/3/50, II/5/18c, Edmonds Papers, KCL.

28 General Sir Anthony Farrar-Hockley, *Goughie,*p.164.

29 Beddington, 'My Life,' p. 24, Beddington Papers, KCL.

30 Stephen Gwynn (ed), *The Anvil of War: Letters between F.S. Oliver & his Brother*, p.144.

31 Beddington, 'My Life', p.24, Beddington Papers, KCL.

32 ibid, p.25.

33 Wilson Papers, 73/1/18, Imperial War Museum (hereafter IWM); A.P.Ryan, *Mutiny at the Curragh*, p.128-134.

34 Richard Holmes, *The Little Field-Marshal*, p.191-194. Gough's later writing (*The Fifth Army & Soldiering On*) glosses over this enmity but his contemporary letters show otherwise.

35 Wavell, *Allenby*, p.123.

36 Gough to Liddell Hart, 9/4/35, LH/1935/72, Liddell Hart Papers, KCL.

37 French to HDF undated 1899, Fanshawe Papers, Peter Fanshawe Collection (hereafter PFC).

38 Edmonds to Sir Ernest Swinton, II/5/18b, & 2/5/1a, Edmonds Papers, KCL; conversation, Jock Stuart to Beddington, 'My Life', p.93, Beddington Papers KCL. Major-General Peyton to Edmonds, III/12/17, Edmonds Papers, KCL.

39 Apart from the French circle, other examples were Lord Roberts (India) who pushed Sir Ian Hamilton and Sir Henry Wilson. Lord Kitchener advanced both Birdwood and Haig.

40 T.H.E. Travers, 'The British Officer Corps 1900-18,' p.532-3, *Journal of Contemporary History*, Vol. 17, 1982.

41 General Sir Hubert Gough, *The Fifth Army*, p.32.

42 Dr Ian Beckett, *Johnnie Gough VC*, p. 203-204.

43 Gough to Edmonds, AWM 3DRL (7953, item 34); Colonel J. F. C. Fuller maintained it was the system, rather than any lack of personal courage, which kept senior Staff officers back, J.F.C. Fuller, *Memoirs of an Unconventional Soldier*, p.14.

44 Robert Blake (ed), *Private Papers of Douglas Haig*, 18 April 1915.

45 Rawlinson commented, 'I would of course, sooner have had poor Johnnie Gough', Beckett, *Johnnie Gough VC*, p.207.

46 Gough to Edmonds, re Official History, AWM 3DRL 7953/34; Gough, *The Fifth Army*, p.84-85; Gough, *Soldiering On*, p.122.

47 Sir Charles Callwell, *F-M Sir Henry Wilson, His Life and Diaries*, 8 May 1915.

48 Canon E. Crosse Papers, IWM.

49 *The Times* 23/3/63. For an examination of the dangers that awaited senior

officers at the front, see Keith Simpson,'Capper and the Offensive Spirit', *RUSI Journal*, 1973, p51.

50 John Keegan, *The Face of Battle*, p. 261.

51 John Terraine, *The Smoke and the Fire*, p. 179.

52 Field-Marshal Montgomery, *Memoirs of Field-Marshal Montgomery*, p.35; 'The General and his Troops', *Army Quarterly*, p.90, Oct.1961.

53 'GOC – His Mark', p.67 , *Army Quarterly*, April 1939; Farrar-Hockley, *Goughie*, p.165-166.

54 For the meetings between the King and the generals see Acc3155/97/9, 24 Oct. 1915, Haig Papers, National Library of Scotland (hereafter NLS).

55 C.R.Cruttwell, *A History of the Great War*, p. 255-256.

56 Haldane Papers, MS20249-ff 117, 30 June 1916, NLS; Fanshawe Papers, PFC; T.H.E. Travers, *The Killing Ground*, p. 22-23.

57 General Sir Anthony Farrar-Hockley, *The Somme*, p.96.

58 Maze, *A Frenchman in Khaki*, p. 135. During the Second World War, Herman Goering discovered Maze's book in a billet. He wrote on the flyleaf, that it was the best book he had ever read on the Great War.

59 Blake, *Private Papers of Douglas Haig*, 1 July 1916; *Military Operations 1916*, p.481.

60 Major the Rev. John Croft, 'A Great Opportunity Lost,' Vol.116 1986, *Defence Journal* .

61 Repington accepted 'Hunter-Bunter's' version of the slaughter. Ironically, Hunter-Weston defended Haig against accusations that he spread the guns too thinly, Colonel Charles Repington, *The First World War*, Vol I, p.266-267; Gough, *The Fifth Army*, p.138-139.

62 Wace to Edmonds, 30 Oct. 1936, CAB 45/138, Public Record Office, London (hereafter PRO).

63 In conversation with Liddell Hart, Gough admitted that he had made himself unpopular by sacking officers too drastically, LH 1935/72, Liddell Hart Papers,KCL.

64 CAB 45/140, PRO.

65 'Memoirs' III/12/16, Edmonds Papers, KCL.

66 Edmonds to Wynne 17/2/44, Edmonds Papers, KCL; Julian Putkowski, *Shot at Dawn*, p.150-155.

67 Farrar-Hockley, *The Somme*, p.183.

68 In 1920 the spelling reverted to 'Welch.'

69 Trevor Wilson & Robin Prior, 'Summing up the Somme', *History Today*,Vol. 41 1991.

70 Blake, *Private Papers of Douglas Haig*, 22 July 1916.

CHAPTER II

The Boys who 'Hopped the Bags'

The banners at home had proudly proclaimed 'Australia Will Be There'. It was an incredible achievement that she was there at all on the Western Front in 1916, for sixteen years before, there had been no Australian Imperial Force, let alone an Australian nation.

After 1901, when the six federal states were grafted into one Commonwealth of Australia, Lieutenant-Colonel William Bridges, a British regular, welded the six militias together.[1] Individual states, some of which had already fought in the Sudan and Boer Wars were represented by particular battalions and brigades, rather like the British regimental system. There was no shortage of enthusiasm for citizen soldiering among young Australians, who had been brought up on Fitchett's *Deeds That Won The Empire* and other stirring tales about British heroes spreading that rash of pink seen on every schoolboy's atlas. It also helped that the leading politicians, Hughes, Cook and Fisher, were all British born.[2] So Bridges' mission was eased by the fact that the four million Australians already considered themselves part of a civilised, educated and white race. They were one and the same with Britain, an extension of the breed on the far side of the world, who would be defended by the Royal Navy and in return would help defend the Empire and, especially, keep Germany out of the South Pacific.[3]

At Gallipoli in 1915, an Australian national identity was forged. There is no question that, due to the compact battle area, and because officers and men shared appalling hardships together, a 'mateship' grew. This camaraderie was further reinforced a year later by their Commander's determination to keep Australian units fighting together when they reached the Western Front. Although this theatre of the war was even farther away than Gallipoli, Australian newspapers kept alive the original cause of 'Plucky little Belgium'.[4] While this campaign sustained enthusiasm for the Empire, the Anzacs' respect for and allegiance to British Command was no longer unquestioning. Those loyalties had been battered by the events at Gallipoli, and more ominously in 1916, splits were beginning to show within the Anzac Command itself, that would seriously threaten its battlefield performance in 1917.

Four AIF divisions (1st, 2nd, 4th and 5th) arrived on the Somme in April 1916 and were divided between Lieutenant-General William

Birdwood's I ANZAC Corps and Lieutenant-General Alexander Godley's II ANZAC Corps. While Godley went north, Birdwood moved south but neither Anzac commander was in place soon enough to control the AIF 5th Division's first fight at Fromelles. It was to prove a disaster.

From the outset, the objectives of Lieutenant-General Richard Haking, the Corps Commander in charge at Fromelles, were wildly different from those of GHQ. Haking had grandiose plans for capturing nearby Aubers Ridge and the fact that he was 'an extraordinarily quick worker and mapper', may have led to cutting corners in the plan of attack.[5] Unfortunately, GHQ had in mind a good full-blown artillery offensive to act as a feint to draw German reserves away from the Somme. Consequently Haking did not have troops adequate for his attack and the Australians lost over 5,500 men and the British 61st (South Midlands) Division suffered losses of 1,500.

'Pompey' Elliott, a brigade commander in the AIF 5th Division, was outraged at the incompetent planning and execution at Fromelles. Further Australian anger was directed at the British troops, but the British 61st Division was only a second line territorial unit, fighting its first major action in France. As in most battles, the infantry plan was based largely on the effectiveness of the artillery and their support was a failure. The fire-plan only allowed for half an hour's registration which was not enough for the inexperienced gunners and few trench strongpoints or enemy gun batteries were hit.[6] The carnage was terrible, especially among the junior officers and NCOs and an eye-witness recalled that the enemy shelling was so persistent that the wounded could not be retrieved, calling out to be finished off by the German machine-guns.[7]

At Corps level, Haking squandered the divisions passing through his control, but at divisional level, Major-General McCay (AIF 5th Division), was responsible for the poor staffwork. Yet both managed to hold onto command positions afterwards. McCay was withdrawn from the 5th Division and given the post of GOC, AIF Depots in England, although Birdwood did ensure that he was not re-appointed to a divisional command.[8] So in this respect, the AIF were as capable as the British Army of hanging onto ineffectual officers, as Charles Bean the Official Australian Historian privately admitted:

> When a Brigadier gets a weak unsuitable officer in his battalions, he has been accustomed not to get rid of him to Australia, but to send him to the Training battalion or to the 6th Division; in due course they have to come back from there and then they find the battalions saddled with them. The COs will not put down on paper a regular reason for their thinking that an officer is defective, or if they do, they water it down.[9]

Poor staff work was widespread. Cancelled orders were not conveyed between British and Australian divisional HQs and this weakness proved to be disastrous for combined operations on the Western Front. Furthermore, it showed little sign of improving. Well over a third of all the British pre-war trained staff officers had been killed by the end of 1915 and their replacements were often inexperienced.[10] Among the Australians, the position was worse as they had started the war with very few of their own staff officers and because, until the Duntroon Officer Training School was opened in 1911, they had no facility to train them. Consequently their divisional and Corps staffs continued often to be an awkward mix of raw British and Australian officers. With these problems, combined with a planning preference for attacks on narrow fronts, Fromelles was a gruesome blueprint for what was to come.

For the next show at Pozières, the Australians were more optimistic. They would be fighting under their own I ANZAC Corps, commanded by Birdwood. Described by Sir Ian Hamilton as 'The Soul of Anzac' for the part he played in the Gallipoli evacuation, 'Birdie' had always displayed courage and a disregard for personal safety, which had been appreciated by the men. In May 1915, at Gallipoli, near the spot where General Bridges was shot the next day, a bullet grazed his skull.[11] He treated danger lightly and was often in close proximity to it. He told Charles Bean what happened when one of his men complained that his bombs didn't go off:

'Surely they do', said Birdwood.'No they don't sir', the man said, lighting one and putting it down – 'See here!' 'That's dangerous. Won't the thing explode?' said Birdie and turned his back quickly. The next second it did explode. By a marvel, Birdwood and the man were not injured. 'The man wasn't a bit worried', Birdie said, 'he simply said, 'Well, it's the first time I've known it do that!' [12]

Birdwood had built a reputation on his informal rapport with 'his Australians' and he played the card for all it was worth, especially for morale purposes. He was not a crusty or 'peppery' general and had none of the remoteness which had dogged Bridges' relationships. Although events in France were to sour this affinity, he was still for the moment 'old Birdie'. Major-General Butler, his GSO2 Intelligence officer, recalled:

The only form of recreation at Anzac was bathing. Shells or no shells, everyone tried to get to the beach, no-one was keener than Birdie. We swam in our birthday suits. Birdie, a rather short little man with quite a tummy on him, was bobbing about in the waves one day. A digger who was close to him, looked at Birdie's tummy and said to him, 'My bloody oath mate, you must 'ave been among the biscuits'.[13]

He could smooth over rough patches and play the diplomat with prickly egos like the French commander, Bailloud, in a way that few could match.[14] However, Birdwood's talents could not disguise his weaknesses, which were clearly evident to his Chief of Staff, Major-General Brudenell White:

> Birdie's sense of proportion is not good. Indeed I am talking confidentially to you Bean, it is often very bad. I remember at Anzac during the last days of the evacuation, General Birdwood came ashore and spoke to me of one thing he had noticed, there was a lot of Signal wire about. 'See you get that reeled up, White', he said. 'We ought to save as much of that as we can'. I thought 'Heavens – what does he think we are doing here'. Why I would gladly have left all the guns behind if we could only get the men off safely.[15]

On 18 July, Haig ordered Gough to attack Pozières. Haig professed a policy of 'wearing down' the enemy by a series of 'bite and hold' operations and the capture of the ridge behind Pozières was vital to enable the British to work up behind Thiepval. Such a cautious approach might have seemed appropriate if the task had been allotted to infantrymen like Rawlinson or Plumer, but Gough was hardly the man for siege warfare. It appeared that Haig still harboured hopes of a big breakthrough.[16]

Gough had at his disposal the British 48th (South Midland) Division and the AIF 1st Division from Birdwood's I ANZAC Corps. The 48th, a territorial division, had been holding sectors of the front line since April 1915 but had not been engaged in heavy fighting. Its commander was fifty-two-year-old Major-General Robert Fanshawe, the youngest of the three Fanshawe brothers. A veteran of 1st Ypres and Festubert, where his 6th Brigade had been on Gough's flank, Fanshawe had rather a 'blimpish' air about him. One man who served under him recalled a typical exchange on the roadside, 'I saluted him and he responded with, "Good morning to you my boy! Good morning. Good morning. Now what's your job? A sapper? Good, splendid. Well good morning to you again. Good morning"'.[17] Such banter makes Fanshawe sound like 'the cheery old card' in Siegfried Sassoon's famous poem, but his manner masked an able mind. Nevertheless, he would not have gone down well with the Australians, who responded better to officers like Major-General Walker, their gritty 1st Division Commander. Known as 'Hooky' because of his large nose, Walker was a British regular who had led the AIF 1st Brigade at Gallipoli with distinction. Ironically he later took over Fanshawe's 48th Division and was one of the last British commanders to leave the AIF in 1918.[18]

In combined operations, the Australians often doubted the fighting potential of their British counterparts. This distrust was usually because of physical comparisons, from which the Australians inevitably came off better. Sergeant Jack Bourke of the AIF 8th Battalion, buoyed by the recent praise from Phillip Gibbs in the London press, wrote:

How the British Tommy ever accomplished anything in history is a mystery. A good heart and a wooden head must have carried him through. As far as physique is concerned, he is a weed. The average height is about 5ft. 4". He shuffles along, not a spring in his body and our chaps chip him continually. Thousands of them are mere boys and how on earth England hopes to push big Germans backward, passes comprehension.[19]

This preoccupation with physique was common in Australian correspondence, and only the Scottish Highlanders and the Irish escaped poor comparison. Invariably the Australians were paired with 1st or 2nd line English territorial divisions for operations in France and because these divisions were used as manpower reserves, they were often under strength and poorly trained. For their part, the British often thought the Australians:

an awfully rough crowd who have already caused a good deal of trouble. They don't seem to have any discipline at all and all their officers have practically no hold over them.[20]

Charles Bean blamed much of the problem on the slackness of NCOs who treated the men as the friends they had known at home. However, other colonial troops, such as the Canadians, were just as capable of excess, but the label didn't stick. An officer of the York & Lancs Regiment recalled that 'the Canadians preceeded us in this district and left a very bad reputation behind them. They broke windows, smashed furniture and paid for nothing'.[21] However, when there was lawlessness among colonial troops, they were never subjected to the same brutal suppression that was the hallmark of the British military police.

Gough was determined to strike quickly against Pozières. On 18 July, instead of waiting for the arrival of Birdwood and the staff of I ANZAC Corps, he immediately summoned Major-General Walker to his HQ in Albert. According to Walker, Gough issued a simple order, 'I want you to go into the line and attack Pozières tomorrow night'.[22] Walker was staggered. One day was simply not enough to organise an attack, especially without his own Corps Commander, and he argued strongly against Gough.

Gough would have none of it, but some of his Army Staff saw the sense in Walker's caution and warned Birdwood and White at ANZAC Corps HQ about the trouble in store. According to Major Thomas Blamey, GSO1 to 1st Division, Birdwood was in the habit of leaving these more delicate problems to White, who then proceeded to pressure Gough to delay the attack.[23] Gough surprisingly relented and the attack was postponed for three days, to allow more time for a thorough fire-plan, for assault practice and for jumping-off trenches to be dug. Walker may have been a tough and resilient character but he was still only a divisional commander and it required leverage from Corps level to bend the will of an Army Commander. Still, they had succeeded in the short term and Walker's account was evidence (as at Aubers Ridge and after the first day of the Somme) that Gough could cancel or postpone suicidal attacks. However, that now seemed to hinge on how often Birdwood and White were prepared to go to the brink with their Army Commander.[24]

Haig, however, seemed to be more reticent about throwing the AIF 1st Division head first into a pitched battle. He had news of the recent disaster which had befallen the 5th Division at Fromelles and was keen for Gough to 'foster' them in their first large assault.[25] After a preliminary British bombardment during the night of 22/23 July, the men of the 1st Division clambered over their trench parapets, described by Bean as 'hopping the bags', and charged the enemy positions. They made good progress at first and captured both the ridge and Pozières village. But few expected the German artillery to respond with a ferocity of fire which exceeded that at Verdun. The enemy howitzers fired shells continuously into the hastily dug Australian trenches at the rate of four per minute.[26]

Pozières was soon reduced to a pile of rubble and brick dust. All features on the surrounding ridge were blasted away but the 1st Division miraculously hung on and fought off repeated German counter attacks. On 24 July, it even managed to consolidate the trenches to the west of the village, which the British 48th Division had partly taken. It had been a considerable achievement and Birdwood was delighted at the fearlessness of the Australian attackers, commenting 'we made about eight really successful raids across no man's land into the German lines, in which we actually bayoneted some 300 of them . . . It does a lot of good in keeping up the right spirit among the men.'[27] This preoccupation with the bayonet, especially if accompanied by the proper 'killing face' in battle, was not peculiar to Birdwood. As a prime weapon in 'the cult of the offensive', it was widely regarded amongst the regulars as a means of keeping men moving forward in an attack, rather than allowing them to stop to fire.[28]

Apart from this success on the first day, no other gains had been made by the British along the eight-mile front, except for Delville Wood. This now left much of the German artillery free to concentrate on Pozières ridge.

Walker's 'one day notice' for the preparation of an attack, is a well known story and it fits easily with the notion of a thrusting Army Commander like Gough. However, Gough was not alone in dispensing with advance warnings. In the enemy camp, or 'on the other side of the hill' as it was known, the German Army Commander, General Wellman was also under pressure. On 24 July, Wellman and his 18th Reserve Division arrived at Pozières to relieve part of the German front. Exhausted after his journey from Artois, Wellman appeared at Haplincourt Château, the divisional headquarters, and was met by the Army Commander General Fritz von Below and the Corps Commander, General von Boehm. Wellman was promptly told, 'You are entrusted with the recapture of Pozières which will take place tomorrow after-noon'. Wellman recorded in his diary that this was 'a nice sort of surprise for me and my staff'.[29] His counter attack subsequently faltered when one of his regiments never got started and the other lost direction, was split up and cut to pieces. Consequently, Wellman's division suffered 50% casualties, proving that chaos and costly mistakes were common to both sides.

Haig now realised that reserves would have to be brought up before any new offensive could continue. On 27 July, the shattered AIF Ist Division was withdrawn, having suffered 5,285 casualties, and their place was taken by the 2nd Division, whose brief was to capture the Windmill on the crest of the ridge. If this could be achieved, the British would have a clear view to Bapaume and beyond, enabling Gough to assault the fortress of Thiepval.

On the night of 28 July, the 2nd Division attacked the ridge. Within a short time, they were caught up in the deep barbed-wire entanglements which their artillery had failed to destroy and were cut down by the withering enemy machine-gun fire. The assault collapsed and the division suffered nearly 3,500 casualties in return for some small gains in the 6th Brigade (Gellibrand) sector.

ANZAC Corps blamed the Army Command, but Brudenell White knew that their own planning was sometimes suspect. It was Birdwood's lack of organisation that really worried White:

I don't think he [Birdwood] ever drew up the plans of an operation, which they [the Australians] carried out. It was not an element in his capacity. Of course he has never been an organiser. When Birdie went out for the day, he never brought back with him a reliable summary of what he had seen. He would spend a couple of hours up at one of the brigades and I have often tried, when he came back, to get a real estimate of the position there from him. I found you could never rely upon it being at all like the fact.[30]

Surprisingly, Haig put most of the blame for the failure on his Army Commander and was for once unimpressed with Gough's performance. He felt that Gough and his Chief of Staff, Malcolm, had 'failed to properly supervise the Australian operation'.[31] He was dismissive of the Anzac commanders, but it was Brigadier-General Cunliffe Owen, Birdwood's GOCRA, whom he chose to sack on account of the artillery's poor showing. The weak counter-battery work had allowed the German guns to deluge the ridge with HE shells and those Australians caught in the open were blown to pieces. Many who sought sanctuary in shallow shell holes or 'possies' (cover holes for one man), were buried alive. Others who emerged without marks on them were shaking and unable to speak. One of the nastier developments in modern artillery was the improved powders used which, on concussion, had a disastrous effect on the nervous system. Although the term 'shell-shock' became widely used to describe all battle fatigue, the direct effect of HE proved the most debilitating.[32]

As part of a shake-up, Haig brought in Brigadier-General William Napier as the new GOCRA of I ANZAC Corps.[33] From a famous military family and with a grandfather, Lord Napier, who had fought at Trafalgar, the fifty-two-year-old gunner appeared a sound bet. A well-known society figure and 'man about town', he gained rapid promotion at the outbreak of war. Napier was wounded at Festubert in May 1915, but more recently had been with Lieutenant-General Horne's XV Corps, where he had commanded the Heavy Artillery with credit.[34]

The General Officer commanding the Corps' Heavy artillery was a more dour character. Brigadier-General Lyons Fraser was a forty-two-year-old British regular who had commanded the 1st Heavy Artillery Brigade under Gough, when Gough was commanding I Corps. Fraser had only been with the Australians since April 1916, so Pozières was his first real baptism of fire with I ANZAC Corps.

Major-General Legge, commanding the AIF 2nd Division, was eager to recover the situation and needed little encouragement from Gough to launch a further attack on 4 August. He carried the ridge but his exhausted division could not reach Mouquet Farm and they were withdrawn.

So far, during their twelve days on the ridge, the 2nd had suffered 6,846 casualties. Birdwood removed Legge from command the following January, with his customary politeness and tact. This was apt to confuse and irritate other colleagues, especially when the retiring commander was told there was nothing wrong with his leadership. On returning to Australia, Legge was 'promoted' to Chief of the General Staff, a position he held until after the war.[35] In some ways he was a scapegoat, for there was much talk of 'inexperienced troops being driven by an over eager GOC'. But as Brigadier-General John Gellibrand told Bean, 'the 2nd were no newer to offensive warfare on the Western Front than the 1st Division'.[36]

Gellibrand, who had been responsible for implementing many of these futile plans of attack, placed much of the blame on the 2nd Division Staff who, he claimed, 'were pretty poor'. Bean had also heard much the same complaint about muddling and the incompetent staff work of I ANZAC Corps.[37] Gellibrand was scathing about the 2nd Division HQ in particular, who appeared 'unduly impressed' by their 7th Brigade, putting them in the vanguard of attacks when they were clearly not 'stormtrooper' material.

For the incoming AIF 4th Division, Gough and his Chief of Staff, Malcolm, promised an unrelenting diet of 'offensive action.' In a memorandum to Corps Commanders and their subordinates on the eve of the 4th Division's arrival, Malcolm emphasised that 'every yard of ground gained has great consequences, both material and moral'. In his directive, he stressed the word 'energy' over and over again, demanding 'relentless pressure everywhere and always'.[38]

The veterans of Gallipoli bedded into their new positions around the site of the old Windmill, and awaited the order to attack. Among them were men of the 48th Battalion (part of Brigadier-General Duncan Glasfurd's 12th Brigade), which was notable for being the domain of one family, the Leanes. It was commanded by thirty-eight-year-old Lieutenant-Colonel Ray Leane, a bull of a man who was wounded winning a Military Cross at Gallipoli, where he earned a reputation for being 'a good leader in a tight corner'. The battalion also contained his younger brother, Major Ben Leane (second-in-command), and two nephews, Captain Allan Leane and Captain Thomas Fairley. The wits in the AIF soon christened it the 'Joan of Arc' battalion, after the patron saint of the French army, as it was 'made of all Leanes'.[39]

Just because the command was something of a family affair, it didn't mean that life in the 48th Battalion was too comfortable. Ray Leane was a forthright and exacting man, expecting the same high standards in his men that he set for himself. His 'tall square-shouldered frame and immense jaw', made him a formidable presence which he used to great effect, especially when squaring up to the equally blunt Glasfurd, his brigade commander.[40]

Leane was ordered by Glasfurd to occupy the forward trenches, on which he knew the German guns had registered. Astonishingly, at first he refused, arguing that it would mean certain death for his men. He then demanded the order in writing so there could be no ducking the responsibility afterwards.[41] With the order in his hand, he reluctantly sent his men forward but the advance collapsed under intense enemy shelling. On 7 August, the Germans attempted to force the Australians off the ridge by launching another counter-attack, but courageous actions by such men as Bert Jacka of the 14th Battalion stemmed the enemy attack and recovered lost ground on the crest, east of Pozières.

The fighting was hand-to-hand, using bayonets, rifle-butts and trenching tools. It was a hard, bitter slog for the Australians across the ridge, but Gough wanted the wedge to be forced right up behind the German fortress of Thiepval. Before that approach could be made, Mouquet Farm, a strategic ruin a mile north-west of Pozières, would have to be captured. Unfortunately, the plan of attack used the usual tactics of assaulting through a narrow salient without the support of an effective counter-battery plan. Barely any cover existed and reinforcements were shot to pieces advancing across the skyline. The grim struggle carried on through August, and even the testing of the new 'creeping barrage' ended in disaster. Scores of men were killed under their own guns when the heavy artillery refused to lengthen their range.

Not even Gellibrand's agile brain could see a way through the labyrinth of craters and collapsed trenches, and his further attacks around 'Mucky Farm' foundered. Finally on 5 September, with no further progress made, the Australians were relieved by the Canadians. I ANZAC Corps had suffered 23,300 casualties in seven weeks of fighting.

It was a relief for the Australians to be out of it, but they were bitter. Birdwood's charm failed to flatter men who been through an inferno with little to show for it and he came in for much criticism.[42] Pozières and Mouquet Farm seriously disillusioned the Australian soldier and his letters home from the Western Front in the Autumn of that year show a deep despair.[43]

What had Gough's Reserve Army HQ been doing, whilst the British and Australian troops battered themselves against the enemy defences? This Army, like other Armies, was purely an administrative unit and, at this stage, comprised about eighty staff. It is true that there were plenty of stories to support the popular notion of 'château generals'. Paul Maze witnessed the extraordinary spectacle of 'red-tabbed' colonels and generals staggering out for an early morning boar shoot, prior to the Battle of the Somme.[44] However farcical this may seem in the middle of a war, Maze was probably not surprised. It was a popular pastime amongst generals in France and Lieutenant-General Sir Alexander Godley confirmed to his wife that 'Rawly's rest is pig-sticking or boar hunting'.[45] It was not exclusive to the Reserve Army. So these activities did not mark out Gough's Army Staff as indolent and neither could the charge be levelled at the Chief of Staff, Neill Malcolm. F.S. Oliver, who saw Malcolm in action at Fifth Army HQ, noted:

> He is often up at 5 o'clock to go and see some outlying division; then he is in his office for an hour before breakfast, and returns to it shortly after 9 o'clock. He is working all day, either in the office or among the divisions, and goes back after dinner, remaining there till midnight or later. I don't believe that any man can work his brain safely for as long hours as this.[46]

However, the charge of staff remoteness does have some truth. Although, before the battle, there was an impressive telephone communication system in place between Army, Corps, Division and other arms right down to battalion level, the moment troops went into action, the system collapsed. Enemy artillery destroyed most of the forward telephone lines and usually runners brought back conflicting and unreliable information. There were competent Army Staff officers and they went forward more often than their French counterparts. But there were still too few going forward to Corps or Divisional HQ, so when information came back that was out of date or inaccurate, it was rarely verified.[47] At the sharper end, too many brigade HQs were kept too far back to respond quickly to changes on the field. The result was poor intelligence summaries and dubious War Diaries which relay little of the scale of the casualties or the slow advance. To compound the problem, too many commanders at corps, division and brigade level had received rapid promotion and were inexperienced in their new commands at 1 July 1916. [48]

In the combined operations around Pozières, the British, New Zealand and Canadian Divisions lost an average of 7,000 men each, nearly equal to the losses suffered by I ANZAC Corps.[49] These grim figures indicate that GHQ did not just single out the Anzacs for impossible tasks.

As Army Commander, Gough was ultimately responsible for the Pozières plan, though neither Birdwood nor White made any prolonged effort to oppose it. Advancing into a narrow salient meant that successive waves of attackers were too close. Together with the congested front trenches, they provided inviting targets for the German gunners, not to mention their own artillery. The lesson was gradually sinking in, that regardless of planning, support and leadership, actions on the Western Front were wasteful of manpower. Even Walker's successful first day at Pozières cost his division dearly.

Sadly, the qualities that Charles Bean had so admired in the 'Digger' at Gallipoli, his bushcraft and his resourcefulness, counted for little on the squalid Pozières ridge. Results on the Western Front increasingly hinged on the power of the artillery. That this artillery had performed so poorly was cause for further anxiety and, despite the later eulogies heaped by General Monash on the commander of the 'Heavies', Brigadier-General Fraser's Pozières record was not distinguished.[50] So poor was the accuracy and gun-laying, that some assaults were only preceded by a desultory six shells, all of which missed the target.[51]

It should be said that the more sophisticated techniques of 'flash-spotting' and 'sound-ranging' were barely developed. Nor was the 106 fuse in use, which would have made wire-cutting by HE more effective. Shrapnel and trench mortar bombs were therefore the mainstay in the gunners' arsenal, but even these were of little use, unless their impact on the wire could be regularly monitored. Throughout the battle, Napier's fire plans for I ANZAC Corps artillery continued to rely on destructive rather than neutralising fire-power.

However, the biggest weakness of the Anzac artillery was the breakdown of cooperation with the infantry. This communication failure was well-known, especially after Pozières, and there were constant attempts to correct it, without success. Consequently, because hostile batteries were rarely promptly identified, counter-battery work was poor.[52]

Bean was scathing about both the Anzac Artillery and Engineers in his private notebook but typically omitted such comments in his Official History:

R.E. and R.A. are worthless. The men by their sheer hard work and ingenuity, will probably make a name for Lotbinière's engineering, but their R.A. will let them down, some day, frightfully.[53]

These were prophetic words. But artillery was the devil the Australians knew and, as 1916 drew to a close, feverish preparations were in hand to introduce a new wonder weapon to the battlefield, about which the Australians knew little. The 'Tank'.[54]

NOTES

1 Charles Bean immortalised Bridges in his biography, *Two Men I Knew*. Bridges was shot in Monash Valley, Gallipoli, in May 1915. After some allegedly careless first aid, he died on the hospital ship 'Gascon'. AWM 92/3DRL 6405/4.

2 Bean Diary, AWM 3DRL 606/114. See also John Moses, 'The Ideas of 1914 in Germany and Australia: A Case of Conflicting Perceptions,' *War & Society* Vol.9 No.2 (Oct. 1991).

3 The formative years of the AIF are well covered by L.L. Robson, *The First AIF – A Study of its Recruitment*, and Bill Gammage, *The Broken Years*. A more comprehensive study of Anglo-Australian relations can be found in E.M. Andrews, *The Anzac Illusion*.

4 Judith Smart,'Poor Little Belgium', *War & Society* Vol.12 No.1 (May 1994).

5 III/2/16, Edmonds Papers, KCL.

6 Hereward Wake to Edmonds, 12/3/37, CAB 45/138, PRO.

7 Gammage, *The Broken Years*, p. 161.

8 *The Official History of Australia in the War*, Vol. IV (hereafter Bean IV), p. 24; Birdwood to Pearce, 12/3/18, AWM 38 3DRL 6673, Item 67. McCay was so unpopular that his headquarters staff were often unwilling to work for him, Andrews, *The Anzac Illusion, p.96*.

9 Bean Diary, AWM 38 3DRL 606 Item 95, p.42.

10 Beckett, 'The Nation in Arms' p.21 in *A Nation in Arms*. For an exhaustive study of staffwork, see Colonel W. N. Nicholson, *Behind the Lines: An Account of Administrative Staffwork in the British Army 1914-18*.

11 Bean Diary, AWM 38 3DRL 606 Item 86, p.68.

12 Bean Diary, AWM 3DRL/606 Item 45.

13   Major-General S.S. Butler Papers, IWM PP MCR 107.
14   Bean Diary, AWM 3DRL 606, Item 60.
15   Bean Diary, AWM 38 (3DRL/606-113) p. 8-9.
16   Paddy Griffith, *Battle Tactics of the Western Front*, p. 20-21; Trevor Wilson and Robin Prior, 'Summing up the Somme', *History Today*, Vol. 41, 1991.
17   John Glubb, *Into Battle*, p.105.
18   *Australian Dictionary of Biography* (hereafter ADB).
19   Bourke to his father, 17/6/16, AWM File 12/11/845. See also Dr Alistair Thomson, 'Living with a Legend: Anzac Memories and Australian National Identity', (Paper, Leeds International Conference, Sept. 1994).
20   Lieutenant W.W.A. Phillips, Liddle Collection, Leeds.
21   Sir Douglas Branson (4th York & Lancs), Liddle Collection.
22   Bean III, p.4 & 68; Bean, *Two Men I Knew*, p.134. Walker was extremely critical of Gough and the Fifth Army, see Walker to Bean, AWM 38 3DRL 7953 Item 34.
23   Bean Diary, AWM 38 3DRL 606 Item 94.p.71.
24   In correspondence with Bean, Gough refuted Walker's allegations, T.H.E. Travers, 'From Surafend to Gough', *Journal of the Australian War Memorial*, no. 27 (Oct. 1995).
25   Blake, *Private Papers of Douglas Haig*, 22 July 1916, p.155.
26   Birdwood to Rintoul, 9/8/16, Birdwood Papers, IWM; Peter Firkins, *Australians in Nine Wars*, p.72.
27   Birdwood to Rintoul, 23/7/16, Birdwood Papers, IWM.
28   Griffith, *Battle Tactics of the Western Front*, p.67-71; T.H.E. Travers, 'The Offensive and the Problem of Innovation in British Military Thought, 1870-1915', *Journal of Contemporary History*, Vol. 13, July 1978.
29   General Wellmann, *Mit der 18 Reserve Division in Frankreich*, p.116.
30   Bean Diary, AWM 38 3DRL/606-113, p.10-11.
31   Blake, *Private Papers of Douglas Haig*, 29 July 1916.
32   Griffith, *Battle Tactics of the Western Front*, p.137
33   Earlier in the war there were no artillery commanders above division, only 'advisers' at Corps and Army level, titled Major-General Royal Artillery (MGRA). Because of friction with other staff levels, they soon became known as General Officer Commanding Royal Artillery (GOCRA). To confuse everyone, for a period in 1916, they became Brigadier-General RA (BGRA). For simplicity they are referred to throughout as GOCRA. Divisional commanders continued to be known as CRA.
34   Napier Private Papers (Margaret Whittingdale).
35   Bean Diary, AWM 38 3DRL 606 Item 70, p.82.
36   Bean correspondence on Official History, Gellibrand to Bean 26/1/34, AWM 38 3DRL 7953 Item 30.
37   Ibid; Bean Diary, AWM 38 3DRL 606, Item 94.15/11/17.
38   AWM 25 305/1.
39   *Reveille*, 31 Oct. 1931. Also *Adelaide News*, 29 April 1926 and *Perth Mail*, 21 July 1932.
40   Duncan Glasfurd was a contemporary of White and Gellibrand at Staff College. He was hit by a shell, whilst out reconnoitring in November 1916. 'The straight clean-minded Scottish boy, grown into a straight honourable man', died after ten hours on a stretcher, being carted back from the front line, Bean, *Two Men I Knew*, p.148; ADB.
41   Bean reported that Leane refused outright, even after written orders, Peter Charlton, *Pozières*, p.217. However in Leane's correspondence to Bean on the

Official History, he implies that he obeyed Glasfurd only after receiving the order in writing.

42   Bean Diary, AWM 38 3DRL 606 Item 60.

43   Leane Papers, AWM IDRL 0411; See also Jack Bourke Papers, AWM IDRL 139 (12/11/845).

44   Maze, *A Frenchman in Khaki*, p.132-133.

45   General Sir Alexander Godley to Lady Godley, 23/2/17, Godley Papers, KCL.

46   Stephen Gwynn (ed.), *The Anvil of War-Letters between F.S. Oliver & his Brother*, p. 225.

47   T.H.E. Travers, 'A Particular Style of Command: Haig and GHQ, 1916-18', p.366, *Journal of Strategic Studies*, Vol. 10, no.3 (Sept. 1987); 'Contacts with Troops: Commanders and Staffs in the First World War', *Army Quarterly*, July 1964.

48   WO 95/518, PRO; Prior & Wilson, *Command on the Western Front: The Military career of Sir Henry Rawlinson, 1914-18*, p.182-184.

49   Amongst the British casualties at Pozières was Lieutenant George Butterworth MC, the famous composer, killed by a sniper on 5 August.

50   General Sir John Monash, *The Australian Victories in France*, p. 173.

51   E. J. Rule, *Jacka's Mob*, p.105-107.

52   AWM 25 75/15, Report on Hostile Artillery Activity. Also 'Cooperation between Artillery and Infantry', 5 Oct. 1916. I ANZAC Corps and Fifth Army records show that this problem persisted throughout 1917/18.

53   Bean Diary, AWM 38 3DRL 606 Item 44 ,p.28. Brigadier-General Joly de Lotbinière was Birdwood's Chief Engineer.

54   Although the original design for the tank would be attributed to the British, there was an Australian contender – a surveyor, Lancelot de Mole. As early as 1912, he had submitted sketches to the War Office for a 'fighting caterpillar vehicle.' Through a combination of accidents and logistics, his plans were not pursued but his contribution eventually received recognition by the 1919 Royal Commission on Awards to Inventors, De Mole Papers, AWM 93; Moore Williams Papers, AWM 43.

CHAPTER III

'Manhood versus Machinery'

Tanks had once been top secret. When the first machines were trans-
ported, they carried descriptions such as 'Water Carriers for Mesopotamia' or other outlandish disguises. The prototype, 'Little Willie', did
indeed look like a water tank and it was probably why the name stuck. It
was not, as is commonly supposed, derived from an abortive design from
a Mr Thomas Tank Burrell.[1] However, now that the tank pioneers, or
'hush-hush crowd' as they were called, had come out into the open, they
were showing pictures of the 'cars' to packed London cinemas in the
early months of 1917. 'The Battle of the Ancre and the Advance of the
Tanks' was the first chance for people at home to see moving pictures of
the 'Amazing tanks'.

The premiere of the film took place on 15 January 1917 and it was
subsequently shown in 107 London cinemas.[2] The film reached its climax
as the HMLS 'Dodo' tank appeared.[3] Cinema pianists pounded on
beneath the screen, and a sequence caption flickered on: 'The Men of the
Tanks – Are they Downhearted?' When the audiences saw the grinning
faces of Lieutenant Swears and his men on the screen, they erupted with
cheering and applause. The new weapon had certainly succeeded in
raising morale at home, especially after the depressing and endless
casualty lists from the Somme in 1916. Across in France, 'the men of the
tanks', some of whom had experienced tank actions in the autumn of
1916, were equally ecstatic. Lieutenant Hugh Swears, one of the
instructors at the new mechanical training school at Bermicourt, wrote:

> One of our officers who was in the stunt you have read about, is in
> hospital here. He is suffering from shellshock and collapse, after his car
> had a pretty thin time of it. Tail blown away etc. I saw him and he was
> very enthusiastic about it all. Don't believe all the drivel the Daily Mail
> have been writing about the 'heroic courage' required to take a tank
> into action. If you have ever seen a Willie and handled one, you would
> never rest until you had taken one into action. It is more a pleasure than
> anything else.[4]

However, the baptism at Flers in September 1916, followed by Gough's
deployment at Thiepval and Beaumont Hamel in November, showed

some of the tanks' potential. But because so few of the Mark I's were being produced, they could only be used in small sections or 'penny packets' over a wide front. Nevertheless, Gough was impressed and noted, 'their co-operation in battle, under favourable circumstances, can be decisive'. But, it was unfortunate that the Report on the Reserve Army Tank Operations listed few defects. Apart from calling for the rear steering wheels to be removed, the report failed to offer constructive advice on tactics which did not bode well for future operations.[5]

The sheer physical presence of the tanks made a great impression on those seeing them for the first time, but it also tended to blind officers to their mechanical limitations:

They resemble some marine monster with caterpillar wheels. They seem to enjoy crunching over wire and trenches and we saw their path through a spinney where they'd simply levelled trees, 30" in diameter. Nice sort of pets to have in the house, but rather noisy! [6]

Among the tank visionaries at the time there was one man who set down on paper definite ideas about the purpose of tanks and how they should be used on the battlefield. Colonel Ernest Swinton was the 'father of tank tactics', and realised that, for tanks to be effective, they would have to be used en masse and in cooperation with the other arms of infantry, aircraft and artillery. He also liked to pronounce that he was the 'originator' of the tank, though this claim should be shared among several other notable pioneers such as Colonel Maurice Hankey, Commodore Murray Sueter and Winston Churchill. In fact no one individual could claim to be the 'inventor' of the tank, as it was a concept derived from many sources, including the original H. G. Wells short story, 'The Land Ironclads', in 1903. Tritton & Wilson subsequently designed the 'Mother' tank but, it would still be up to the 'Landships Committee', to develop its use.[7]

Swinton had published his 'Notes on the Employment of Tanks' and 'Tank Tips' in an effort to explain to GHQ the real potential of tank warfare. These notes were indeed visionary and explained how a breakout could be achieved using about 100 tanks. However, Swinton failed to take his projection further to convince GHQ how the breakout might be exploited. Perhaps he felt this was moving into the area of 'grand tactics' for which GHQ should be responsible, for they subsequently sidelined his proposals. GHQ felt his ideas were too ambitious, given that the production of tanks was proceeding at an alarmingly slow rate. Consequently, they produced their own slimmed down guidance notes which, in the short term, advocated that tanks should be employed as auxiliaries to the infantry, mainly in destroying enemy strongpoints.[8] Swinton became bitter about the rejection and believed his advice was being deliberately pigeon-holed. There was no question that his proposals were not buried, for even Hugh Elles, GOC Heavy Branch, later confirmed that he never saw Swinton's notes until 1918.[9] Writing to his old friend Edmonds after the war, Swinton raged:

My plan for the use of tanks en masse was carried out at Cambrai on 20/11/17, of which 3 (or 5) printed copies were sent out to G.H.Q. in March 1916, in order to tell the bloody fools something about the new machines, their powers and limitations. It was never sent onto the Tanks Corps. This action of GHQ is inexplicable except on the grounds that the Gen. Staff was not going to accept any advice from that bloody fellow Swinton. This was very largely Butler[10] but not entirely. My intrusion was resented from the beginning by most of GHQ, especially the 'cavalry spirit'. [11]

Swinton was reviving the old argument that some cavalrymen had a grudge against machines. Even H. G. Wells, in his prophetic story, had told of a newspaper headline warning of the perils of 'manhood versus machinery'.[12] But Swinton was incorrect in alleging that GHQ, as a body, was against tanks. They would continue to support mechanised warfare through to the final months of the war, but they would swing back behind the old infantry/artillery combination for the closing operations of 1918.[13] For the moment, there were elements who opposed Swinton's personal influence, but there is also much evidence to confirm that both Haig and his Chief of Staff in 1916, Lieutenant-General Kiggell, were impressed with the tanks, especially after their baptism in September 1916.[14] Conditions and battlefield tactics on the Western Front were evolving and some of Swinton's assumptions were being overtaken. For one thing, the terrain, in which the tank was designed to operate, was changing rapidly. Swinton had the 1915 Loos battlefield in mind when he devised his brief for the tank, but these conditions were already out of date because of the dramatic increase in artillery power. The battlefield of the Somme had received three times as many shells as Loos and, 'when the ground was dry, it was like aerated soft sand and when wet, it was a quagmire'.[15] Another problem, and one that highlighted Swinton's breakthrough dilemma, concerned the German defence system. In its simplest form, this shallow system originally comprised a front firetrench and rear support trench, with reserves to the rear. Should the tanks break through, they would by then be too weak and too few to exploit the breakthrough. A suitable force had still to be found for this.

After the Somme, the Germans were experimenting with a new 'elastic, defence in depth' which meant a deeper system going back some five miles and comprising trenches with inter-linked strongpoints and a 'killing ground', a trap for the attackers.[16] Achieving a breakthrough against this defence, let alone exploiting one, would thwart the ablest tactician.

Ultimately, the deepest concern, and one which Swinton stressed, continued to be the tanks' vulnerability to artillery fire:

Tanks will be destroyed by a direct hit of any type of howitzer shell. They will probably be put out of action by all except the most glancing hits of hi-explosive shells, fired by field guns. Since the chance of success lies with surprise, it follows that these machines should not be used in driblets.

The artillery should concentrate as heavy a counter-fire as possible on the enemy's main artillery position and on any field or light guns whose situation behind the first line is known. The necessity for the co-ordination of all arms to work together in the offensive generally requires no remarks here.[17]

The artillery commanders had their own ideas, but integrating their 'fire-plans' with tank operations was not a high priority. Even infantry commanders found it difficult to conceive that tanks, like machine-guns, should have a tactical logic of their own.[18]

It has been argued that, by using the first tanks too quickly in September 1916, Haig had sacrificed tactical surprise. However, it is difficult to see how improvements could have been made and new marks developed, unless the tank had first been subjected to battle conditions. No new fire-power technology comes to its units already tried, tested and perfected.[19]

While this debate was fizzing, what did the Germans make of it? The German OHL were far less interested in the possibilities of the tank than GHQ. They did not rush into tank production upon first sight of the Mark I's and neither did they hurry to develop serious anti-tank weapons. Their reaction was curiously rather lame. General Ludendorff, who had assumed joint command with Hindenburg in August 1916, seemed happy to rely for the moment on artillery as an antidote. 'For defence against tanks, the 06 field-gun which penetrated them, was sufficient; all we had to do was to turn it out in sufficient quantities.'[20] One other anti-tank weapon was the Mauser rifle, but this was unpopular with the troops for the large number of shoulders it broke, and it was not used in any quantities until 1918. However, the Austrian 'K' bullet, with a tung-sten-carbide core, had been used by German machine-gunners and snipers since 1915 against long-range targets and for penetrating sentry protection plates. These were occasionally used against tanks but their devastating effect against the boiler-plated Mark I and II was not realised until 1st Bullecourt in April 1917.

The Heavy Branch had grown out of the Machine Gun Corps and by the winter of 1916/17 had a full-blown staff. In England, Swinton the great pioneer had been removed as Administrative Commander and replaced by Brigadier-General F. Gore-Anley, an infantryman uninspired by tanks. Major J.F.C.Fuller, GSO2 of the new outfit, summed up his new Commander in typical style:

> I thought him a pleasant little man, the problem was in inverse ratio to his size. He may have been a good infantry Brigadier but he knew nothing about tanks. On one occasion I heard him say, 'Little Anley is like a small china pot, floating among a lot of big iron ones; little Anley is not going to get cracked'.[21]

Some of the 'big iron pots' had meanwhile established themselves beyond Anley's reach, at the new French HQ at Bermicourt. This Château had been a British billet in 1815. It lay just three miles away from another reminder of former glory – Agincourt. Despite its proximity, Evan Charteris, attached to HQ, was surprised that no one from the Heavy Branch ever visited the battlefield or commented on it. Perhaps the Staff Officers were preoccupied with their own fast-moving events. There was still no tank representative at GHQ and this probably added to the feeling among the Bermicourt staff that they were the ones to push the bounds of tank tactics. Commanded by Lieutenant-Colonel Hugh Elles, the Heavy Branch HQ had a Staff packed with fertile brains and combative spirits. Elles was the ideal choice to control the 'loose cannons' on the Staff and embody the young Branch with an *esprit de corps*. Major J.F.C Fuller and Captain Gifford Martel were in charge of Operations. Both men were intelligent advocates of tank warfare but both were very strong personalities and the old Château regularly shuddered with the sound of their arguments.[22]

'D' Battalion, one of the founding units of the Heavy Branch, was split into three companies, each fielding twelve tanks. The battalion was commanded by the charismatic Lieutenant-Colonel John Hardress Lloyd, described by Fuller as 'a man of big ideas' and a *beau sabreur* who always kept a good table and a fine stable. Hardress Lloyd had been with Gough on the Tirah expedition of 1897 and commanded the 1st Inniskillings at Gallipoli. He was certainly an excellent rider, having played polo for both England and Ireland before the war and this prowess still counted for something, even in a new technical arm like the Heavy Branch.[23] He was conversant with the latest in tank technology but his supreme confidence, whilst inspiring his men, would overstretch his battalion in the coming Spring offensive. Evan Charteris, based at Bermicourt, recalled:

> He [Lloyd] had a great vogue in the corps and was a chief favourite of Wills [Elles]. Tall, and the last word in 'smartness,' a polo player and big game shooter but with more character than brains. He was aware that his cards were not all trumps but that much could be done by bluff,

in legitimate tactical ways. A man of much practical common sense, not easily perturbed. In fact, it was not easy to imagine him bewildered either by what he could not understand or by the occurrence of unforeseen contingencies. When a bomb made a hole in the roof of his hut while he was in bed, his only comment to his aide-de-camp inquiring if he was all right was, 'Yes, as long as it doesn't rain'.[24]

Although Hardress Lloyd affected the manner of 'gentleman amateur', he should have been aware of the tank's handling ability and more importantly, its limitations. He had attended the Oldbury tank trials with Elles and collaborated with Fuller in tactical exercises.[25] As for the hardware that Lloyd would be controlling, there were only sixty Mark I training tanks in France at this time. However a large proportion of these were usually in the tank workshops at Erin, and this acute shortage of serviceable machines to practise on meant that improvisation was called for. In the lanes and fields around Blangy-sur-Ternoise, where No. 11 Company, D Battalion were billeted, strange shapes started appearing. Major William Watson recalled the 'pantomime' tanks:

A large canvas box was stretched over a wooden frame about six feet high, eight feet long and five feet wide. Little slits were cut in the side and six men got inside and lifted it by the cross-pieces. It would then waddle out of the gate to be surrounded by a mob of cheering children. Some were mounted on wagons drawn by mules with the crews tucked in with their Lewis guns. The contraption, a cross between a fire-engine and a triumphal car in the Lord Mayor's Show, would gallop past targets which the gunners would recklessly endeavour to hit.[26]

These charades, amusing though they were, caused concern among the senior commanders, who knew that time was running out for the arrival of new tanks. The Arras offensive was planned to start shortly. At the beginning of March 1917, the War Office had made assurances that, 'the 60 machines of Mark I, II and III are really practice machines (without armour plating) and will be returned as soon as they can be replaced by delivery of the new Mark IV'.[27] Major Albert Stern of the Landships Committee, who knew more than anyone about tank production, had heard these bland promises before. He sounded the alarm:

I consider it more than unwise to use practice Tanks in action under any circumstances. They have all the faults that necessitated the design of last year being altered to the present design of the Mark IV. In addition, the training of the men is being delayed by this action.[28]

Most of the officers and men of D Battalion, who had only begun their training in January 1917, were totally unaware of this production problem. Virtually all training had been carried out in mock-ups of the Mark II, for the few practice tanks that were available were used for the driving school. Consequently the crews had little idea about the environment inside a tank, let alone the protection they could expect. When they finally went into action, they never realised that it would be in practice tanks, which had no armour plating and hulls of 6mm and 9mm boiler plate. This plate would at best only afford protection against SAA and shrapnel.[29]

Lieutenant Hugh Swears, who was one of only two officers in No. 11 Company, 'D' Battalion to have ever seen action in a tank, lectured the young subalterns. 'The idea,' he wrote, 'is to train all the officers of the brigade in driving and mechanism – no light task as some of them don't know the first thing about it'.[30] Even the officer commanding No.11 Company, twenty-five-year-old Major William Watson, was 'a new boy'. He had just arrived from commanding a cyclist battalion and was bursting with new ideas and enthusiasm. He was assisted by his second-in-command, Captain Richard Haigh, late of the Royal Berkshires, who had already been wounded twice at Loos and on the Somme.

Since each of the company's tanks was usually commanded by a junior subaltern, drafts of 2nd Lieutenants were received during December 1916 and January 1917. Most were in their mid twenties, had received their commissions in the Kitchener Service Battalions and seen action with their infantry regiments on the Western Front.

It was hoped that each of these junior officers would bring some skills to No.11 Company. 2nd Lieutenant Harold Davies could lecture the men on the Lewis gun, which was now issued to tanks in place of the Hotchkiss. Lieutenant 'Fany' Field who had come from the artillery, gave instruction in the use of the 6 pounder gun and Lieutenant Eric Money, who had been with Watson in the Cyclists Corps, passed on his knowledge on mechanics. But for most of the others, like 2nd Lieutenant Harold Clarkson, their experience was almost exclusively as infantry officers. Clarkson had been wounded with the Northumberland Fusiliers on the first day of the Somme and 2nd Lieutenants Cuthbert Birkett (3rd Mons.), Arthur Bernstein (4/North Staffs.) and Hugh Skinner (3/Royal Scots) had all seen action in the trenches. As infantrymen, it was expected that these new tank commanders would have at least some skills of map-reading and navigation, but it soon became clear to Elles that they still had a lot to learn:

These commanders were completely overburdened with instructions ... It took weeks of training to instruct them in picking up landmarks. It is not a thing you can teach a boy by telling him; it requires a great deal of practice.[31]

Tank commanders had to learn to steer the tank by a primitive mechanism, direct the fire and command the crew within the tank, whilst maintaining contact with those outside. The wireless had yet to be put into tanks and so communication between the machine, tank section Commander and Battalion HQ could only be by Aldis Lamp and flag signals. These usually got lost in the heat of battle and, although pigeons were carried, it was only a one-way message to the brigade loft, several miles to the rear. So in practice, a 'volunteer' runner was chosen and it was a case of 'out through the sponson door and run like hell'.[32]

Crew training suffered because of lack of practice on real tanks. Davies, the Lewis gun instructor, could tell his men how to retract the gun inside the mock-up to avoid the casing being damaged by shellfire. But, unless they had practised this from inside a tank, they would not realise what an awkward and lengthy operation this was. So awkward in fact that, in action, most crews left their guns hanging out of the loopholes, where they were ripped open by incoming fire.[33] With the few real tanks available, the drivers found it difficult (despite the manufacturer's claims) to change gear without stopping the tank. The gunners on the 6 pounders were happy enough with this, as it allowed them to get a steady aim on their targets, but it was to prove a lethal defect in battle. The tank would become a sitting duck to enemy artillery, who could range on it at will. Had the time and tanks been available, the drivers and gearsmen could have been trained to keep the tank moving, and the gunners trained to fire on the move.[34]

Even before the lessons from the tank actions in 1916, it was recognised that it was essential for the infantry and artillery to liaise with the Heavy Branch in their training programmes.[35] Tank liaison officers from the 1st Brigade were supposed to be despatched to Divisions which they would be fighting with. Yet, the 'Report on Preliminary Training' shows that this link was a shambles:

> Section and Tank Commanders and NCOs attended some infantry attack rehearsals using banners marked 'Tank' to indicate positions of tanks. A few infantry officers, Divisional and Brigade Staff Officers, attended schemes carried out by Tank battalions. Some 'Notes on Tanks' giving a brief general description of tanks was issued from HQ Heavy Branch.[36]

Cooperation between arms was simply not given priority by either the Heavy Branch or infantry and artillery officers. And while much preference has been given in recent years to the concept of the tank as a 'neglected war winner', what was more important was the failure to recognise the role of the tank in the 'all-arms' doctrine.[37]

The endless boxing and soccer competitions, designed to promote *esprit de corps*, could have been sacrificed to learn one last important lesson. Travelling to the battlefield was a gruelling and frustrating business. During the latter stages of the battle of the Somme, the railway system in France had broken down and, despite the efforts of the newly formed DGT, moving a company of tanks from their base at Erin up towards the Arras front was a time-consuming job. As well as the problem of constant delays, new railheads and unloading ramps had to be constructed off the main network. Once off the railway, to avoid detection, the tanks drove at night. The tank commanders would then lead their tanks on foot by the aid of a lamp, averaging only 1½ mph cross country. The routes in original operations orders had to be reconnoitred beforehand and fuel dumps established ahead. There were usually three of these dumps along the way to the front line, containing petrol, oil, grease, ammunition and water, and as the tank only had an operating distance of twelve miles, these dumps were its lifeline. Tapes were then laid cross country for the drivers to follow. However, constant last-minute changes in a battle plan would throw all this organisation into chaos. It was therefore, extremely optimistic to expect reliable rallying times for these machines.[38]

The men of No.11 Company had, like their officers, come from a mix of regiments. Invariably from large families and industrial cities, most of the men had answered Kitchener's call and enlisted in their local regiment. Benjamin Bown was typical of them. One of ten children from a mining family in Nuneaton, Warwickshire, he had enlisted under age, in 1914. He passed through the Warwickshire Regiment and into the Machine Gun Corps where he was badly gassed. He then returned to the front, hoping that his short height and machine-gun skills would gain him a transfer to the 'Tanks'.[39] He was not disappointed. Together with Private Basil Gardner and Private Henry Leat, he was snapped up by the Heavy Branch in 1916. Leat himself was something of a celebrity within No. 11 Company, as he was one of the few 'tankers' to have been in action. He was in the crew of the first tank ever to go into battle at Flers-Courcelette on 15 September 1916.[40]

Of the others, a sprinkling of men had joined from the RFA and RHA to man the male tank 6 pounder guns. Most of the drivers came across from the Army Service Corps but the majority of the crews comprised infantrymen.[41]

In a crew of eight, two men were trained as left and right gearsmen. Crouching at the rear of the tank, they would in turn engage the gears when the commander banged on the engine casing. This had the effect of steering the tank by having one track in a high gear, the other in low. Heaving a lever, the commander could alter the direction by degrees, but the whole driving and steering operation was a thoroughly exhausting business. The engine and main gearbox were positioned in the middle of the tank with the driver and commander sitting up at the front. Both could look out forward through a hinged port, the commander instructing his driver by sharp taps on the shoulder. The driver, if he was lucky, could pick up speed to walking pace. Behind them, in the sponsons on either side of the tank, would be two machine gunners (in a female tank), or a 6 pounder gunner and his loader (in a male tank).[42]

Life inside the hull of the tank was noisy, dark and fume-filled. The arrival of the Mark II at the end of 1916 did little to improve the lot of the crew, or their combat effectiveness. Fifty Mark II's were rapidly produced to fill the demand for training tanks, whilst production of the improved Mark IV got under way. The Mark II looked very similar to its predecessor, except that the cab was slightly narrower and iron 'spuds' had been put onto its tracks to improve traction.

When it was realised that the Mark IV's would not be ready for the Arras Spring offensive, all eyes fell on the Mark II training tanks.[43] Together with a small number of Mark I veterans from the 1916 actions, they were to form the entire fighting force of the Heavy Branch. Sixty were scraped together for the whole Arras offensive of which Gough's Fifth Army received two old Mark I's and ten Mark II's.[44]

During March, constant shifts in the strategic plans with France and Italy meant tactical changes for the Arras front. The role of the tanks in the plan was being regularly reviewed. As No.11 Company were to play a special part in the coming offensive, operations orders from brigade HQ were coming at Hardress Lloyd thick and fast.[45] For the first time they were to use their tanks 'en masse' against the Siegfried Line, surrounding the stronghold of Bullecourt but, despite representations from Fuller, the allocation of twelve tanks to the Fifth Army was not to be increased.

Then, at the end of March, the limited training programme finished and No. 11 Company prepared to leave their billet in the old Abbey St Berthe. Many of the men scratched their names into the soft Abbey walls as a premature memorial. Private Basil Gardner, who was helping to pack the wagons, was handed a letter telling him his father, George, had died. However, all compassionate leave was cancelled and Gardner had to fall in for the long march up to the front. 2nd Lieutenant Harold Davies, his instructing done, was allocated a crew together with a male Tank, no. 799. He wrote in his diary. 'I have now joined the "Tanks". I wonder how it will all end?' It was his last entry.[46]

NOTES

1   de Mole Papers, AWM 43/206.
2   Geoffrey Malins, *How I filmed the War*, pref. xx.
3   Lieutenant Hugh Swears' tank was No. 712. He named it 'Dodo', after the pet name for his adoring younger sister, Swears Papers, Anne Davison.

4   Hugh Swears to his mother, 20 Sept. 1916, Swears Papers.
5   CAB 45/200, PRO; Gough, *The Fifth Army*, p. 147.
6   d'Arcy Legard to Major-General Hew Fanshawe, 22 Sept. 1916, Fanshawe Papers, PFC.
7   J. P. Harris, *Men, Ideas and Tanks: British Military Thought and Armoured Forces 1903-1939*, p.33-39.
8   'Notes on the Tactical Employment of Tanks 1916', WO 158/834, PRO.
9   Hugh Elles to Edmonds, CAB 45/200, PRO.
10   Lieutenant-General Sir Richard Butler, DCGS, a favourite of Haig's. Haig continually pushed for his appointment as CGS. It went to Kiggell instead, as Butler was not popular at home. Despite Swinton's 'swipe', Butler recommended the expansion of the Heavy Branch, LH 11/1935/72; lunch with Lloyd George and Hubert Gough, LH11/1936/31, Liddle Hart Papers, KCL.
11   II/5/12a in file 2/5/1a-22, Edmonds Papers, KCL.
12   *The Strand Magazine*, 1903; The Tank Corps Journal, May 1919.
13   T.H.E. Travers, *How The War Was Won – Command and Technology in the British Army on the Western Front 1917-18*, p.145-174.
14   Harris, *Men, Ideas and Tanks*, p. 70-72.
15   Elles to Edmonds, 4/9/34, CAB 45/200, PRO.
16   For an analysis of this system, see Timothy Lupfer, *The Dynamics of Doctrine: Changes in German Tactical Doctrine during World War I* ; Harris, *Men, Ideas and Tanks*, p. 89-90.
17   'Notes on the Employment of Tanks', E. Swinton, Stern Papers, KCL.
18   Travers, *The Killing Ground*, p. 73.
19   Sir Eustace d' Eyncourt to Edmonds, 7/5/35, CAB 45/200, PRO; Bidwell & Graham, *Fire Power, British Army Weapons and Theories of War*, p.68-69.
20   General Erich Ludendorff, *My War Memories, Vol.II*, p.337.
21   Colonel J.F.C. Fuller, *Memoirs of an Unconventional Soldier*, p. 93.
22   Captain the Hon. Evan Charteris, *HQ Tanks*.
23   Fuller, *Memoirs of an Unconventional Soldier*, p.94; Capt. E. Miller, *Modern Polo (1911)*.
24   Charteris, *HQ Tanks*.
25   WO95/91, PRO.
26   Major W.H.L. Watson, *A Company of Tanks*, p.23; also Archie Richards to author; letters & recollections, Sergeant D. Dennison (family collection).
27   In fact no Mark IIIs ever went to France.
28   Stern to Dr Addison 12/3/17, Albert Stern, *Log-book of a Pioneer*.
29   Examination by the author of the numerous tank parts found on the battlefield, shows that most plate was riddled with 'K' ammunition rounds.
30   Swears to his mother 3/1/17, Swears Papers.
31   Elles to Edmonds 4/9/34, CAB/200, PRO.
32   Author's interview with ex Tank NCO, Edward Wakefield, 5/11/93.
33   Minutes of Heavy Branch Conference 26/4/17, WO95/91, PRO.
34   'Report on Tank Operations 9-13 April 1917', WO95/91, PRO. The Heavy Branch had used the 6 pdr sparingly. In Gough's allocation of 6 tanks for the attack at Martinpuich (15/9/16) not one of his 3 male tanks fired its guns, Reserve Army Summary, CAB 45/200, PRO.
35   GHQ to Reserve Army, 16/8/16, OB/83, CAB 45/200, PRO.
36   'Report on Preliminary Training with Infantry', WO95/91, PRO.
37   *Battle Tactics of the Western Front*, p.6.
38   *Army Quarterly*, July 1924, p.304; Harris, *Armoured Warfare*, p.11.

39 Interview with M. Drakeley and Clara Hayles (sister of Ben Bown).
40 Commanded by Captain Harold Mortimore, tank no. 765 did excellent work near Delville Wood before being put out of action. For a detailed account of the battle, see Trevor Pidgeon, *The Tanks at Flers*.
41 Research into the background of No.11 Company casualties reveals that over 75% were ex infantrymen, with little or no mechanical experience.
42 'Arras Operations Report-Tank Design', WO95/91, PRO; author's interview with tank NCO Edward Wakefield, 5/11/93; also David Fletcher, *Landships*, p.16-19.
43 WO 161/24, PRO. Tank development was accelerating but production could not keep pace. The Mark IV's would not arrive in France until the end of April 1917. On 1/2/17, the 'Whippet' light tank was tested at Lincoln, attaining a speed of 7.7 mph. It would be 1918 before it saw action.
44 *RTC Journal*, Feb. 1934; Tank serial register,Bovington Tank Museum (hereafter TM); Brigadier-General C. Baker-Carr, *From Chauffeur to Brigadier*, p.216.
45 1st Brigade HBMGC, Daily Operations Orders, March/April 1917, WO 95/91, PRO.
46 H. P. Davies, Private Papers.

CHAPTER IV

The Advance to Bullecourt

While tank training was under way in France, out in the English Channel the German U-Boats were hunting. They could now gorge themselves on any prey since Ludendorff had declared unrestricted U-Boat warfare on 1 February. Commanders like Ernst Hashagen would no longer have to exercise restraint against neutral shipping, recording in his War Log:

2.00 am. Wind W.N.W., fresh breeze. Dived for attack. Took up position for stern attack. Enemy altered course too short a time before the shot. Retired at 10 fathoms.

3.30 am. Surfaced, got ahead again and dived for second attack. Wind W.N.W. Light breeze. Clear. Fired from No. 2 tube, range 800 metres, track angle 80 deg.; hit aft.

3.40 am. Surfaced to give vessel a second torpedo.

4.00 am. Vessel sinking noticeably by the stern and listing heavily to starboard. Did not fire again. Left her sinking. Vessel was a large freight steamer deeply laden, apparently British: [1]

These early months of 1917 saw an alarming rise in the toll of allied shipping. The U-Boats had sunk 24,000 tons in January and during February they sank a further 115,000 tons.[2] There were now five times as many U-Boats as in 1915, and the English Channel and Mediterranean had become infested with them. This state of affairs was causing grave concern in London, where Admiral Jellicoe, the First Sea Lord, warned that, if the wastage continued, Britain could be forced to the peace table by the summer of 1917.[3] It was an alarming prospect and there seemed little hope that the threat from either enemy U-Boats or surface ships could be countered.

However Ludendorff needed to buy time while he starved Britain into submission and before America was drawn into the war. That meant stalling allied pressure on the Western Front, for what he feared most of all was a continuance in 1917 of the draining battles of the Somme. The British artillery, despite its poor showing in certain battles, did inflict serious damage on the German infantry. Ludendorff realised that he did not have the resources for the *materialschlacht* (battle of material) if Haig persisted with his 'wearing-down' policy.[4] Defeats in the field were looking increasingly likely, especially after such shocks as Verdun in December 1916, when a relatively junior French commander, General Robert Nivelle launched a brilliant and successful counter-attack. If the German front line troops continued to be drawn into prolonged combat, revolution in the streets of Berlin could well finish the job for the Allies.

Ludendorff's official title was Quartermaster-General, but in the German Army this meant far more than the mundane responsibility for supply. While his partner, Field-Marshal Paul von Hindenburg provided the authority and gravitas, Ludendorff contributed the tactical genius. He devised a plan whereby the German army could retreat twenty-five miles to a new defensive position, which would effectively straighten out the bulge in the German line, by getting rid of the twenty-seven-mile-long Noyon salient and thereby save at least ten divisions, which could then be used for a reserve against the anticipated British Arras offensive.[5] It was a brave departure from the idea, prevalent on both sides, that possession of territory was paramount, whatever its value. On the British side, Major-General Neill Malcolm, Gough's Chief of Staff had issued a memo to all units of the Fifth Army:

> It is conceded that preparation must be thorough and careful, but once that condition has been fulfilled, it must be impressed on all leaders that rapidity, energy and offensive action are now of the utmost importance to our cause. <u>Every yard of ground gained has great consequence, both material and moral.</u>[6]

Malcolm felt that this policy was vindicated when Gough pulled off a well rehearsed plan in November 1916, to capture Beaumont Hamel and the rest of the Thiepval ridge. Likewise, German troops were exhorted 'not to abandon one foot of ground and if one foot is lost, to retake it by immediate counter-attack at all costs.'[7] This obsession with holding ground at all costs was debated fiercely within the German OHL (High Command) during the winter of 1916/17. Eventually, the 'Here I stand and here I die' school of thought lost out to those who favoured more flexible ideas of defence and this enabled Ludendorff to put his overall plan for the *Ganzer Entschluss* ('great decision') into effect. [8]

First Ludendorff had to organise the construction of the rear defence line. In fact it was to be a number of trench systems, each acting as a brake to check the Allied advance. With his grim humour, Ludendorff named these constructions after characters in his favourite cycle of operas, Wagner's Ring. However he completely missed the irony of his choice, involving as it does, a tale which shows how the lust for power destroys those who strive to possess it.[9]

The main and most famous trench line was called the Siegfried Stellung ('Siegfried Position'), which the British later called the 'Hindenburg

Line'. Work had started on this massive civil engineering project in September 1916, using 12,000 German and 3,000 Belgian labourers and, in clear contravention of the Hague Rules, 50,000 Russian prisoners of war.[10] It stretched for eighty-five miles, running from Arras, down through St Quentin to the Aisne, just east of Soissons. Containing numerous deep dugouts, tunnels, gun emplacements and vast stretches of barbed wire entanglements, it was a formidable project. But it was so ambitious that it could not be completed by the end of 1916 and bad frosts in January 1917 stopped concrete construction altogether. Many of the planned concrete gun emplacements, especially surrounding Bullecourt, were never completed and their concrete foundations continued to confuse British aerial reconnaissance.[11]

Meanwhile, in order to provide a second line of defence facing Arras, the Wotan Line was traced on 4 November 1916, to branch off from the Siegfried Line at the village of Quéant and run north behind the old 1915 battlefields of Vimy and Loos. Work was not expected to begin on this branch until Siegfried was finished, and the final completion of Wotan was not expected before March 1917. Also known as the Drocourt-Quéant 'switch line', it was to lie just to the west of the plain surrounding Douai, a strategic town for the Germans, where Baron Manfred von Richthofen and his famous *Jagdstaffel* ('hunting squadron') were based. The close proximity of this airfield seriously hampered attempts by the RFC to monitor the progress of the German lines.

However, the Wotan Line had some serious defects. It was sited under the tactically important foothills near the villages of Chérisy, Monchy and Roeux. Should these fall to the British, then they would provide excellent artillery observation positions for bombarding the Wotan Line from the west. The other danger for the Germans was the junction of the Siegfried and Wotan Lines near the villages of Quéant and Bullecourt. If the British attacked from the south and occupied this axis, they could 'roll' up the Wotan Line at the same time.

This was exactly what the British had in mind for a Spring offensive. As they had gradually advanced eastwards on the Somme, so they had pinched the enemy into a bulge between the Somme and Arras. The Allied plan was for the Third Army to attack Arras, while the Fifth Army worked up from the south and cut off the German army in the bulge. Gough's Fifth Army was to strike 'as strong and vigorous a blow as possible', on the front between Gueudecourt and Beaumont Hamel, breaking the enemy's line in the direction of Achiet-le-Grand and attracting his reserves. The sole purpose of this operation was to facilitate Allenby's Third Army attack around Arras, planned for 15 March. Then, as a second objective, the Fifth would join hands with the Third Army near St Léger and envelop the enemy.[12] The Germans would be put under further pressure by the French attacking simultaneously on the Aisne.

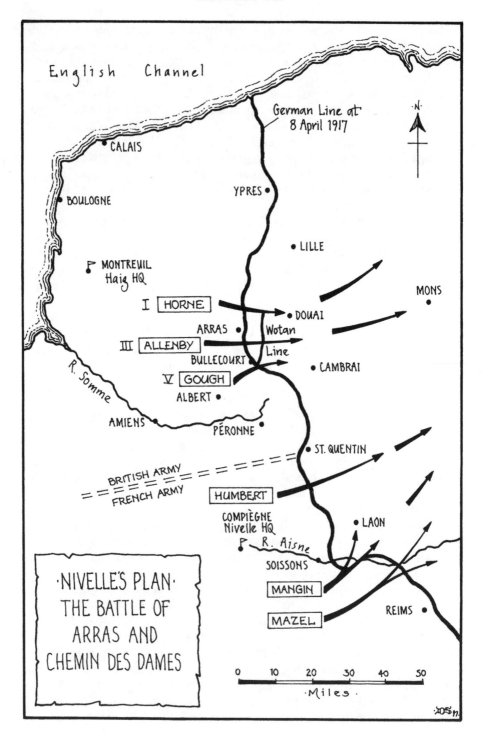

·NIVELLE'S PLAN·
THE BATTLE OF
ARRAS AND
CHEMIN DES DAMES

Gough was pushing on in February, using his British V Corps and I ANZAC Corps in a series of small but bitter village clearing operations at the bottom of the Ancre valley. During the evening of 24 February, the relative peace of the 187th Brigade dugout was shattered by the sudden arrival of the Army Commander. Gough, with Malcolm in tow, was making one of his regular rounds of the line and had come to see the GOC, Brigadier-General Taylor.

Gough, who was in a jocular but impatient mood, was keen to hear the day's patrol reports. He was astonished to learn that a company of the 2/4th York & Lancasters had covered 1,000 yards towards the stronghold of Serre, without challenge from the enemy.[13] This confirmed other similar reports that the Germans were withdrawing wholesale and on a wide front. How far back they would retreat Gough was not sure, but he immediately ordered Lieutenant-General Fanshawe, GOC V Corps, to maintain contact with the enemy by pushing forward strong patrols towards Pusieux and Pys.[14] Such was the extent of the German retreat that, by nightfall on the 25th, the enemy's old defensive front running from Gueudecourt to west of Serre was occupied by British troops.

In fact, the *Ganzer Entschluss,* codenamed 'Alberich' after the spiteful dwarf in *Das Nibelunglied,* had been underway for some weeks. The operation was controlled by Crown Prince Rupprecht, Commander of the Northern Group of Armies. Son of King Louis III of Bavaria, Rupprecht was fond of recounting that, as a descendant of Charles I and head of the House of Stuart, he was the rightful heir to the British Throne. However, despite his imperial air, he was a competent tactician and was always determined to prove himself against the Prussian dominated OHL. He delegated his Chief of Staff, General von Kuhl, to supervise the plan for the withdrawal, which allowed thirty-five days from 9 February for the removal of all material and artillery back behind the new Siegfried Position. Then, on 16 March, the infantry would be allowed three 'marching days' to get back, whilst covered by rearguards. The whole retreat was to be carried out by bounds from one defence line back to the next, with the OHL directive that German engineers and sappers were to lay waste the territory given up.

Von Kuhl promptly gave the order that all buildings were to be razed, trees felled and roads ruined. In fact anything that could give succour to an advancing enemy, such as water and food supplies, was to be destroyed. Although this would have created a wasteland little different to parts of the Somme, Rupprecht erupted when he heard of the order, fearing that such destruction would be a bad public relations exercise.[15] However it was the resulting breakdown in discipline that caused concern among the German officers. Ernst Jünger, a lieutenant with the 73rd Hanoverian Fusiliers, was horrified by the effect on the troops' discipline:

Every village up to the Siegfried Line was a rubbish heap. Every tree felled, every road mined, every well fouled, every cellar blown up or made into a death-trap with concealed bombs, all rails ripped up, everything burnable burned. In short, an orgy of destruction was going on. The men were chasing round with incredible zeal, arrayed in the abandoned wardrobes of the population, in women's dresses and with top hats on their heads. [16]

Secrecy was nonetheless important, and the forced transportation of 126,000 civilians from the area had to be left as late as possible. Troops were not to be told until the last minute and air defences were strengthened to limit allied observation. The Dutch border was closed and false rumours spread about a German offensive. To reinforce this deception, Amiens and other important railway stations were bombed in early February.[17] In the end, the operation would only be successful if the Germans continued to offer stubborn rearguard resistance, to slow the British advance and allow the Siegfried and Wotan Lines to be completed.

The enemy plan certainly succeeded in throwing the British off balance. Further disruption awaited Haig when he attended an Anglo-French conference at Calais on 26 February. At this meeting, General Robert Nivelle, the recently promoted French Commander-in-Chief, managed to assume overall command of the allied forces. He did this with the connivance of the British Prime Minister, David Lloyd George, with the result that the main offensive would now be the French assault on the Chemin des Dames. The British would play a subsidiary role in their offensive at Arras, aimed at drawing the German reserves away from the French. After much wrangling, it was agreed that Haig would only be subordinate to Nivelle for the duration of the Arras/Aisne offensive.[18]

However, these changes in strategic planning did not alter the main tactical problem facing Gough in the field. He still did not know how far the enemy would retire. When they eventually stopped and dug in, he would have to be up with them to launch an attack to assist Allenby's Arras offensive. Because GHQ were unsure of enemy intentions, they could not give clear orders to Gough as to what sort of operations were in store and his role became confused. Writing a memorandum to Kiggell on 3 March, Gough stated: 'I shall be able to employ the bulk of my troops in a vigorous offensive against the enemy's rearguards, should it be decided that this is the correct role for my Army.'[19] One week later, Kiggell still had to admit that GHQ didn't know what the enemy was up to, or whether or not the British should speed up their offensive actions.[20]

GHQ might be making conflicting noises to its Fifth Army Commander, but he was pressing on. For all this uncertainty, 'Goughie' relished a challenge and was now in his element. The cavalryman was on the scent, in open country for the first time in a year and he was not going to lose the enemy by hanging back. He was certainly not going to be cautioned by his Staff:

> The German withdrawal worked General Gough to a pitch of feverish energy. His general instructions were – 'Everyone to push ahead hard'. I got myself disliked by suggesting that we should co-ordinate our advance with that of Third and Fourth Armies, but he would have none of this. Until we were established in the H.L., the operations of Fifth Army were characterised by the same method of 'On Brave Boys', without real co-ordination of formation.[21]

To the 'brave boys' of the 62nd (West Riding) Division, this pursuit was their first taste of warfare and they found it exhilarating. They had only landed in France on 13 January, together with another 2nd Line Territorial Division, the 58th (London), to boost the number of British divisions to sixty five.

Although the Yorkshiremen had been formed into a division as long ago as the summer of 1915, the cream of their officers and men had been transferred to the first line 49th West Riding Division. The men who remained in the 62nd were nonetheless hardy and spirited. They had been drawn from the mills, furnaces and mines of the great Yorkshire industrial cities of Sheffield and Bradford, as well as from the farmlands between Leeds and York. They were well aware that the smarter, regular 7th Division in V Corps considered them the 'country cousins' and they were keen to prove themselves quickly.

The 62nd Division was commanded by Major-General Walter Braithwaite, who had been 'treading water' in England following his return from the disastrous Gallipoli campaign in 1915. There had been much criticism of Braithwaite's autocratic style as Hamilton's Chief of Staff during the debacle and he was fortunate to pick up a subsequent divisional command, even if it was with the 'Pelicans'.[22] He owed that to Sir Douglas Haig, who pushed his Chief of Staff, Kiggell, to lobby the War Office in London, to send Braithwaite out to France as soon as possible:

> Would there be any chance of getting Braithwaite out? The Chief would be very glad to get him and I am writing with his permission to ask if there is any hope of being able to do so. Our idea would be to arrange an exchange, giving you someone with experience.[23]

Quite why Haig was so determined to acquire a divisional commander with little knowledge of the Western Front, at the expense of an experienced man, remains a mystery. Haig certainly rated Braithwaite from the time the latter came onto his staff, when he was Director of Military Training. Haig would also have remembered Braithwaite's contribution to the Haldane Army reforms.[24] But, his later record at Gallipoli, culminating in a hasty return with Hamilton in October 1915, was controversial. Charles Bean privately fumed at Braithwaite's 'arrogance' as Chief of Staff on the expedition, but later published an appreciation of him stating he was 'steeped in the principles of sound tactics and procedure'.[25] Bean's fellow Australian, Keith Murdoch, never revised his opinion of Braithwaite whom he derided in his notorious report to the Australian Prime Minister. With the Dardanelles Report being published on 10 March 1917, it may have been expedient to have Braithwaite tucked away in France. But with such enmity still smouldering in the Australian camp, he did indeed seem a strange choice to place beside I ANZAC Corps.

Described by one of his brigadiers as 'tall and lean, handsome with a hawk eye, immaculate in dress and manners', Braithwaite however carried a terrible personal burden. His only son, Valentine, had been reported 'missing, believed killed' at Beaumont Hamel on 1 July 1916. It was ironic that Walter Braithwaite was now in that same ruined and desolate spot eight months later. As his division advanced, he spent all his spare hours walking alone over the craters, hoping to find some trace of his son. It was a fruitless search, and like many bereaved parents of 'the missing', he turned to spiritualism to bridge the terrible void. [26]

Although Valentine Braithwaite was never found, there were countless sons of Britain and Australia still spread over the old Somme battlefields, unnamed and unburied. Sergeant Jack Bourke of the 8th Battalion, AIF was on the same quest, looking for his lost brother Geoff, as his unit advanced towards the front line:

> I have been over a great deal of the Somme battlefield and hundreds and hundreds of bodies lie still unburied – the poor fellows lie as they fell, for as they charged over these slopes and plains, there was no such thing as stopping – no time to bury a comrade, so for miles and miles, you will find them, all the one way with their heads towards the German trenches and face downwards as they fell. [27]

The hard frost of February had given way to wild and wet weather in March. The thaw turned the tracks and unmetalled roads to rivers of mud, reducing the advance of supplies and ammunition to a crawl. By demolishing all buildings in the retirement zone, the Germans had unwittingly provided a ready source of material to repair the roads. Frustratingly, the British engineers were still faced with a stalemate, for the traffic needed to bring up the road metal caused damage at the same rate that the pioneer gangs effected the road repairs.[28]

Without doubt, the biggest problem facing the Fifth Army was pushing the artillery forward. No large-scale attack could be contemplated without 'the heavies' in support, but the appalling state of the roads made their progress agonisingly slow. It was a problem not always appreciated by Staffs in the rear, as the GSO2 of II Corps found out:

> GHQ Staff telephoned to me angrily one night, complaining that our artillery was all behind schedule in moving up to the new area. My reply was that as all the 60 pounders were stuck in the mud on the old front, there were only two ways of getting them out, (1) by hitching on double teams of horses, which strained them and caused them to be unable to do the schedule marches on the following days, or (2) by dragging each gun out onto a metalled road with a caterpillar tractor. His reply was, 'I do not understand what you are talking about'.[29]

Even Gough and Malcolm had to be persuaded to come and see the mess for themselves. Ammunition had been ordered forward during February in preference to engineers' supplies and, now that the thaw had started, the guns had plenty of ammunition but were too far back to fire at anything. Haig soon realised this folly and priorities were reversed, but the delay was critical.[30]

Charles Repington, *The Times* correspondent, gossiped that Haig had told him to publish the line that Gough had got the Germans on the run, but 'off the record' he confided that with 14,000 horses short, Gough's advance was slowing.[31] And with many of the horse teams required to haul the larger guns and howitzers killed off by the hardest winter in memory, there were no replacements.

By 13 March, Fanshawe's V Corps had reached the outskirts of Bucquoy, the village protecting the left flank of the latest German defence line. The occupation of the village seemed a straightforward operation, like many in the last week. Aerial reconnaissance reported few enemy in the village, so Fanshawe ordered Major-General Barrow, commanding the 7th Division, to take it immediately. Brigadier-General Hanney Cumming, who was charged with carrying out the attack, was horrified to find from recent patrol reports that the mile-long village was strongly held, bristling with machine guns and protected by three belts of wire. He protested but was told to get on with it. The British preliminary bombardment went off three hours too early and then silence. The Germans scrambled out of their dugouts, settled into their positions and waited. The 91st Brigade attacked at zero hour and were cut to pieces, losing over 262 men while a sister brigade suffered 312 casualties. Two days later the Germans decided to withdraw.

Gough was furious with Barrow, the divisional commander, and 'marked his card' for his lukewarm approach to the whole operation.

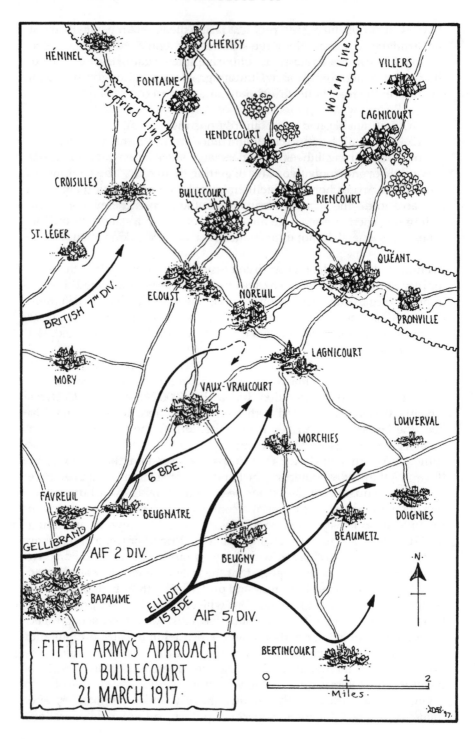

FIFTH ARMY'S APPROACH
TO BULLECOURT
21 MARCH 1917·

Barrow, a cavalryman, was very much an Allenby man having been his GSO1 in the 1st Cavalry Division and this hardly helped him in Gough's eyes. If Barrow failed to display 'offensive spirit' again, he would be out. Barrow's brigade commander, Cumming, was also in Gough's sights and any more arguing about future plans of attack would see him on a boat home. Bucquoy was bad for careers and, despite its limited objective, it was a demoralising check to Gough's progress.

Whilst the 1st and 4th Australian Divisions were taken out of the line for rest and training, the remaining 2nd and 5th Divisions were taking the advance beyond Bapaume. This was the Australians' first prolonged experience of open warfare and their success was entrusted to two of the most imaginative, but wilful, brigade commanders in the AIF

On the right, Major-General Hobbs of the 5th Division ordered Brigadier-General 'Pompey' Elliott to advance his 15th Brigade, supported by some field artillery and light horse towards Morchies and Beaumetz. It was vital that he didn't outdistance his support, in case the enemy suddenly counter-attacked and swamped the isolated advance guards. The same rules applied to Brigadier-General Gellibrand, advancing his 6th Brigade on the left towards Vaulx-Vraucourt. By the evening of 18 March the German 26th Reserve Division had evacuated Vaulx and Gellibrand quickly covered the two miles from Bapaume to occupy the ruined village. He was now the nearest commander to the enemy lines.

Gough was looking to thrust forward, and on receipt of intelligence reports that fires were burning beyond the Siegfried Line, he ordered the Lucknow Cavalry Brigade on the Army's left flank to chase the Germans out of Ecoust St Mein and Croisilles, two miles away. Gellibrand's 6th Brigade was to support the cavalry and push the Germans back to the Line. Gough believed these fires resulted from more villages being destroyed and that the Germans were withdrawing even farther back beyond the Siegfried Line. He wanted to 'wrong foot' them before they were ready to leave.

After Gough paid a personal visit to the front on 19 March, his Army Staff telephoned I ANZAC Corps urging them on towards Lagnicourt and Noreuil, but fatally without detailing the measure of force to be used. ANZAC Corps passed the message on to 2nd Division Staff who, still without a written order, passed it on to Gellibrand. He took it as an order to attack without delay; after all, 'where the divisional HQ are concerned: they know my views that the harder the Bosch are pushed, the better for us in eventual casualties'.[32]

The village of Noreuil was some two miles directly ahead of Gellibrand's column and, like its neighbouring villages of Lagnicourt on the right and Ecoust St Mein on the left, it lay at the head of a shallow valley. Gellibrand's plan was to steal up the spurs that ran between the villages and, using his young engineer Gilchrist as a guide, the leading company would encircle Noreuil. The twenty-eight-year-old Gilchrist had already made a name for himself and was one of Gellibrand's most trusted men. He had been responsible for mining operations at Lone Pine, Gallipoli and had since won the MC at Pozières. Noreuil, however, was supposed to be 'a sitter' and after the failure of a previous creeping barrage before the attack on Grevillers, Gellibrand decided to dispense with any artillery cover. [33]

On 20 March, Gellibrand's Victorian troops set off into the cold, drizzly night to attack the village. But one raiding party after another ran into enemy traps and as dawn broke, Captain Gilchrist telephoned Gellibrand to tell him the position was hopeless. The botched attack cost thirteen officers and 318 men and even Gellibrand's close friend Bean could not condone his gamble.[34] Brudenell White concluded that:

Dear old Gelly had one of those contrary fits, which periodically affected him, and he rushed into it. He had a similar 'going bush' with Bridges once and it looked like being serious. He is a soldier of rare quality but some contrariness which caused him on odd occasions to take up impossible attitudes.[35]

Gellibrand confessed privately to Bean that it had been a nightmare but urged the Official Historian to mention that 'the 6th Brigade took the chances in a decent Godfearing sort of Victorian way'. [36]

This abortive attempt on Noreuil cost Gellibrand the full confidence of the senior Anzac command. White would remain loyal to his old friend 'Jellybean', but thereafter Birdwood always harboured doubts about him. Bean observed:

Birdwood and White make no allowances for anything but success – are inclined to open their eyes at the casualties. But if you say you 'want Noreuil & Lagnicourt & Longatte [Ecoust] occupied' you cannot expect this to happen without the risk of casualties. If you don't try hard, they blame you quite rightly. If you do make a serious attempt there is no royal road for avoiding casualties – I daresay White could plan these things to happen without casualties if he had time, which Gelly hadn't. Birdwood couldn't. [37]

The rebuff at Noreuil was enough to slow Gough down. Some days before, General Godley had reported him 'flourishing and quite fat', but now he was in a more subdued mood. On the evening of the 20th, when the full casualties were known and reports digested, Gough called a Corps Commanders' conference at his HQ, a red brick building, patched with sacking and boards, in the town of Albert. As Birdwood, Fanshawe and their staffs were arriving, to the north-east the first British 4.5mm howitzer shells were landing on Bullecourt, the nearest part of the Siegfried Line. Gough's advance columns were within three miles of the Line, so he decided that his role in the Arras offensive could be expanded. In addition to providing just artillery support to the Third Army on his left, he felt he was strong enough to press an infantry attack on the Siegfried Line itself. The best point for the Fifth Army attack was at Bullecourt, where he could penetrate the Siegfried Line and also turn the Wotan Line. To get there, he would first have to take the string of outpost villages directly in front. However Gellibrand's 'bloody nose' at Noreuil convinced him that caution was required for the home straight:

> Preparatory to attacking the Hindenburg Line, guns to be brought up and attacks thoroughly prepared. It is evident that we cannot 'rush' the defence any further than we have now done.[38]

Such caution, however, did not sit easily with 'Pompey' Elliott, the commander of the Australian column advancing on the right. The swashbuckling brigadier may have been an avid student of military history but rarely felt himself constrained by military convention. Bean noted:

> He is a regular Napoleon – and an optimist. He has little judgement. As they say – he puts his big thumb on the map (and his thumb covers about 3 miles of country) and says, 'My men will take that', without realising that he is committing them to the work of an Army Corps.[39]

This one-time Melbourne solicitor had nevertheless earned the respect and devotion of his men to the extent that they would follow him anywhere. He combined a massive frame with fierce independence, but this did not always endear him to higher command. He had clashed with Birdwood over the selection of his battalion commanders in March 1916, and a further, more serious argument followed with White after a disastrous attack near Flers, in October 1916. He was constantly at odds with Birdwood and White.[40] However, Elliott and Gellibrand were allotted their tasks because of their records as hard-driving and ingenious commanders. Like Gough, they still had to be kept on a tight rein in open country.

Elliott, working up the right wing, was four miles beyond Bapaume and weaving his 59th and 60th Battalions around the forward villages of Morchies and Beaumetz. He promptly collected another reprimand from Birdwood over his occupation of Bertincourt, a village on his right flank which lay in the neighbouring Fourth Army sector. He had wanted to secure it before attacking Beaumetz but failed to notify his divisional commander, Hobbs, that he was going to attack it. Nor did he notify the British XIV Corps HQ, whose cavalry was closing on the village.

Fortunately the cavalry didn't attack but Elliott was shocked by the reaction of his superiors:

Gen. Birdwood resented this in the most extraordinary manner. I visibly remember being well straffed by Gen. White. He used the expression which I resented and still resent very much, viz – 'You will have to learn to modify your Napoleonic ideas'.[41]

By 22 March, Elliott was in possession of Beaumetz. But that night the Germans counter-attacked and drove out the Australians. Brudenell White recalled that Elliott could 'erupt like a volcano' if events didn't go as he wanted them to, and this situation was no exception. Elliott was furious at the audacity of the enemy. 'I'll teach these beggars to leave me alone', he stormed, and promptly ordered an attack for the following morning on Doignies and Louveral.[42]

Eight hours later it was daylight and the two villages just over a mile in front could be clearly seen. It was obvious that they formed part of the string of outpost defences, but Elliott's blood was up and he intended to attack without flank or artillery support. At first he even refused to inform Hobbs of his plan of attack, but a subordinate forced him to relent. When Hobbs was notified of the plan, he immediately cancelled the un-supported attack and tore up to the front line to find Elliott. It would have finished Elliott's career on the spot, had Birdwood found out, but Hobbs needed him to finish the immediate task and declined to report the incident. Thereafter Elliott was passed over for the divisional command he so dearly longed for and he never forgave Birdwood or White.[43]

The advance to the Siegfried Line was proving costly, not only in men and time but also in military reputations. The discord among senior commanders was not just among the Australians. On the left of the Fifth Army advance, Gough was becoming impatient with the slow progress of Major-General Barrow's British 7th Division attempting to take the outpost villages of Ecoust and Croisilles.

Barrow, who had earned Gough's displeasure over Bucquoy, was not happy about advancing 1,200 yards across open country under the eyes of an enemy well dug in behind uncut wire. So he delayed the attack while he arranged meetings with the commander of the adjacent 58th Division, Major-General Hew Fanshawe, to organise artillery support.

Gough was furious when he found out and accused Barrow of 'fussing about'. He told him to attack Croisilles immediately. Despairing, Barrow put in Cumming and his 91st Brigade, but the two battalions of South Staffordshires and Manchesters failed to take the village.[44]

It was the familiar story of not enough time for preparation. Gough, however, was not minded to listen to excuses especially from a faint heart like Barrow. He sacked him straightaway, sending him home to England.

Had it not been for Barrow's influential friends in England, including the CIGS Sir William Robertson, he would have been one more smouldering enemy of Gough. Barrow was eventually found a job in Palestine but, there was a clear warning to his successor, Major-General Thomas 'Harry Tate' Shoubridge.[45] He came into the line on 29 March, under no illusion that the Army Commander would tolerate anyone failing to show 'offensive spirit'. Nor was the message lost on Major-General Hew Fanshawe:

> One cannot help feeling as David Campbell [GOC 21st Division] said when he told me about Barrow having been sent home – we all feel that we are sitting on a volcano out here. I have just heard that we are to go to H. Gough – I wonder how long I shall last.[46]

To be fair to Gough, the relentless pressure he was applying could well bring dividends. The Germans were working flat out to complete the Siegfried Position and, if Gough could reach it before they made it impregnable, he stood a chance of breaching it. And while there is no doubt that Gough induced fear in many divisional and brigade commanders, fear was always an element in command and Gough had a better grasp of the concepts of command than many generals on the Western Front. Brigadier-General Carruthers, who had been with Haig in India, recalled that the C in C (Haig) could inspire more dread in regular soldiers than Kitchener and they could be panic stricken in his presence. Although this fear existed in the German Army, any defeat in the field was usually followed by the dismissal of the most senior staff officer, rather than the GOC. A general could only be removed after consent from the Kaiser, which was inevitably complicated.

There was also another reason why Gough had to turn in a high profile performance. During this period of political intriguing, he was talked about as a possible successor to Haig should the latter fall foul of Lloyd George. Lord Esher, the aesthetic and well informed founder of the CID, noted:

> The talk was that Lloyd George had come over to France to put Douglas Haig under Nivelle; that D.H. would in all probability go, and that Gough would be Commander-in-Chief.[47]

To be in the picture at all, Gough had to ensure that his Fifth Army was far enough forward to assist the Third. Failure to provide that support by zero hour on 8 April would leave the Third Army's right flank hanging in the air and it was Gough who would be responsible.[48]

It was not a situation he was ready to contemplate.

NOTES

1   Ernst Hashagen, *Log of a U-Boat Commander*, p.67.
2   Sir Leo Money, *Table of Losses-British Steamships*,15/2/7.1, Liddell Hart Papers, KCL.
3   Crutwell, *A History of the Great War*, p. 381.
4   Lupfer, *Dynamics of Doctrine*, p.7.
5   The original impetus for this troop reduction came from Lieutenant-General Fuchs at the German Western Front conference, Cambrai, 8 Sept. 1916., *Militär Wochenblatt* 27 Feb. 1937.
6   AWM 25 305/1.
7   General von Falkenhayn, *Der Weltkrieg 1914 bis 1918*, Vol.X p.355.
8   Foreword to *The Principles of Command in the Defensive Battle*, 1 Dec. 1916, translated by Gen. Staff Intell. BEF 1/1/18, IWM.
9   Wagner adapted the old folk tale, *Das Nibelunglied*. Some of the limited number of German tanks produced in 1918 were also named after its heroes – Siegfried (no.525) Hagen (no.543) and Wotan (no.563).
10   Captain Wynne, The Hindenburg Line, *Army Quarterly*, Jan. 1939.
11   *Der Weltkrieg*, Vol. XII, p. 164.
12   OAD 258 issued by GHQ, Appendix 6, Military Operations, Vol. I, 1917.
13   Everard Wyrall, *History of 62nd (West Riding) Division*, p.22; *Military Operations 1917*, Vol. I, p.96 The credit for the very first report on 22 February must go to Lieutenant F. L. Lucas (7/R. West Kents) II Corps, who observed the crest near Miraumont had been evacuated, Jonathan Nicholls, *Cheerful Sacrifice*, p.7.
14   Fifth Army Operation Order no.44, 10.15 pm. 24 Feb. 1917, WO95/519, PRO.
15   Field-Marshal Crown Prince Rupprecht, *Mein Kriegstagebuch*, p. 118.
16   Ernst Jünger, *Storm of Steel*, p.126. Jünger became one of the most influential writers of the later Weimar period.
17   *Der Weltkrieg*, Vol. XII. p. 196.
18   II/4, Clive Papers, KCL; VI/3, Kiggell Papers, KCL.
19   'Mem. on Future Operations by Fifth Army', 3 March 1917, WO 95/519, PRO.
20   OAD 329 to all Army Commanders 10 March 1917, WO 95/519, PRO.
21   E.M.Birch (GSO1 Fifth Army) to Edmonds, 22/7/37, CAB 45/116 (B), PRO.
22   The emblem of the 62nd Division was a pelican.
23   Kiggell to Lieutenant-General F. Davies (Military Sec. War Office), 19 Sept. 1916, V/44/108, Kiggell Papers, KCL.
24   John Terraine to author, 8/3/95.
25   C. E. W. Bean, *The Story of Anzac, Vol. I* , p.231.
26   Brigadier R.C. Foot, 'Reminiscence', 86/57/1, IWM.
27   Lieutenant Bourke Papers, Feb. 1917, File 12/11/845, AWM 1DRL/0139.
28   Gilbert Frick to Cyril Falls, 16/2/39, CAB 45/116, PRO.
29   Lieutenant-Colonel Lord Stanhope to Falls, 27/11/38, CAB 45/116, PRO. For an appreciation of the problems facing artillery commanders, see Griffith, *British Fighting Methods in the Great War*, p.34-39.
30   Montgomery to Falls, 7/7/37, CAB 45/116, PRO.
31   Charles Repington, *The First World War 1914-1918*, Vol I, p.535.
32   Gellibrand to Bean, 30 March 1930, AWM 3DRL 606 Item 260 (1). Gellibrand, in his comments on the Official History, concludes that the 2nd Division staff work was at fault and that there was no excuse for the delay by Lieutenant-Colonel Forbes, OC AIF 21st Battalion.
33   Gellibrand to Bean, 12 May 1936, AWM 38 3DRL 6673 Item 492; I ANZAC Corps Summary of Operations, WO95/982, PRO.

34 Bean to Gellibrand, 2 March 1930, AWM 3DRL 6405 Item 4.

35 White to Bean, 15 Jan. 1930, AWM 38 3DRL 6673 Item 258.

36 Gellibrand to Bean, undated, AWM 38 3DRL 606 Item 260.

37 Bean Diary, March 1917, AWM 38 3DRL 606 Item 73(2).

38 Proceedings of Fifth Army Conference, W095/519, PRO.

39 Bean Diary, AWM 38 3DRL 606 Item 95.

40 Elliott to Bean, AWM 38 3 DRL 606 Item 260 (1).

41 Elliott to Bean, AWM 38 3DRL 606 Item 260 (1).

42 Bean, *Two Men I Knew*, p.168; *Military Operations Vol. I*, 1917; Bean IV, p. 169.

43 The antagonism between Elliott and the high command got worse after he was unjustly critical of neighbouring units in a report after Polygon Wood. He accused Birdwood of destroying the report and even after the war had finished, he continued his battle against Birdwood and White in the Australian Senate. *White Diary*, April 1921, Lady Derham. See also AWM 38 3DRL 6673 Item 258, White to Bean 17/6/32. Also *Commonwealth Parliamentary Debates*, Vol. XCV 27th/28th April 1921, NLA.

44 Cumming, *A Brigadier in France*, p.58-61.

45 In Palestine, Barrow's caution even exasperated 'Lawrence of Arabia', with whom he worked on several operations. He was promoted to Adjutant-General of India after the war, Barrow Papers, IWM.

46 HDF to AF, 31 March & 2 April 1917, Fanshawe Papers, PFC.

47 Oliver Esher (ed), *Journal of Viscount Esher IV*, 9 March 1917.

48 At this stage, this was the presumed date for the offensive to commence. It was later changed to 9 April.

CHAPTER V

A Horseshoe for Haig

As news of Gough's rapid advance reached the German Northern Army Group HQ in Cambrai, Crown Prince Rupprecht realised he was in trouble. He had received another depressing visit from his First Army Commander, General von Below and his Chief of Staff, Colonel von Lossberg, to tell him that work on the Siegfried Line was behind schedule. Anxious that the German troops would retire and find only a weak indefensible line, they had authorised the construction of extra trench lines from Bellicourt up to Croisilles, to run in front of and behind the existing line. In a rear battle zone stretching back three miles, they laid out strongpoints to slow any British attack while Reserves lay waiting to counterattack. It was a classic example of the new German 'elastic defence'.

The problem for the Germans was that they had barely started the Bullecourt sector when Gough was on top of them. It was quite likely that the British would attack this sector and yet Bullecourt was one of the few stretches which had not been 'improved'. Von Lossberg decided it would have to be defended, under simpler, rigid *Geschlossen* ('closed') defence principles. Therefore, the original plan for concrete shelters in the fire bays and machine-gun emplacements to the fore had to be abandoned, leaving foundations that were to perplex British intelligence for some time.[1] For cover, the defenders would have to resort to the old idea of large dugouts in both the fire and support trenches. But these were now so designed that, if captured, the entrances would be fully exposed to German bomb and trench-mortar fire.[2] To introduce at least some of the new tactical thinking, a general who was conversant with the ideas of 'defence in depth' would be appointed to command Bullecourt.

General Otto von Moser, Commander of the XIV Reserve Corps (known as *Gruppe Quéant*), arrived on 18 March 1917. At this time, the Corps was still under von Below's First Army, but when this Army moved south to Rheims, the Corps came under General Freiherr von Falkenhausen's Sixth Army just before the Battle of Arras. He was indeed a trusted exponent of the new ideas, having been the first Director of the *Divisionskommandeur-Schule* at Solesmes, a school devoted to teaching the new tactics to divisional commanders of the Northern Group of Armies.[3]

Von Moser at once set about consolidating his defences around Bullecourt and in front of the neighbouring village of Riencourt, a mile to the east. Realising that it was lunacy to pack the front trenches with men, most of whom would be slaughtered in the first bombardment, he garrisoned the front-line with a trip-wire of men, behind which lay a network of machine-guns ready to lacerate any British attack. If the British achieved a foothold in the line, they could be winkled out by small groups of highly trained stormtroops, springing forward from the rear.

Furthermore, the creation of two strongholds out of Bullecourt and Riencourt was no accident. Both villages were superbly sited on the crest of a semi-circular ridge. Bullecourt, projecting from the line, created two deadly re-entrants on either side and Riencourt protected the junction of the Wotan and Siegfried Lines. Standing on the Riencourt ridge, on the site of the old Moulin Sans Souci, the German observers had superb uninterrupted views of the Wotan Line, snaking its way north past Cagnicourt. It was a position the Germans were unlikely to surrender, and to further protect the junction, a *Balkon* ('balcony') trench was constructed in front of Quéant, a village half a mile south-west of the junction and hidden in a valley. It was a brilliant defensive position joined by a double trench system, much of which lay out of sight to the British on reverse slopes. Riencourt in particular benefited from plenty of underground cellars and catacombs near the village church, useful for stores and the billeting of troops.[4]

One key weapon in the German defence was the machine-gun. Although the light Mark 08/15 was not yet widely distributed, the Germans realised the tactical value of their existing machine-guns and used them as main, rather than support infantry weapons. Relatively few troops would occupy the front 'firetrench' in this stretch of the Line and Australian survivors would later testify to the high ratio of machine-guns to enemy infantry. Von Moser established them where possible, on the reverse of the ridge that ran from Bullecourt, round in front of Riencourt and Quéant.[5] In keeping with the new defence ideas, few of these machine-guns were fixed so that most could be used as mobile units to fight in the open or to support local counter-attacks. If further support was required, regiments of the *Eingriff* ('intervention') divisions would be brought up from the village of Cagnicourt, two miles to the rear. The commanders in the rear would have to judge finely the direction and timing of their counter-attacks. Many would also remember the lessons of the Somme, where small, well organised detachments succeeded, while forces engaged en masse were shot to pieces.[6]

While the Germans were frantically trying to complete the Bullecourt defences, Gough was preparing to use his V Corps to attack Croisilles and Ecoust, which lay one mile in front of the Siegfried Line. Meanwhile, to the south-east, I ANZAC Corps was moving up its 4th Division. This unit was commanded by Major-General Holmes, the first 'citizen soldier' to rise to divisional command. He had led the Rabaul expedition in the early months of the war and attracted some criticism over his handling of the occupation of New Guinea. German officers had been flogged and there were outbreaks of looting while he was in command, but his subsequent war record, including the attacks on Stormy Trench two months earlier, had been exemplary.[7]

Holmes' division, who were to spearhead the Fifth Army assault on Bullecourt, were in fine form. Twenty-year-old Captain Allan Leane, a company commander in his uncle's 48th Battalion, was definitely 'in the pink'.

> The Company are all below ground and we are all set up. Writing to you at 9.45 pm, everything in the garden being lovely. It is the best H.Q. I have ever had and I am just tickled to death with it. I reckon that it's just spiffing. I am fit and well, Ben and Charlie are ditto.[8]

Meanwhile the Third Army was moving up around Arras to launch its attack against the Siegfried Line from the west. Its task was to break through and push the Germans back towards their second line of defence on the Wotan Line. If the Fifth Army could come up quickly enough from the south-west, they could provide artillery flank support or even catch the Germans in the rear, and hinder their retreat. If Gough had the time to assemble sufficient artillery support, there was always the chance that he could even attack the junction of the Siegfried-Wotan Lines and roll up this second line of defence. This would severely hamper the enemy and help the Third Army achieve an extraordinary victory. The man entrusted by Haig with the bulk of the planning was the Third Army Commander, Lieutenant-General Sir Edmund Allenby.

Haig knew Allenby well. They were Staff College contemporaries but hardly the best of friends. Allenby rapidly rose from Cavalry Corps to V Corps Commander, and in October 1915 was appointed Third Army Commander, the last big appointment that Sir John French made before he was removed. This association, similar to the one that tainted Hew Fanshawe, did not endear Allenby to Haig.[9] But in spite of their obvious lack of rapport, Allenby was unswervingly loyal to his Commander-in-Chief and GHQ, and would not countenance any criticism of their plans by subordinates.[10] Haig, in turn, appeared to trust Allenby's judgement, especially over the 'degumming' of certain Corps commanders like Lieutenant-General John 'The Toreador' Keir. Nevertheless, Allenby was often at loggerheads with GHQ. One notable disagreement was over the timing of the preliminary Arras bombardment, which was only resolved by the removal of the Third Army MGRA and an extension of the bombardment to four days.[11]

Edmonds, who also knew Allenby from Staff College days, recalled that he was a popular officer but adopted the air of a 'fox-hunting squire'.[12] Unfortunately, on the Western Front, Allenby overplayed the bluster:

> When later, Allenby became a general, to our great amusement he tried to play what he thought was the part and assumed a roughness of manner and an abruptness of speech which were not natural to him – and became 'The Bull (of Basan)'. To give an example which I myself witnessed when trench walking with Allenby (Army commander) and Snow (Corps commander): we came to a shell hole in which a dead man was lying with nothing on but his khaki. His comrades were waiting for a chaplain to read the burial service. Allenby roared, 'did I or did I not issue an order that no man was to go up to the trenches without a steel helmet and a leather jacket?': 'you did sir': 'Then why has that man not got them on?': 'Beg pardon, sir, the man is dead and awaiting burial.': 'Did I or did I not, issue an order etc'. [13]

It was vintage Allenby in full flight. He was never as eccentric as Edmonds portrayed him but he was always ready to pronounce on any subject, even berating subordinates on their use of the English language:

> One day Allenby arrived and asked to have the situation explained. Taking him to a point of vantage, Bulfin [later General Sir Edward] said, 'Do you see sir, that tree on the near horizon?': 'There is no such thing as a near horizon'. [Allenby] 'Beg your pardon, sir, I have just read a book called "The Far Horizon". After a pause, Bulfin began again, 'Do you see, sir . . .', to be again interrupted by the Bull with arguments to prove that there is only one horizon.[14]

Edmonds does not tell us whether this conversation took place with shells flying overhead but it shows that Allenby was a man not always diverted by priorities. Yet despite Edmonds' caustic and sometimes exaggerated observations, Allenby was widely respected and admired (though perhaps not always loved) by those who knew him well.[15]

Although Arras was going to be 'the Bull's plan', he found that the timing and location of the offensive were constantly being altered by GHQ, as they tried to anticipate enemy intentions. It was agreed that on a front of nearly eleven miles, running from the edge of Vimy Ridge just north of Arras to Croisilles in the south, ten infantry divisions would assault the Siegfried Line. To protect Allenby's left flank, Lieutenant-General Horne's First Army would first secure the high ground of Vimy Ridge. To the south, Gough's Fifth Army would support the right flank and assist when the Third Army broke through the important village of

Monchy. This high vantage point to the south-east of Arras, was a first day objective which was essential for control of the artillery battle and to create a breach, through which the cavalry could rush.[16]

That old idea of a cavalry breakout was stubbornly hanging on in British plans even at this stage in the war. Haig and Allenby, both cavalrymen, envisaged mounted brigades dashing through the gap on fast roads past the villages of Monchy and Chérisy and across Gough's front.[17] The 4th Indian Cavalry Division (operating directly under Gough) would then gallop through the breach made on the Fifth Army front between Ecoust and Quéant. Once beyond the Siegfried Position, all cavalry would join up and come directly under GHQ, and would then dash towards Cambrai. [18]

So far, so good. But there were indications that Gough was moving onto a different tack from Haig and Allenby. Even though Gough was a cavalryman, he had doubts about using Major-General Kennedy's mounted division. But Haig insisted that the Third Army front was too congested to assemble any more cavalry in its forward area.[19] More alarmingly, he also threatened Gough with the transfer of twenty of his thirty-five siege howitzers to the Third Army, unless he could advance them quickly enough to be of use within his own sector.[20]

Gough was becoming increasingly worried that he might not be able to play a major role in the overall plan. At the same time, Allenby was determined to assert his control, especially at conferences where Gough was present. Brigadier-General Baker-Carr recalled the atmosphere:

> Allenby turned to one of his principal Staff Officers, a Major-General and asked him whether a certain order had been carried out. 'I think so, sir', replied the Staff Officer. 'What the deuce do you mean by that?' burst Allenby, turning on the unfortunate man. 'You're not paid to think. You' ve got to know. Find out immediately.'[21]

Allenby had a violent temper and could explode at a moment's notice, but just as suddenly, sit down and calm down.[22] He realised that at the Army Commanders' conferences before Bullecourt, Gough was more composed and, as a most fluent speaker, could hold Haig's attention. Gough, for his part, was concerned that Allenby was indifferent to his participation and lukewarm to the idea of the Fifth Army playing a larger part. Gough recalled:

> The idea of a subsidiary attack by my Army was born in my brain and not in Haig or Allenby's. Haig jumped at it – Allenby took no interest in it whatever. But everything was then left entirely to me.[23]

It was Gough's old beef that, once Haig had considered the options and set the objective, he no longer interfered with his subordinate Army commanders, or 'knocked heads together'. When Gough later argued with General Plumer over the Menin Road plan at Passchendaele, Haig again refused to get his Army commanders 'round the table for a frank discussion'.[24] Gough was not alone in these views and other commanders like Henry Wilson and Aylmer Haldane were also concerned at Haig's and GHQ's isolation. Unfortunately, it was not as simple as Haig determining strategy and setting objectives, leaving his Army commanders alone to devise tactics. Haig was just as liable to intervene at a lower level and direct the depth of objectives. For Army commanders who had already planned their own tactics, this was a confusing and unwelcome complication.[25] Communication was also hindered by Haig's Chief of Staff, Kiggell, who failed to deal with the commanders on anything like a personal level and was invariably too timid to put strong representations to his chief. Like Haig, hampered by the lack of a sense of humour, Kiggell could never get through to the quick-witted Gough. Consequently, the Fifth Army commander felt the responsibility for this lack of cooperation between the Armies lay fairly and squarely at Haig's door. It was a problem that kept surfacing from Arras to the Spring 1918 German offensive.[26]

> Either Haig should have commanded the operations of the two Armies himself from an advanced GHQ – or he should have appointed a chief of the two Armies with a small staff – exactly the same wretched failure occurred again in March 1918, between the Third and Fifth Armies – each Army operating independently, and as regards the Third Army (& GHQ), without any regard to the position and operation of the Fifth Army.[27]

While there were routine conferences of Army commanders, held at each HQ in turn and chaired by Haig, there were few meetings between commanders for explicit operations. Gough later complained that there were no meetings or consultations directly between himself and Allenby.[28] This omission would prove disastrous, since the Fifth Army subsidiary attack depended on the success and advance of the Third Army, so the timing and location of Gough's attack should have been dictated by Allenby's day-to-day position. If Gough was as independent of GHQ as he claimed, he could of course have arranged these meetings himself, but the personality clashes between these Army Commanders defeated any hope of close cooperation.[29]

Ironically, Allenby had once been a supporter of Hubert Gough. Although he kept out of direct involvement in the Curragh Incident, Allenby approved of the stand made by the Gough brothers back in 1914.[30] But Gough's criticism of Allenby's command of the Cavalry Corps during the early part of the war soon put paid to any mutual admiration. Gough recalled:

> Unlike Haig, he [Allenby] rarely had any ideas of his own, although he was good in taking them from a subordinate and generous in accepting responsibility for any failure, but he had no grip on the situation in France.[31]

In August 1914, Gough had become so disillusioned with Allenby's command of the Cavalry Division during the retreat from Mons, that he detached his 3rd Cavalry Brigade from Allenby's control. Setting himself up with I Corps (under Haig's command), he had relished a new order where Brigade commanders were actually informed about operations. [32]

Current relations between Chief Staff Officers were hardly any better. At the top, Kiggell was not a man to encourage discussion with the Army Chiefs of Staff, so there was little feedback to GHQ from this source. However, it was well known that, in the Third Army, Allenby and his new lively Chief of Staff, Major-General Louis Bols, complimented each other. The same relationship did not exist within the Fifth Army, for Gough and Malcolm were too similar in temperament. Malcolm, the brusque Scot, was a competent administrator and, like Gough, had a good grasp of the concept of command. But he was apt to explode at the slightest provocation, and most staff officers tended to keep out of his way. Even Gough conceded later to Liddell Hart that they were not a good pairing:

> Despite Neill Malcolm's good brain, he had not been an ideal Chief of Staff; too impatient with those who are slow, and showed it. Gough felt he had made a mistake in always going around with Neill Malcolm, who thought it was his duty simply to endorse his Chief's opinion. It would have been better if they had gone round separately, so that junior commanders would have been free to ventilate their troubles to Malcolm.[33]

In practice, few junior commanders were prepared to discuss problems with Malcolm, even in private. Brigadier-General Jerry Boyd, Fanshawe's Chief of Staff in V Corps, made a habit of by-passing Malcolm whenever he could, and dealing with the more junior Beddington in Fifth Army GHQ. Although such contact was irregular, it kept the wheels in motion and even appeared to have the tacit approval of Fanshawe.[34] Over at I ANZAC Corps HQ, now moving forward to Grevillers, Birdwood and White had built up an understanding since Gallipoli, that made them a good match. White's administration had proved itself, particularly in the Gallipoli evacuation and he could provide dependable staffwork behind

71

Birdwood's rather broad brush. It was a style of command not lost on their Australian troops:

> Old Birdy – he was fair enough
> When things was going good
> E'd 'oof it round the trenches
> And e'd ask bout our food
> No rooster was more game than him
> E'd go where no man goes
> But e's too enthusiastic
> In offering us for shows
> And when a stunt's fair started
> Old Birdy didn't mind
> You'll find him pottering around in front
> Or possibly be'ind
> T'was plain to us the clever 'ead
> That's needed for a fight
> Was planning in the old Chatoo
> Our Major General White.[35]

As far as the Army Commander was concerned, 'Birdwood was always easy to work with.' [36] But Birdwood was no tactician and the task now facing I ANZAC Corps needed shrewd handling.

By the beginning of April, Allenby's vast Third Army plan was on schedule, but in the Australian sector of the Fifth Army front, only Lagnicourt had been captured and then at a cost to the 7th Brigade of 377 casualties. The AIF 26th Battalion had carried the village on 27 March, with Captain P. H. Cherry winning a posthumous VC. Among the casualties evacuated by the field ambulance units were a number of German infantrymen and the unusual prize of a German pilot. Private E.C. Munro of the 5th Field Ambulance was even more surprised to find that this pilot was a member of the German Royal family:

> One night, Prince Frederick Charles was brought in, pretty badly hit in the stomach . . . He was a German airman and talked splendid English and had a charming manner. He was a noted tennis player and enquired after Anthony Wilding who he had known. He wore an Iron Cross of the 1st Order. Since leaving us, I heard he died. [37]

Prince Frederick of Prussia had not been allowed to fly in a fighter sqadron but asked special permission for one patrol. Inexperienced in formation, he was soon shot down by RFC No. 32 squadron, a few hundred feet above the Lagnicourt valley. Attempting to escape from his crashed plane, he was shot by men of the 26th Battalion.

Swapping personal details often happened when an enemy no longer posed a threat. A camaraderie could develop, especially between wounded men who had been enemies a moment before, but now found themselves suffering the same fate. Private Roy Hankin, an infantryman with the AIF 12th Battalion, was wounded in the early hours of 8 April, in the assault on Boursies, one of the outpost villages. He was shot through the left arm, the bullet lodging near his spine and he lost consciousness. When he came round, he attempted to move but was shot at again from the enemy lines. The only help he received at this stage was from a wounded German nearby, who commiserated with him and they swapped tokens. Although badly wounded, Hankin just managed to reach out and accept the German's One Deutschmark note between his congealed fingers.[38]

However, the Germans who were dug in around the remaining outpost villages of Doignes, Louveral and Noreuil, were in no mood for reconciliation and still posed a very real threat to Birdwood's ANZAC Corps. On the British V Corps front, Ecoust and Croisilles still held up Fanshawe's progress.

Behind them, the Anzac engineers were going flat out to make the approach roads passable for the lumbering heavy artillery, most of which had to be hauled forward by traction engines. Although the weather had dried up towards the end of March, the volume of traffic had increased dramatically and the congestion on the Albert-Bapaume road was appalling. It had only been made fit for transport on 18 March and in many stretches was only single carriageway. In addition to artillery, the road had to accommodate the advance of the AIF 4th Division together with its straggling divisional train. This 'train' was the means by which the 19,000 men of the 4th Division were supplied with food, fuel and baggage and kept in fighting trim. The convoy, comprising large numbers of horse-drawn wagons, motor lorries and carts, was supplemented by transport bringing up medical supplies for the Field Ambulance units and Casualty Clearing Stations. Adding to the throng were Postal wagons (carrying the all important mail to and from home), mess carts, veterinary supplies and assault stores. There was also a stream of service vehicles loaded up with spares and tools for the wheelwrights, carpenters and farriers to maintain the transport itself. As the inevitable breakdowns increased this monumental traffic jam, the whole advance assumed the pace of a funeral march. It was fitting for what was in store.

Most of the SAA ammunition for the infantry and shells for the artillery were normally brought forward by railway. But the German retreat had created yet another problem for, as well as the destruction of roads, the railway system had been torn up. The British engineers had managed to re-lay much of the track, but the main railway junction of Achiet-le-

Grand had only been reached by 28 March, and no concentrated artillery bombardment could commence before the ammunition arrived. The railway disruption also affected the arrival of another offensive weapon – the tank.

At the beginning of April, the role of tanks in the Arras offensive had been decided by the Army Commanders. Essentially, they were just to support the infantry and destroy designated enemy strongpoints that might hold up the attack. Forty out of the sixty available Mark I's and II's were allotted to the main Third Army thrust, whilst eight tanks were to assist the Canadian attack at Vimy and the remaining twelve were to join the Fifth Army attack at Bullecourt. Because of the railway problem, each tank consignment was taking at least two days longer than planned to reach railheads from the central tank workshops at Erin, twenty-five miles to the rear.[39]

Despite the obstacles, at dawn on 1 April, the train containing two old Mark I's and ten Mark II's arrived at the railhead at Achiet-le-Grand. But the time and effort needed to detrain the temperamental beasts was not built into the timetable. Drivers were inexperienced at this craft and the chore of detaching and re-attaching ill-fitting sponsons again hindered progress. One Mark II had to be left behind and it took two further days to get the remaining eleven tanks to No.11 Company 'D' Battalion's HQ at Behagnies, two miles to the west.

Captain Richard Haigh, second in command of no. 11 Company, was riding ahead towards the Siegfried Line, checking positions for forward dumps to store fuel and supplies for the tanks. Being so close at last to the enemy was enticing:

> The fields across which we rode had been ploughed the preceding autumn by the French civilians. We could see where the ground had been torn up by the horses of a German riding-school, 10 days before. Here and there were places where the Bosch had had his watering troughs and also traces of scattered huts and tents on the ground.[40]

Haigh organised tank routes and observation posts, whilst back at Behagnies the tanks were overhauled and then covered in camouflage to 'lie-up' and await their final orders.

On his mission, Richard Haigh rode back past Shoubridge's 7th Division preparing to go up to the V Corps front to attempt another attack on Croisilles. This tough nut had been Barrow's undoing, but Shoubridge was now allowed the support of the Third Army's 21st Division (Major-General David Campbell) who would pinch Croisilles from the north-west, as the 7th attacked from the south. There was also sufficient heavy artillery in place at last to provide a creeping barrage to cover not only the 91st Brigade's attack on Croisilles but also the simultaneous 20th

Brigade's attack on Ecoust-Longatte, two miles south-east of Croisilles.

Brigadier-General Cumming did well to clear Croisilles by 3 April as the attack had got off to a bad start. Lining up behind their 'jumping-off' tapes at 5.00 am on 2 April, the centre battalion comprising the 21/Manchesters were hit by their own artillery barrage. Despite the carnage, the Manchesters rallied and resumed their place in the attack, going in just as dawn was breaking. Almost instantly, they met a hail of machine-gun fire issuing from the railway embankment, some forty feet above the village. Working around the village was now out of the question, as support from the neighbouring division had not materialised. So it took a day for the Manchesters, together with the 2/Queen's and 1/South Staffs, to secure Croisilles. [41]

As groups of escaping Germans vaulted the rubble and made off across the open ground back to the Siegfried Line, two miles down the road, the 20th Brigade were mopping up in Ecoust. This village and its 'annexe', Longatte, lay about a mile in front of Bullecourt, on the same slight rise that allowed observation for miles around. The 8th and 9th Devons were determined to shake off the recently acquired divisional label of 'sticky' and charged into Ecoust with Lewis guns blazing. The battle soon devolved into dogged house-to-house street fighting at which the Devons proved surprisingly adept. But, attempting to outflank the enemy, many were caught and slaughtered by German machine-gun fire in the village cemetery. [42]

It took most of the day for the 2/Gordon Highlanders to get in and fight their way through the ruins of Longatte but, by nightfall on 2 April, as snow began to fall, Ecoust, Longatte and fifty-two Germans were in British hands. Major Richard Foot and an artillery colleague, advancing over the ground the following day found evidence of the inevitable bill to be paid for capturing the ruins:

The Gordon Highlanders had evidently been caught here by heavy and well-aimed machine-gun fire, and thirty or forty of them lay out dead on the exposed slope. Face downwards, rifle and fixed bayonet still gripped in an outflung hand, their corpses lay as they had fallen, the powdery snow dusting their dark tartan kilts, and their buttocks blued with the chill of death. Kenneth stopped suddenly in his tracks, looked at me with a pea-green face and threw up all his breakfast in a single convulsion. 'Sorry, Major', he said as he recovered, 'but I've never seen a dead man before'. [43]

One mile away lay many more dead, the result of the simultaneous Australian assault on Noreuil. Among them was Lieutenant W. Hoggarth who eight months before, had been the first Australian to reach Mouquet Farm. He was one of over 600 casualties suffered by the 13th Brigade in close-quarter fighting. The losses of the defending German 119th Regiment were only half those of the Australians. I ANZAC Corps and the British V Corps had finally achieved all their objectives for 2 April and, when the remaining smaller villages to the south were taken by the Australians in the next few days, the way was at last clear for Gough's attack on the Siegfried Line.

As for the exact point of his attack, Gough was still restricted by the directions laid down for the cavalry advance. The original GHQ order had specified a Fifth Army attack somewhere between Quéant and Ecoust.[44] The cavalry under his command were to make for Hendecourt, a mile and a half behind the stronghold of Bullecourt. Then, in the event of a Third Army breakthrough on the left, Gough's cavalry would wheel right towards Cagnicourt, a garrison village to the east on the Wotan Line. [45]

This operation posed many problems for Gough. The line either side of Bullecourt could be breached to push cavalry through. A main strike to the left of the village by the British, across even but exposed terrain, was attractive, but it would ignore the important Siegfried/Wotan junction near the old Moulin Sans Souci. The Germans were well aware of the importance of this junction, as General von Moser noted in his diary:

> Successful enemy penetration or breaching of the XIV Corps lines would have been of great consequence strategically, as it would have given the foe clear access to the rear flanks of the Arras front.[46]

Alternatively, a main strike to the right of the village could secure this junction for the British, but the fortified stronghold of Quéant lay only a mile away. Although it was in the fold of another shallow valley and not visible from the approach to the junction, Quéant's recently dug frontal defence or 'balcony trench' was dangerously close. Furthermore, any assault in this re-entrant would subject the Australians to enemy fire from both the Bullecourt and Quéant flanks, not to mention artillery shelling from the rear. Gough did not have the resources to attack Quéant itself and anyway, the farther east he went, the less chance he had of converging with the Third Army breakthrough.

Meanwhile, in the Siegfried Line, von Moser brought fresh troops into Bullecourt to relieve the outgoing 26th Reserve (Württemberg) Division. The new 27th Division was another tough Württemberg unit that had proved to be one of the best during the Battle of the Somme. Now rested but alert from a recent training programme, it was a division von Moser knew well as he had been its commander up until his promotion to XIV Reserve Corps in March. Now General von Maur took over as divisional commander and set about installing Infantry Regiments Nos.120, 123 and 124 in the front line with No. 127 in reserve at Cagnicourt.[47]

Fifth Army Intelligence were receiving frequent reports from prisoners that the number of concrete dugouts and blockhouses was increasing and that foundations for concrete machine-gun and trench mortar emplacements now existed in many regimental sectors. Work was not expected to be finished on these fortifications, at least to the east of Bullecourt, for some weeks and there appeared to be a good chance of interrupting the enemy before his plan was complete. However these intellegence reports were still conflicting. Constant reports of fires in nearby Pronville and Cagnicourt and Riencourt, fuelled talk of another retirement, yet POWs talked of the Germans wanting to hold their lines at all costs.[48]

Day after day, Gough pored over maps and daily reports at his HQ in Albert. His Corps Commanders and their Chiefs of Staff would appear for hastily convened conferences, to crowd around their superior. The elegant Fanshawe, the trim Birdwood and the lanky frame of Brudenell White all dwarfed Gough around the map table. But what the chief lacked in stature, he made up for with his extraordinary willpower and zest.

The Fifth Army Operations Order of 5 April had originally directed I ANZAC Corps, on the right, to assault the re-entrant between Moulin Sans Souci and Bullecourt and make a breach. The stronghold of Bullecourt itself was to be initially by-passed by the British V Corps on the left flank, who would seize a similar section of the German line; in both cases, the cavalry were to push through and join up with the Third Army advance. But now, by 7 April, Fifth Army Order 51 had largely swept the cavalry off the board, relegating them to a supporting role.[49]

It was the infantry who were now to spearhead a push beyond the Siegfried Line, to objectives over a mile away. Once through the Line, I ANZAC Corps on the right were to attack Riencourt and swing right towards Cagnicourt. The V Corps on the left were to go through the Line and on to Hendecourt. Bullecourt was now to be bombarded the night before, using the new Livens projectors to hurl gas shells into the village. At zero hour, attacks were to be made on the left and right sections of the Line while Bullecourt received a further hour's shelling followed by a pincer assault to capture it. V Corps and I ANZAC Corps would each receive five tanks each to assist in their attacks on the enemy trenches but only one tank per Corps would be required to help capture Bullecourt itself. Clearly Army HQ had little idea of the number of enemy strongpoints within the village.[50]

These were indeed optimistic objectives and, given that the front for each Corps to attack was no more than 1,500 yards, there was a limit to the number of assaulting battalions that could be squeezed in, let alone the number of artillery brigades to support the attack. It was a plan for deep penetration on a narrow front, which would leave the British open to easy enemy counter-attacks which could cut off the attacking force.

The assault would hardly be helped by the two re-entrants on either side of the village. The right-hand re-entrant facing the Anzacs was three times the width of the left, but the V Corps' brief on the left was just as desperate. Although it involved an assault in a shallower re-entrant, the men would have to move over 'land as flat as a tennis court' and scramble through thicker wire. In the Anzac sector, there were three belts of wire in front of the Siegfried Line, with further belts between the fire and support trenches. The 'balcony' trench was protected by two belts of wire. In the V Corps sector, some chicanes comprised four belts. In all, it was a terrible prospect for the attackers.[51]

It was therefore a plan which included all the risks that the old Staff College lesson had cautioned against and would provide the enemy gunners with concentrated targets.[52] To counter these risks on the Anzac side, Gough left Napier, the GOCRA of ANZAC Corps, to deal with the threat from Quéant – 'artillery instructions for the attack will be issued separately. Special attention will be paid to the right flank'.[53]

Time was at a premium, but Gough unexpectedly obtained a short breathing space. Several days before, on 4 April, the Third Army artillery had commenced their four day bombardment on the Arras front, but to the south the French were behind in their preparations for the main offensive on the Chemin des Dames. General Micheler, Nivelle's second-in-command, asked for the British to delay their offensive for forty-eight hours. Haig was happy to allow twenty-four hours because of the snow falls, but no more. So the date was finally set for the main attack at Arras and Vimy on Easter Monday, 9 April. Gough's Fifth Army, unable to cut the enemy wire in time, would then assault the Siegfried Line forty-eight hours later. [54]

The plan was laid and Haig found time to attend church on Easter Sunday, the eve of the great offensive. Lieutenant-General Sir Sidney Clive, head of the British mission at the French GQG, accompanied him:

> I caught up with the C In C who was walking back from Church. A glorious Easter Sunday morning. D.H. very quiet but confident that the attack has a very good chance. We passed a horse shoe which he picked up and dropped over his shoulder.[55]

NOTES

1   Fifth Army Intell. Reports 7-16 April, WO 157/209, PRO. These foundations can be clearly seen in contemporary aerial recce. photographs.
2   I ANZAC Corps Intelligence, WO95/565, PRO; Fifth Army Intell. Report, WO157/209, PRO.
3   The Wotan Position, p. 240, *Army Quarterly*, July 1939.
4   Item 254, 10/4/17, WO 157/565, PRO. Information from German POWs.
5   German map of defence positions prior to 11 April 1917, Ref M.C.21, IWM.

These machine-guns, especially those placed over the ridge near Quéant, wrought terrible havoc amongst the AIF 5th Brigade, attacking on 3 May.

6   Bidwell, *Gunners at War*, p.39.
7   AWM 3DRL/2803 and AWM 33 10/1.
8   Allan Leane to his mother 28 March 1917, AWM 1DRL (0411). 'Ben' refers to Major B.B. Leane, brother of Ray and second-in-command of the 48th Battalion.
9   Hew Fanshawe followed in Allenby's footsteps, taking over command of the Cavalry Corps in Aug. 1915 and V Corps in Oct. 1915.
10 Blake, *Private Papers of Douglas Haig*, 8 August 1916.
11 Allenby to Spears, 31 Oct. 1934, 2/3/1, Spears Papers, KCL.
12 Allenby 'changed for the better when he went to Palestine.' Edmonds to Liddell Hart, LH 11/1934/41, Liddell Hart, KCL.
13 Edmonds Papers, III/2/14, KCL. It is not surprising that Wavell used few of Edmonds' anecdotes for Allenby's biography.
14 Edmonds Papers 111/2/14, KCL. Edmonds could be extremely fickle in his portraits of contemporaries. Prior to publication, his Official Histories also swung dramatically. Overall he settled for a pro GHQ stance. See Brian Bond, (ed), 'Sir James Edmonds and the Official History', *The First World War and British Military History*.
15 Edmonds' caricatures of his Staff College contemporaries were colourful but often overdone. A Chief of Staff, Brigadier-General Jeudwine, described Allenby as 'a great man and a great soldier', II/3c, Allenby Papers, KCL.
16 GHQ Letter OAD 350, 26 March 1917, Appendix 26, *Military Operations Vol. I*, 1917.
17 As late as January 1918, Haig was still trying to persuade the War Cabinet that the cavalry could be of great service for offensive and defensive purposes, G. A. B. Dewar, *Sir Douglas Haig's Command, Vol. II – Cavalry Studies*, p. 45.
18 Fifth Army OAD 381, WO95/519, PRO.
19 *Military Operations, Vol I, 1917*, p. 181.
20 Instructions issued to First, Third & Fifth Armies 9/3/17, 2/1/11, Spears Papers, KCL.
21 Baker-Carr, *From Chauffeur to Brigadier*, p. 215.
22 Major-General J. Shea, IWM Sound Archives.
23 Gough to Falls, 25 Nov. 1937, CAB 45/116, PRO. Haldane commented, 'The tail wagged the dog'.
24 Graham & Bidwell, *Coalitions, Politicians & Generals*, p.114.
25 For an analysis of GHQ/Army Commander relations, see T.H.E. Travers, 'A Particular Style of Command: Haig and GHQ, 1916-18', *Journal of Strategic Studies*, Vol 10, no.3 (Sept. 1987).
26 Hubert Gough talking to Liddell Hart and Lloyd George, 27/1/36, referring to Passchendaele and the 'Michael' offensive, LH 11/1936/31, Liddell Hart Papers, KCL. Haig was also betting 'each way' on Gough. If he broke through, Haig would get the praise and if Gough failed, he could be sacrificed, Eric Andrews in 'Second Bullecourt Revisited', *Journal of the Australian War Memorial*, no.15, Oct. 1989.
27 Gough to Liddell Hart, LH 11/1936/31, Liddell Hart Papers, KCL. Gough refers to the disaster that befell the Fifth Army during the 1918 German Spring offensive.
28 John Terraine, *Haig: The Educated Soldier*, p. 179.
29 T.H.E. Travers agrees with Gough – 'Gough was absolutely correct here:

GHQ simply adopted a hands-off policy with army commanders and failed to find out what was happening at the front', 'From Surafend to Gough', *Journal of the AWM* no. 27 (Oct. 1995) See also E.M. Andrews, 'Bean & Bullecourt: Weaknesses and Strengths of the Official History of Australia in the First World War', *Revue Internationale d'Histoire Militaire*, no. 72, 1990.

30 Dr Ian Beckett, *The Army and the Curragh Incident*, p.23.

31 Gough in discussion with Liddell Hart, 9 April 1935, LH 11/1935/72, Liddell Hart Papers, KCL.

32 It also helped that Gough's brother, Johnnie, was Chief Staff Officer.

33 Liddell Hart in conversation with Gough and Lloyd George, Reform Club, 27 January, 1931, LH11/1936/31, Liddell Hart Papers, KCL.

34 'My Life', p. 102, Beddington Papers, KCL.

35 Box 11/63, Brudenell White Papers, National Library of Australia (hereafter NLA).

36 Gough, *The Fifth Army*, p.145.

37 Private E. C. Munro Diary, AWM 1DRL /0526; Bean IV, p.190.

38 Private Hankin was later brought in by stretcher bearers to a casualty clearing station. Like most seriously wounded AIF men, he went on to Rouen Hospital and was then evacuated to Southwark Hospital, London. He was invalided home to Tasmania in December 1917. He is still alive at the age of 102 years and lives at Erina, NSW. The bullet is still lodged in his back; Melba Alexander to author, 25/4/95.

39 Tank HQ records, WO95/ 91, PRO. For tank transportation problems, see *Army Quarterly* July 1924, p.304.

40 Captain Richard Haigh, *Life in a Tank*, p.64-65. This memoir was published unusually in Boston USA in 1918, after Haigh 'toured' the city in a Mark IV tank.

41 WO95/1632, PRO; Cumming, *A Brigadier in France*, p.63-69.

42 C. Atkinson, *The Devonshire Regiment 1914-18*, p.243-248.

43 Brigadier R.C. Foot, 86/57/1, IWM. The 20th Brigade suffered over 300 casualties taking Ecoust and Longatte.

44 OAD 26 March 1917, WO95/519, PRO.

45 Fifth Army Order no. 50, 5 April 1917, WO95/519, PRO.

46 Von Moser, *Feldzugaufzeichnungen*, p. 267.

47 *Württemberg Heer Im Weltkrieg Die 27 Division*, p.112-115.

48 Fifth Army Intell. Summaries 1-8 April 1917, WO 157/209, PRO. When the author visited the site of the Siegfried Line to the west of Bullecourt in 1996, a series of completed blockhouses were being excavated. They were subsequently broken up to allow access for farm machinery.

49 Item 292, WO 158/248, PRO; Item 297, Army order to Cav. Corps, WO 158/248, PRO. The cavalry were to follow ANZAC Corps and veer off towards Vis-en-Artois should the VII Corps (Third Army) need assistance.

50 Fifth Army Orders 50 & 51, WO 158/248, PRO.

51 Fifth Army Intell. captured German map, IWM Q52949; trench maps, 'Bullecourt-Riencourt corrected to March & April 1917'.

52 Intelligence Notes (File 3), Durrant Papers, AWM PR88/009.

53 Fifth Army Order No. 50, WO 158/248, PRO.

54 Hand written note by Lieutenant-Colonel Cannings GS, Item 294, WO 158/248, PRO; I Anzac Corps Order no.123 8/4/17, WO95/982, PRO.

55 Clive Diary 8 April 1917, II/4, Clive Papers, KCL.

CHAPTER VI

The Buckshee Battle

As dawn broke on Easter Monday, 9 April, the German outpost defenders on Vimy Ridge braced themselves against the rasping wind and sleet. Down below them, barely 100 yards away, the leading companies of Lieutenant-General Byng's Canadian Corps were assembling undetected for the attack.

It was to be a carefully prepared attack with nothing left to chance. The four Canadian Divisions had practised the assault with mock-ups of the terrain, using General Currie's new 'firepower and movement' tactics. This enabled platoons to pin down enemy defenders with Lewis guns, whilst using bombers and riflemen to swiftly outflank them. The plan also allowed for recent innovations, such as the rolling barrage and divisions 'leapfrogging' each other to the next objective.[1]

At 5.30 am over 1,000 British and Canadian guns bombarded the enemy positions coinciding with the infantry assault. It was an incredible preliminary bombardment that was nearly treble the density of the one prior to the First Day of the Somme. At Vimy, one heavy gun was employed for every twenty yards of front. And as the barrage moved forward in 'lifts', so the Canadians advanced, quickly taking Farbus Wood, Thelus and Hill 135 before the morning was out. The Germans were surprised in their dugouts and their attempts to mount local counter-attacks were smashed by the incoming allied artillery barrage. General von Falkenhausen, the German commander, had made the fatal mistake of placing his larger reserves one day's march to the rear. They were out of range of the British artillery but too far away to help their beleaguered colleagues. As the defenders in their 'island fortresses' were quickly surrounded, Ludendorff's elastic defence system collapsed. It was a great Allied success story, with only the highest part of Vimy Ridge, the notorious Hill 145 on the left of the sector, holding out for a further day.

Meanwhile, to the south of Vimy, Allenby's Third Army was enjoying mixed results. Lieutenant-General Fergusson's XVII Corps, on the left of the attack and above the river Scarpe, made good headway. Here the 4th Division leapfrogged the 9th during the afternoon and captured Fampoux, a stronghold in the last German defence before the Wotan Line. But below the Scarpe, where the ground was boggy, the progress faltered and Haldane's VI Corps met stiff resistance at the Railway Triangle. On his right, Lieutenant-General 'Slush' Snow's VII Corps was held up by a stubborn enemy defending Telegraph Hill and the critical high ground of Monchy-le-Preux. Nonetheless, with advances of over three miles on certain sectors of the Third Army front, the attacks of 9 April 1917 achieved the deepest penetration since trench warfare began.[2]

On this first day, there had been high hopes that the tanks could play a useful supporting role in following the infantry and crushing enemy strongpoints. But against all advice from gurus of the Heavy Branch like Major Fuller, GHQ allocated the forty-eight available tanks in 'penny packets' all the way across the front. The morning had started badly for the 'tankers' when their chief intelligence officer, Captain Hotblack, was nearly killed. He had arrived at the Old Citadel in Arras to find the tank plan in shambles, with most tanks 'ditched' shortly after starting off. A shell fell between Hotblack and his popular staff officer, Captain Tommy Nelson, killing Nelson instantly and severely wounding Hotblack.[3] Even more depressing news came from the north at Vimy, where the eight tanks of 'D' Battalion never even got within range of the enemy artillery. The burly Canadian Major 'Roc' Ward, commanding a company of tanks from 'D' Battalion, found that all his machines ditched in the loamy soil, churned up by the heavy artillery bombardment.[4] The tanks fared marginally better in the southern sector, where the ground was firmer and eighteen tanks were employed against the bastions of 'Telegraph Hill' and 'The Harp'. Walking across 'The Harp' after the battle, Fuller realised for some it had been a tragically short baptism of fire:

> I found one tank standing out of a trench with its tail end resting on the bottom of it. On looking through the sponson door, I saw the driver sitting upright in his seat. He was beheaded.[5]

Whilst a tank afforded more protection to a soldier than an infantryman in the open, the fate that awaited many tankers was particularly nasty. If an incoming shell failed to find its way through the observation flap in front of the driver, small arms fire could always ignite the two petrol tanks situated in the track frames either side of the head of the tank commander and his driver. Direct hits on a tank usually resulted in internal explosions as the fuel and ammunition went up, buckling the sponson exit doors. Should any of the crew escape the flames and noxious fumes, they would stumble out disorientated, and present easy targets for the enemy machine-gunners.

Pacing up and down the tank battalion HQ at Behagnies on the morning of the 9th, Hardress Lloyd hoped for better news. Although two companies of his 'D' Battalion had been in action, the 'star turn' of Major William Watson and his eleven tanks at Bullecourt would be delayed for some days. So it was with some surprise and delight that he received Watson, who arrived on horseback bearing news of a scheme to bring forward the attack on the Fifth Army front.

Watson, OC no.11 Company, had used his fertile brain to devise a plan using the best tool in the armoury – surprise. Since it was taking so long to cut the wire for a conventional attack at Bullecourt, he argued that the eleven available tanks could be used 'en masse' to steal up to the enemy wire undetected, flatten it and then allow the infantry to sweep through under cover of the artillery. The tanks would be a substitute for a rolling barrage. More importantly, dispensing with an artillery bombardment could keep British intentions secret for the last vital twenty-four hours before zero hour.[6]

Hardress Lloyd was keen to prove the capability of the tanks and heartily endorsed Watson's plan. During the afternoon of the 9th, Lloyd and Watson hastily motored down to Gough's HQ at Albert, to see if the Army Commander would adopt the plan. Gough had received news of the Vimy success that morning and was in an excitable mood. However, he had not heard the latest reports of the stiffening enemy resistance near his army boundary.[7]

Watson, being only a company commander, was of course flattered when Gough took to his plan. Gough wanted the attack to be made the next day, but when he failed to get confirmation of RFC support for moving the tanks in daylight, alarm bells should have rung. Watson knew that his men had little night-time training with tanks and, with the probability of snow showers, a twelve-hour timetable for moving them forward was too optimistic. Yet Gough knew that, if Allenby's cavalry suddenly broke through near Monchy and Chérisy, he would have hours rather than days to rally his support for them. As the exercise would only work if the tanks advanced in a close group, the Anzac 're-entrant' front of 1,200 yards was selected for the main attack. Gough then packed off the two 'tankers' to confirm the fine detail with Birdwood and White at their Corps HQ at Bihucourt Château.

The plan met with a mixed reaction from I ANZAC Corps. White seemed happy for his infantry to follow the tanks as long as Hardress Lloyd was confident of success.

Birdwood was less enamoured of the plan but, with reservations, gave his consent to I ANZAC Corps being used.[8]

Zero hour would have to be no later than 4.30 am on 10 April, which would allow one and a half hours for the objectives to be taken before sunrise; there would be no repeat of the daytime Fromelles disaster. Although Heavy Branch HQ had not seen Swinton's 'Notes on the Employment of Tanks', the start time for tanks would be in line with his recommendations – 'The best moment for the start will be just before dawn, so soon as there is sufficient light in the sky to distinguish objects to some extent.'[9] Machine-guns would be detailed to fire continuously, to drown the noise of the advancing tanks, while the right flank would be protected from the enemy in Quéant by a smokescreen and on the left, Bullecourt would be drenched in gas prior to the attack.[10]

There still seemed doubt as to the enemy's resolve to stand on their present line and both the British V and I ANZAC Corps were to keep up strong probing patrols towards the wire. Both Corps were aware that each would be sending forward patrols and of the importance of notifying each other if events changed.[11] Meanwhile, the AIF 4th Brigade (Brigadier-General Brand) and 12th Brigade (Brigadier-General Robertson) were to move their battalions up from Favreuil to spearhead the attack. There were now so many men and supplies bunching up in the Noreuil valley that space had to be found beyond the railway embankment for the eventual 'jump off' point. The HQs of the attacking battalions were established in dugouts in the railway embankment, whilst Brand's and Robertson's brigade HQs were set up in Noreuil, a mile to the rear. Communication would be maintained between brigade and battalion HQs by buried cable, pigeon or runner.[12] For Brand in particular, there remained the exciting prospect of commanding a full brigade on the Western Front rather than piecemeal battalions.

At 9.50 pm on 9 April, while the assault equipment and ammunition were being moved up, Captain Bert Jacka, the Intelligence Officer of the 14th Battalion, was assembling a reconnaissance patrol behind the embankment. He moved off with two other officers and a small party of men, creeping out 200 yards to the sunken road where the leading waves were to jump off. Out in no man's land it was bitterly cold with driving rain and snow. The sky was lit with white and orange flares and the 1,200 yards of the re-entrant echoed to the sound of sporadic machine-gun fire and incoming artillery shells.

Jacka and his patrol reached the enemy wire within fifteen minutes, and moved along the centre section checking the extent of damage to the wire. Jacka found 'the wire to be very badly broken and cut to pieces by the bombardment'.[13] He further endorsed the results of Fraser's howitzer bombardment on the enemy lines, confirming, 'our heavies also shelled Riencourt very effectively'. Bean further recorded that Jacka was concerned that 'other parts of the wire were intact', but there is no evidence of this in Jacka's handwritten report. However, the Germans seemed alarmed enough to report that 'the wire was shot to pieces, a sure sign of a coming attack and even Riencourt received strong fire of calibres up to 24 cm'.[14] When a German patrol came too close for comfort, Jacka had to abandon any further reconnaissance. Retiring to their lines, the recce party noticed that the enemy was stepping up his shelling of the railway embankment. Moreover, the shelling appeared to be coming from a number of enemy field guns in the direction of Quéant.[15]

When the party returned before midnight, Lieutenant E.J. Rule recalled being told by Jacka that he had 'warned all the heads it was pure murder to attempt the operation'.[16] However, Jacka's written report was passed to 4th Divisional Intelligence who took up his comments on the broken wire with some enthusiasm. In their Intelligence Summary[17], they confirmed that the Germans still manned their front line trenches but ignored Jacka's remarks on the artillery shelling coming from Quéant. Despite later denials, the 4th Division Staff did not appear to be unduly worried about the wire. A similar situation was reported by patrols of the 12th Brigade operating in front of the left-hand sector. They confirmed that 'several gaps twenty yards wide, had been cut in the wire' in the re-entrant but the wire around Bullecourt remained intact.[18]

It was not enough to postpone the attack. The two infantry brigades received their written orders at 7 pm and 9.30 pm respectively that evening and elements of the 14th and 16th Battalions were already out in the sunken road beyond the embankment. Some six miles to the rear, in an old quarry near Mory, Lieutenant Swears received his final orders from Heavy Branch HQ at 6.30 pm. The eleven tanks, split into three sections, were to make their way across country and up the Noreuil valley to rendezvous behind the embankment. They would then be guided forward by AIF Intelligence Officers to taped starting points in front of the assembled troops.

Out of the three section commanders, only Swears had any experience of actual tank warfare. In addition to commanding his section of four tanks on the left, he would also liaise with the AIF battalion HQs. Captain 'Fanny' Field, the ex-gunner, would command the centre section of three tanks and Captain Wyatt the right section consisting of four tanks. The company waited until the sun had set at 7.30 pm, to avoid enemy spotter planes, before moving off.

Swears went on ahead to meet the Australians. Meanwhile Wyatt, the only officer to have reconnoitred the latest route to Noreuil, led the way with each tank commander guiding his tank on foot with the aid of a hurricane lamp. The crews, sweating in the intense heat inside the tank cabs, could barely see their commanders outside. Darkness soon came over the straggling party and a biting wind swept down the Mory valley. It began to snow heavily.

Two miles to the north, the other part of the British element in the plan, the V Corps, were preparing for their attack on Bullecourt Village. Lieutenant-General Edward Fanshawe received encouraging news at 8.40 pm that the 21st Division, barely two miles away on his left flank, had breached the Siegfried Line.[19] In accordance with the Army plan, Braithwaite's 62nd Division had to wait for the Australians and the tanks to enter Bullecourt. Then, only on receipt of a signal, would the 62nd attack and consolidate the capture of the village. But first, to test the enemy's strength, the 62nd Division would send forward strong patrols 'at any time after the 10th instant, on receipt of orders from Corps HQ'.[20] At 11.50 pm, the Staff of the 62nd Division accordingly issued the following confirmation to its attacking brigade and its neighbours on the right flank – the Anzac 4th Division:

> Unless it is discovered that the enemy have evacuated the S.L. during the night on our front, the 185th Brigade in conjunction with the 4th Australian Division, will push forward strong patrols under a barrage as per order 32.[21]

Brigadier-General Vigant de Falbe, commanding the British 185th Brigade, knew there was no chance of an enemy withdrawal. He scribbled in his diary – 'Excitement of higher command believing Bullecourt evacuated. We on the spot know the enemy are still holding the line strongly'.[22] He immediately warned both the 2/7th and 2/8th Battalions West Yorks to assemble three strong patrols to advance towards Bullecourt at 4.30 pm (zero hour). He knew the odds were stacked heavily against them, for his intelligence reports had recently shown that the wire around Bullecourt 'was intact, as all artillery shells had fallen some 20 yards short of the wire'.[23] These rounds had come from the 2nd Heavy Artillery Group, operating from Vaulx–Vraucourt, three miles to the rear, and were an early indication that the artillery support was going to be erratic. The Group comprised four British siege batteries, which were under Fraser's Anzac command. The 6" howitzers were hurling shells towards the village of Bullecourt at the rate of one per minute for eight and a half hours until zero hour.[24] At this 'normal' discharge rate, the Forward Observation Officers should have had ample time to confirm registration with their batteries.

However, the gunners had their share of obstacles. Pre-determined landmarks for the artillery to register on in Bullecourt and Riencourt were rapidly disappearing as the Germans blew them up. British reconnaissance planes, vital to the recording of targets and troop movements as well as to observing the success of bombardments, were being shot down in large numbers by Richthofen's squadron – the month soon became known as 'Bloody April' by the RFC as the Germans gained air supremacy.

Next, there was also the problem of shell fuses. Although the '106' instantaneous fuse, which burst on grazing the ground, had been used at Vimy Ridge with success, most ANZAC and V Corps shells were unfortunately still equipped with delay fuses. This meant that shrapnel shells buried themselves in the ground before they exploded, losing most of their impact. The problem was also compounded by the resistance of CRAs to the use of HE shells, which would have been more effective.[25]

Most importantly, Major-General Herbert Uniake, the GOCRA of 5th Army and expert on heavy artillery, went away on sick leave just before Bullecourt, leaving Fraser to refer to other senior staff officers at Army HQ, for ultimate sanction for his orders. This question of sanction was a lengthy procedure and one which Uniake campaigned to streamline, in the hope that artillery could be handled at the highest level that control is possible. Had he been on duty, it was conceivable that he would have provoked a quicker response from Army HQ to daily artillery problems.[26]

Despite the failure of the artillery to crush the wire defences, the Germans were not impregnable in Bullecourt. At 1.00 am, sentries of the 120th Württemberg Regiment on night watch crouched low as a short barrage of incoming artillery shells hit the ruined houses behind them. There was no warning smell and they were suddenly asphyxiated by phosgene gas. There were no tell-tale clouds of gas released from the British lines beforehand and those Germans caught within 200 yards in the open or in shallow dugouts, were soon retching and gasping for air.

The 'Livens Projectors', which were fired by electrical charge by a company of the Royal Engineers from behind the embankment, had a deadly effect on the German garrison. These mortar-like contraptions now delivered gas by shell instead of being filtered out of canisters and taken by an unpredictable wind. They had been used during the last few days on the Arras front to terrible effect and, in the narrow communication trenches of Bullecourt, they wreaked havoc among the 1st Battalion, 120th Regiment, who suffered nearly 200 casualties in this attack. These Projectors were also capable of delivering irritants like cold tar or even sewage, but phosgene gas, ironically first developed by the Germans, had the most debilitating effect. When the enemy garrison eventually recovered, they responded with an angry fusillade of machine-gun fire.

The fire from Bullecourt was not heavy enough to interrupt the mission of Captain Jacka out on patrol again, deftly crawling towards the enemy in the re-entrant to the east of the village. Shortly after 2.00 am he was ordered to lay white 'jumping off' tapes as guides for the infantry who would soon rise up from their temporary positions in the sunken road. He started to lay the tape, working back towards his own lines. Looking back after completing his task, he suddenly saw the extraordinary sight of Lieutenant Reich of the 124th Württemberg Regiment, cane in hand and orderly in tow, hanging on to the other end of the tape – the event had an almost comical air about it.[27] Jacka promptly had the Germans encircled and captured, pistol whipping the officer who was reluctant to return with him.[28]

As zero hour approached, the two brigades of Australians, lying out in the sunken road in the re-entrant, were still undetected by the enemy. But they were concerned that there was still no sign or noise of the tanks that were to spearhead the attack. Back at Brand's Brigade HQ at Noreuil, the tank company commander, Major Watson, was becoming anxious. The attack was postponed for half an hour and then at 4.15 am the telephone rang. It was Wyatt, the exhausted tank guide. He reported that the column of tanks had failed to keep together in the snowstorm and they had only just reached Noreuil. It would take at least another hour and a half to reach the jump-off points.[29] Soon it would be dawn and it was obvious that both tanks and infantry would be massacred in the daylight. Watson conferred with Major-General Holmes and it was decided to call off the attack and quickly get the infantry back from no man's land before the Germans spotted them.

But in the rush to organise the withdrawal, no-one on the 4th Division Staff told the neighbouring 62nd Division the attack was cancelled, some even claiming ignorance of the 62nd Division's orders to send out patrols.[30] Consequently, at 4.30 am as arranged, six strong patrols of the West Yorks moved forward to probe the west of Bullecourt. The 2/8th on the left and the 2/7th on the right made swift progress across the open approach. By 4.45 am the 2/7th were up to the wire and under the first belt, but they soon realised something was wrong. There was still no sign of the tanks or the Australian attack on their right.

As the Lewis gun sections struggled through the wire, they were suddenly illuminated by falling flares. Then the German machine-guns erupted. Those caught outside the wire were quickly cut down, the survivors taking refuge in a nearby sunken road. Their sanctuary was short lived. The author of the West Yorks War Diary despaired at what happened next:

> The sunken road was an extremely good position to occupy. It is regretted that our own 6" Howitzers then shelled the sunken road and ended up with an intense bombardment. Nothing would apparently induce them to lengthen range onto the wire which was their target.[31]

Most of the Yorkshiremen sheltering in the road were blown to pieces. It was just as wretched on the German side of the wire, where the British Lewis gun teams who had crawled through were desperately fighting off the enemy. But, just after 5.00 am their gunfire finally ceased. The patrols had been decimated and the West Yorks lost 162 men.[32]

Oberst von Gleich, the German commander of the 120th Regiment in Bullecourt, thought this action was the prelude to a large-scale attack and immediately called for an artillery bombardment of the British positions in the embankment. But it was the sector of the neighbouring AIF 48th Battalion that took the full brunt of the shelling, with twenty-one casualties around their HQ. Lieutenant-Colonel Ray Leane soon arrived at the smouldering dugout to find the body of his younger brother and second-in-command, Major Ben Leane. The great bear of a man was devastated – he had only recently lost an elder brother at Delville Wood. He gently picked up his brother's remains and carried them away to a quieter place where he personally dug the grave and set up a cross.

When the forward AIF battalions received the message, 'the stunt is off', at 5.00 am, there was concern that the activity of a withdrawal would bring down the most terrible enemy bombardment.[33] It was just becoming light, but by a stroke of luck, a heavy snowstorm came down and the Australians' retirement was shielded from the enemy trenches. Some of the battalion commanders assumed that the Germans knew what was happening but, as Bean privately noted, 'the German unit histories show that if some Germans saw them, the knowledge did not get through to their HQ'.[34]

As the exhausted tank crews threw tarpaulins over their stationary tanks in the Noreuil valley and awaited their next orders, the Australian infantry were marched the six miles back to Favreuil, cursing the British 62nd Division and the tank battalion in equal measures. They felt that the game had been given away.[35] However, feelings also ran high in the 62nd Division over their needless losses, due to the failure of the staff of both the AIF 12th Brigade and the 4th Division on their right, to notify them of the cancelled attack.

The 'Buckshee Battle' as it became known was a bad start and the day's events did little to foster cooperation between the British and Australians. That relationship was to be strained to breaking point the following day, when Gough ordered a repeat of the attack.

NOTES

1 Haldane claimed that Crutwell elaborated the 'leapfrogging'. 'I only had one division, the 37th, which was available to do the leaping,' Haldane to Spears, 31 Oct. 1934, 2/3/52 – 2/3/56 Spears Papers, KCL.

2 Trevor Wilson, *The Myriad Faces of War*, p. 450-456. For an excellent account of the Battle of Arras, see Jonathan Nicholls, *Cheerful Sacrifice*.

3 Nelson, a Scottish publisher, was a close friend of both Paul Maze and John Buchan. Buchan immortalised him in his memoir of six friends killed, *These for Remembrance*.

4 'Report on Arras operations', 1st Brigade HBMGC, WO 95/91, PRO.

5 Fuller, *Memoirs of an Unconventional Soldier,* p. 106.

6 This paid particular dividends at Cambrai (1917) and Amiens (1918), Griffith, *Battle Tactics of the Western Front*, p.34.

7 Watson, *A Company of Tanks*, p. 44-46.

8 I ANZAC Corps War Diary, WO95/982, PRO; Bean IV, p.273. There are no formal written objections to the plan by Birdwood, in either PRO or AWM archives.

9 'Notes on the Employment of Tanks', (Feb. 1916), Stern Papers, KCL; Harris, *Men, Ideas and Tanks*, p.56-58.

10 Operations Orders No. 11 Co. 'D' Battalion, 9 April 1917, WO95/91, PRO;

Fifth Army telegram 5.50 pm 9/4/17, WO 158/248, PRO.

11   I ANZAC Corps Order 123, WO95/982, PRO.

12   4th Australian Division Signals Instruction, WO95/3443, PRO.

13   Jacka's signed hand written intelligence report 10/4/17, Appendix 8, WO95/3494, PRO. See also E.J. Rule manuscript, AWM 92 PR MSS 1380.

14   The History of the 124th Württemberg Regiment, p.66, seems to confirm this.

15   Jacka's report, WO95/3494, PRO.

16   Bean IV, p. 276; Rule, *Jacka's Mob*, p.167. Bean's and Rule's accounts are at odds with Jacka's written report.

17   Intell. Summary No. 124, WO95/3443, PRO.

18   Bean IV, p. 277.

19   V Corps Intelligence Summary, 9 April 1917, WO95/748, PRO; 185th Brigade Operations Orders No.18/19, WO 95/3082, PRO. This report, like so many others of the next 24 hours, proved to be inaccurate.

20   Copy of V Corps Order no. 134, WO95/748, PRO.

21   General Staff, 62nd Division Order 33, WO95/3068, PRO.

22   de Falbe to Falls 3/7/37, CAB 45/116, PRO.

23   Intell. Report 2/7 West Yorks, WO95/3082, PRO. See also Patrol Reports by Lieutenant-Colonel K. James, WO95/3068, PRO.

24   War Diary, Commander Heavy Artillery; Operations Order 42, WO95/993, PRO. The 2/ HAG fired a total of 1,758 shells on 10/4/17. At 4.30 pm the barrage was to be lifted to the Quéant salient.

25   For an analysis of the artillery's performance at Arras and Bullecourt, see Birch to Falls 22/11/37, Broad to Falls 14/11/37 and Vickery to Falls 11/2/39 – all CAB 45/116, PRO.

26   Broad to Falls, 14/11/37, CAB 45/116, PRO; Bidwell, *Gunners at War*, p. 43-45.

27   Jacka's hand written report, WO95/3494, PRO.

28   For his brave work in the enemy lines, he was awarded a bar to his MC.

29   Watson, *A Company of Tanks*, p. 48.

30   Colonel D. Bernard to Bean, 23/10/30, AWM 3 DRL 7953 item 34.

31   WO 95/3082, PRO.

32   War Diaries 2/7th& 2/8th.West Yorks, WO 95/3082, PRO; Wyrall, *History of 62nd Division* Vol I, p.42-43; *Das Württemberg Kaiser Reg. no. 120*, p. 65.

33   Signals message to 14th Battalion. WO95/3494, PRO.

34   Bean's margin notes on Leane's comments on the Official History, AWM 38 3DRL 7953 item 30.

35   Intell. Report, WO 157/565, PRO. In fact both the 120th and 124th Württemberg Regiments had been warned by the 27th Division staff to expect an attack from 9 April onwards.

CHAPTER VII

The Real Stunt – 11 April

At noon on 10 April, General Gough convened a full meeting at his Albert HQ. He told his Corps Commanders, their Chiefs of Staff , artillery and tank commanders that another attack on Bullecourt was to be made that night.

General Allenby's Third Army was to push forward its line to the villages of Fontaine, Cherisy and Vis en Artois before dawn on 11 April. Gough was to assault Bullecourt at the same time and push through to join them. The plan had barely changed except that now the tanks were to move forward at zero hour (4.30 am) and the 4th and 12th AIF Brigades were to attack in their wake at 4.45 am, without having to rely on any signals from the tanks. Because of the complete failure to cut the wire around Bullecourt itself, V Corps were not to attack until it was clear that elements of the 12th AIF Brigade had seized Bullecourt from the west.[1]

This time, Birdwood and White were determined to counter the optimism of Gough and Hardress Lloyd, who had absolute control over the tanks, without reference to 1st Brigade (Baker-Carr) Heavy Branch. During the meeting the Anzac commanders argued with Gough for a postponement to allow more time for preparation. Suddenly, Gough was called away to receive a telephone call from Kiggell, Haig's Chief of Staff. One of the staff officers witnessing the scene was Major Jack Churchill, the younger brother of Winston. He had seen many stormy meetings before, having been on both Sir John French's staff and subsequently General Hamilton's staff at Gallipoli. He had been with I ANZAC Corps for nearly a year and, as well as keeping his prominent brother briefed, he had become something of a mainstay of the Staff.[2] Churchill told Bean that during the telephone call, it was really Haig, through Kiggell, who forced Gough to implement the plan. However, Brudenell White didn't believe it, countering that 'there is no question that it was Gough who wanted to attack. He was anxious to do something – he was up against Allenby'.[3] White believed that Gough had made up the account of Haig's direct order, to cut off the argument. After all, when Birdwood was faced with an order from his Commander-in-Chief, he either carried it out or he was sacked. Although he had persuaded Gough to postpone an attack at Pozières the previous year, Birdwood was not known for his resolution when dealing with GHQ. The year before, he was put up by other

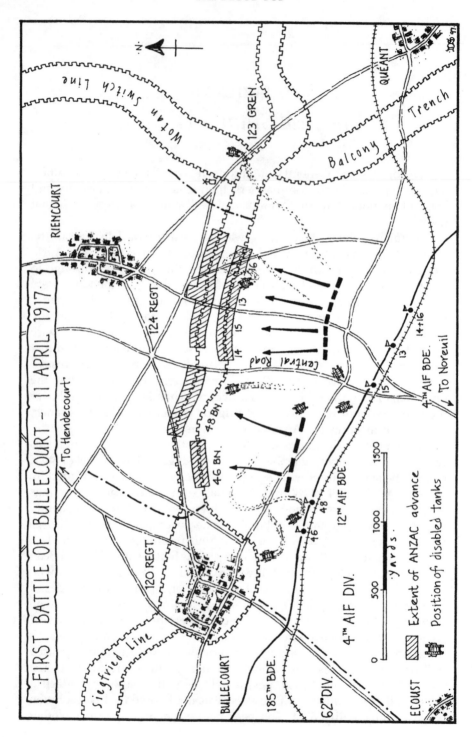

FIRST BATTLE OF BULLECOURT – 11 APRIL 1917

commanders to alter a GHQ pamphlet, 'Haig raged at him, "I won't have anyone criticising my orders". Birdwood collapsed and the others said nothing'. So Birdwood was unlikely to provoke either Haig or Gough over the plan for Bullecourt, despite White's later comment to Bean that Birdwood should have resigned. In practice, it was hardly an option, but Birdwood could have pursued the argument that the Third Army was not far enough forward.[4]

So the order was finally given to Robertson's 12th Brigade and Brand's 4th Brigade at 4.00 pm that same afternoon. During the evening, even as the assault troops were moving up, the plans were constantly being modified and adjusted so that the final details were not known to the battalion commanders until midnight, barely four and a half hours before zero.

By 3.00 am, out on the left flank south-west of Bullecourt, the men of the 46th Battalion (Denham) and the 48th Battalion (Leane) were lying out in the snow-covered no man's land. Five hundred yards to their right lay the leading waves of the 14th Battalion (Peck) and 16th Battalion (Drake-Brockman). Peck, the solitary and poetry-reading commander of the 14th, was blessed with a Victorian battalion full of 'splendid and spirited' young officers as well as determined men. For them, it was another bitterly cold night with sleet and snow showers and, despite Haig's dictate of a '200 yard dash', the Australians were over 500 yards from the enemy wire. In the time it would take to cover this distance, the Germans could easily sweep the attackers with machine-gun fire.[5] They shivered as they waited in their jumping-off trenches, for they were not allowed greatcoats which would have proved a hindrance in hand-to-hand fighting. Even without these greatcoats, they had enough weight on them as their ample tunics were stuffed with Mills bombs, ammunition and all kinds of unofficial kit. However, the two emblems that marked them out as 'Diggers' and of which they were most proud, could not be worn into combat. The famous slouch hats were stowed away in favour of the more protective 'brodie' helmets and with them the large General Service hat badge of the AIF.[6]

Five hundred yards in front of the Diggers lay their enemy, the Württembergers of the 124th Regiment, highly regarded veterans of the Somme battles who, in the past, had produced rising stars like Oberleutnant Erwin Rommel. Rommel had won the Iron Cross 1st Class with his battalion in 1915 but had now moved on to a Württemberg mountain regiment. However, the regimental HQ still took the opportunity of stiffening the resolve of their men by putting a bounty on the capture of the Australian commanders. The Germans knew the names and characteristics of all the Australian Commanders and gave the 4th Brigade in particular 'a very bloodthirsty chit'. They broadcast that 'it was the constant policy of the AIF brigade to kill all prisoners, except a few samples'.[7] No doubt this had some effect on the German ranks, especially on the younger recruits from Ulm, nervously cradling their 7.9mm Mauser rifles in the forward trenches. They were told their rifles could loose off 10 to 15 rounds a minute, but the 'old sweats' knew that they would be lucky to discharge half that, once the Diggers were through the wire. They had their *Stielhandgranate* ('stick grenades') to rely on, which could be thrown fifty yards and were ideal trench weapons, relying more on blast than fragmentation. But most placed their trust in the 24 Maxim pattern machine-guns which each regiment had mustered. Belt-fed and firing nearly 500 rounds a minute, this weapon could be relied on to devastate an attack.

By 3.00 am, the eleven tanks of No. 11 Company, 'D' Battalion Heavy Branch should have been in position, 150 yards beyond the infantry. But despite a short journey from the Noreuil valley, they were only just reaching their rendezvous point at an old level-crossing behind the embankment. The order for machine-guns to drown the noise of the tank engines was not carried out and the Australian infantry not only heard the tanks but could see them coming in the night, from the shower of sparks rising from their exhaust baffles.[8]

Captain Jacka was assigned to lead the tanks out to their positions. The section on the right, commanded by Captain Wyatt, comprised four tanks. Two (Puttock and Morris) were to advance towards the junction of the Siegfried Line and Balcony Lines and put a 'stop' at the end of the trench, to hold off enemy counter-attacks from the Quéant direction. They would then move down the Balcony Trench on the right, flattening the wire and smashing any resistance. Meanwhile, the other two tanks would attack OGI and OG2, the front fire-trench and support trench of the Siegfried Line (named after 'Old German Line' 1 & 2 at Pozières). The tanks would then split, with one (Clarkson) attacking the left of Riencourt and the other (Davies) attacking the right of the village. All the tanks in this section were in place at zero hour except for Morris who had temporarily ditched at the embankment.

Captain Field's centre section of three tanks (Money, Bernstein and MacIlwaine) were to attack the middle of the re-entrant, advancing across a slight depression. Major-General White had left this part of the objective solely for the tanks to capture, as this part of the line was too well covered by enemy machine-guns to allow an infantry assault. The tank section was to press on across OG1 & 2 and then continue northwards to Hendecourt. Of these three tanks, only Money's was in place at zero.

Swears' section of four tanks on the left (Skinner, Birkett, Sherwood and Richards) were to attack the line in front and then wheel leftwards to attack Bullecourt, two skirting the south of the village and two entering the village assisted by the 12th Brigade. Once Bullecourt was seized, the tanks would come under control of the 62nd Division which would be ordered forward to attack Hendecourt to the north. Again none of the tanks were ready at zero hour.

It was a hopelessly optimistic plan for the Mark II tanks. At all stages, operations depended on the small number of tanks not only keeping going mechanically, but also avoiding the German gunners. Furthermore, Fifth Army Intelligence had known for some time that the Germans had made anti-tank preparations, and it was known that there were over forty gun and howitzer batteries in and behind the enemy lines. It was also anticipated that many of these batteries, clustered in the area between Riencourt, Hendecourt and Cagnicourt, would be firing over open sights.[9]

Out on the German 27th Division's left flank, the forward observation posts of the 123rd Regiment, concealed in dugouts within the wire, had already heard the tank engine noises at 3.00 am. They reported this to their local KTK ('Company HQ') who immediately informed Major Freiherr von Lupin at regimental HQ in Cagnicourt. He put all twelve marksmen and machine-gun companies of the 123rd on alert. Lieutenant Schabel, commander of the No. 3 Machine-Gun Company behind the Balcony Trench, particularly relished the task before him. His guns had been equipped with new armour piercing rounds or 'K' Bullets which had yet to be tested against tanks but it was hoped they would have spectacular results.[10]

At 4.30 am (zero hour), as the Anzac artillery continued their normal rate of bombardment, the tanks of Davies, Clarkson and Puttock moved forward on the right and Money's tank advanced into the depression in the centre. The four waves of the 4th Brigade infantry waited fifteen long minutes before following.

> Punctually at zero hour, after grim and silent handshakes of farewell, and perhaps with some foreboding of the result, the first wave clambered up over the side of the sunken road. [11]

The first two waves followed the tanks, which were crawling forward at about 2 mph and, after fifteen minutes, reached them just before the wire. Inside the tanks, the conditions were appalling. Davies's tank no. 799 was a 'male' Mark II, armed with two 6 pdr guns and a crew of eight. There was no suspension, so as the tank lurched from one shell hole to another, the crew were tossed around against hot exhaust manifolds. The heat from the uncased engine was unbearable and the noise was deafening. Private Basil Gardner and his fellow gunner in the opposite sponson squinted through the narrow aiming slits but could make out few targets in the dim light. The cab was already filling with carbon monoxide and cordite fumes which made some of the crew vomit. At the front, Davies wrestled with the primitive braking system, directing his driver towards

OG1. But he was losing his way. The tank veered off to the right moving up the Riencourt-Quéant ridge and out of sight of the British observers on the railway embankment. Behind the tanks, Sergeant W. Groves waited with the fourth wave of the 14th Battalion, in the sunken road, each man displaying a flash on his helmet to signify his wave:

> By now the first wave must have been 300 yards ahead. Over goes the fourth wave – out about 20 yards, bending low and half stumbling forward. The whole line stops. The three perfect waves ahead have stopped – everyone kneels – save that here and there an officer moves about whispering. It's bitterly cold now in spite of the warming tot of rum.[12]

It was at this point that the Germans detected the Australian attack:

> With startling suddenness, the silence ceases. With a fury of hell, the enemy machine-guns spit out incessant fire. The chaps try frantically to find a way through the frightful network of barbed wire. The enemy had left zigzag passages here and there into which the men pour in dense columns, only to be mown down so that their shattered bodies pile up at the entrances.[13]

The attacking waves of the 14th were getting to the wire and finding there was still no support on their left flank. The advance of the 46th and 48th had so far failed to materialise and the three tanks responsible for suppressing the centre of the Hindenburg Line had had little success.

At 5.15 am, the artillery lifted its barrage on Quéant, to allow the tanks of Puttock and Morris half an hour to sweep the enemy parapets and suppress any threat from the Balcony Trench. Unfortunately, Puttock's tank developed clutch trouble and could hardly move. He soon had to retire, closely followed by a rain of enemy shells and he evacuated the tank near Noreuil.[14] With Morris engaged in hauling out another ditched tank by the embankment, the Balcony Trench remained untouched by the tanks. More worrying was the fact that Quéant was now left unscathed by the artillery, as ordered, for a critical half hour.[15] The reticence of field artillery in the Great War in the use of smoke was widespread – they normally complained that the capacity of the shell was too small to be of value. Unfortunately, Bullecourt was no exception, and the artillery failed to shroud Quéant in smoke. Now the numerous German batteries around the village could operate unhindered.[16]

The first waves of the 16th, bunching at the wire behind Clarkson's 'female' tank, were suddenly urged on by the arrival of their commander, the redoubtable Major Percy Black, an old prospector and Gallipoli veteran. The German guns were now firing into the re-entrant from both

Bullecourt and Quéant, and the tanks firing in front of the wire were attracting a great deal of SAA. It was vital that the attack push on, as waves of infantry behind would soon join them. 'Come on boys, bugger the tanks', Black shouted, pushing his men on through gaps in the wire.[17] Dawn was now breaking and the German machine-gunners could easily pick up the dark bodies struggling through the wire against a white background of snow. Black made it into OG1 and was soon climbing out over the parados and into the support zone. One uncut belt of wire protected OG2 in this zone and, as soon as Black and remnants of his company approached this last main defence, he was shot through the head, collapsing into the wire.[18] Behind him, groups of the 16th followed by the 13th staggered through gaps created by Clarkson's tank but soon received the same deadly treatment. Everywhere there were wounded and dying men hanging on the wire.

Meanwhile over on the left, there was continued confusion surrounding the advance of the 12th Brigade. The tanks which the infantry were to follow had not arrived by 4.45 am, and Lieutenant-Colonel Denham commanding the leading 46th Battalion had orders to advance at that time, regardless of whether the tanks had started. But fatally the leading 46th still hung on to wait for the tanks to pass in front of them. It was another half hour before a tank passed them and only then was the order finally given to advance. That half hour was crucial, for it was fast becoming light and the enemy artillery observers in Bullecourt could easily make out the approaching Victorians.[19] The resulting bombardment, together with cross-fire from machine-gun detachments, cut great holes in their lines as they advanced across the flat ground, south-west of Bullecourt.

By 5.30 am, the attack was well underway and all the tanks except for 2nd Lieutenant Skinner's had finally struggled out beyond the embankment and onto the battlefield. But their arrival had been a shambles. In the approach, one tank mistakenly fired into an Australian trench, and another accidentally killed a mortar crew. These tragedies were sadly not unusual in night fighting; the previous evening, a returning Australian patrol had been shot up by its own battalion sentries.[20] However, such accidents did not travel well in the telling and it was not long before the tank crews were the object of much bitterness among the Australians.

It was two hasty tank crew evacuations that drew the ire of the Australian battalion commanders. In Field's centre tank section, operating near the combined HQ of Peck and Drake-Brockman, a shell hit MacIlwaine's tank track shortly after starting and the crew evacuated before it received a direct hit. In Swears' left section, 2nd Lieutenant Richards' tank engine cut out and he evacuated his crew. They made their way back to the embankment and Richards went looking for his section leader for further instructions. Leane's staff stopped some of the crew who refused at first to go back to the tank as they had no-one in command, which infuriated Leane, a man who always exercised initiative and expected it in others.[21]

Whilst there was undoubtedly panic among some of these tank crews, there was also bravery of the highest order among others in the tanks still operating. In the centre section, Lieutenant Eric Money's tank had reached the third belt of wire and was still firing its machine guns when it suddenly stuck fast. Money screamed at the driver to reverse but the 'spuds' on the tracks had caught fast in the tangled wire. The driver and gearsmen tried everything to free it as the Germans moved up a trench mortar and machine-gun with belts of 'K' ammunition. The tank, with Privates Charlie Barrett and Ben Bown still firing their machine-guns, rocked back and forth as it took four direct hits from the enemy mortar in quick succession. A stream of armour-piercing rounds followed which easily cut through the tank's 9mm hull boiler plate, rupturing the fuel tank which then exploded. Flames engulfed the machine and Money, his driver and two others were burnt alive, but Private Ben Bown, being small enough, managed to scramble out through the sponson door. However, his escape was short-lived as he was met by a hail of gunfire and died against the side of his tank.[22] Money's tank, now blazing in the third belt of wire, had created an enticing opening through the first and second belts. The right hand column of the 46th made a dash for this gap, those with wirecutters leading the rush. The wirecutters had a green sign on their helmets, so those coming up behind knew who to follow but inevitably they were the first to be picked off by the enemy snipers. As the rest of the 46th tore into the gap, the enemy machine-gunners, who had already anticipated the charge, swept the new killing ground and swiftly crushed the attack, killing all but three of the men.

2nd Lieutenant Bernstein's tank, following Money into the central depression, was soon knocked out when a shell came through the front cab flap, taking off the driver's head and exploding inside the cab. A second shell hit the tank on the roof and the stunned survivors evacuated with their wounded commander. So with MacIlwaine's tank also out of the reckoning, the only force trusted with capturing the centre of the Siegfried Line had now been destroyed. Even if the 4th Brigade on the right and the 12th on the left succeeded in capturing their objectives, there would still be a gap of some 300 yards between the Australian troops.

By 6.30 am, the 46th had secured 250 yards of the front trench OG1, while the 48th under Captain Allan Leane had captured 400 yards of the support trench OG2. Unfortunately, the two captured sectors were not in front of each other and the Germans kept up counter attacks all around the Australians. Meanwhile, a tank had finally arrived to support them, commanded by 2nd Lieutenant Birkett. Moving backwards and forwards firing its 6 pdr guns, it drew much of the fire away from a company of the

47th who were advancing in support. But Birkett was moving too far to the right, and Swears, his section commander, ran out from the embankment to order him to move back towards Bullecourt. Shells were falling all around but Swears made it to the tank and passed his order on. He then jumped into a shell hole to dodge the enemy fire but was never seen alive again. [23]

Birkett silenced a trench mortar but, with his section commander dead, he needed further targets and his tank toiled up towards Leane's HQ in the embankment to get further instructions. He was then sent off to silence a troublesome machine-gun in Bullecourt which he did successfully, but on returning, his tank was hit by a shell. Birkett evacuated the survivors but, as he stepped out of the door, another shell landed at his feet and blew both his legs off. Stretcher-bearers ran out to bring him in and he was wounded again. While he was lying on a stretcher outside a dressing station, shrapnel hit him for the third time. [24]

Birkett's smoking tank on the high ground was drawing so much artillery fire on Leane's HQ that Captain Fairley, a nephew of the battalion commander, rushed out to try and restart it. But Fairley presented an easy target and was soon wounded by a sniper. Ray Leane had already lost a brother at Bullecourt, and now a nephew was wounded, while his other nephew Captain Allan Leane was fighting for his life, leading the 48th in the thick of the action. To make matters worse, there was no protective artillery barrage around the Australians and 'Bullecourt, Riencourt, Hendecourt and the snowfield beyond the Siegfried Line lay undisturbed by a single shell'.[25] Reports coming from the Australian FOOs had indicated that the attack was going well, but any bombardment of Bullecourt might kill friendly troops. However, the actual position was desperate. By 8.00 am, the 46th holding OG1 were almost out of bombs and ammunition and only the arrival of carrying parties of the 47th with fresh supplies enabled them to hang on.[26] Some of the 47th also reached the rear OG2 trench where they found Captain Leane's 48th down to 240 men. It was out of the question to try and join up with the 4th Brigade on the right and they now attempted to hold what they had captured even with the help of cases of German egg bombs.[27]

Towards 9.00 am, the last of Swears' tanks came into the battle. It had initially 'ditched' at the start, but had finally been towed over the embankment by Morris's tank. After receiving instructions to silence a machine-gun in Bullecourt, which had been enfilading the 46th, Lieutenant Skinner took his tank towards the village. It negotiated the thick wire and managed to get to the edge of OG1 near the south-east of the village, firing its 6 pdr guns. In return, the tank was showered with German machine-gun rounds, many of them finding the gaps in the boiler plate and splashing the crew inside with molten lead. Skinner withdrew his wounded crew just as the Germans brought forward a trench mortar which soon scored a direct hit on the tank and knocked it out.[28] This last tank casualty signalled the end of any mechanical support for the 12th Brigade.

To the observers on the railway embankment, the situation by 9.00 am was very confusing. The white battlefield was dotted with burning tank carcasses and corpses but the fighting in the Siegfried Line was barely visible. Captain Richard Haigh, second-in-command of the company of tanks, confirmed how difficult it was to make sense of the action:

> One who has never seen a modern battle doubtless forms a picture of masses of troops moving forward in splendid formation with cheering voices and gleaming bayonets. This is quite erroneous. To an observer in a post, no concerted action is visible at all. Here and there a line or two of men dash forward and disappear. A single man or a small group of men wriggle across the ground. That is all.[29]

The white background and early light further conspired to deceive the observers who were finding it difficult to judge distances to the horizon. Even today the landscape plays the same trick on the eye, for the fields to the front of the Siegfried Line appear to be close up to Riencourt. In fact, the trench line was on a reverse slope and these fields were half a mile in front of the village. Accordingly, there were reports that on the right of the battlefield, the tanks of Clarkson and Davies together with groups of infantry were seen approaching Riencourt. By now, only Clarkson's tank was still in action, moving up and down in front of OG1 but the misleading news was enough to stay any artillery barrage on Riencourt.[30] This tank received a direct hit soon after, which killed Clarkson and four of his crew.

Unfortunately, the false rumours of success were bolstered by the arrival of an exhausted runner at 14th Battalion HQ. He reported that 'both objectives were taken and our troops are 400 yards north [of the SL support trench] and still going'.[31] Four hundred yards would have taken them to the edge of Riencourt, so to allow a bombardment of the village at that stage was out of the question.

In fact the 4th Brigade had captured some 800 yards of front trench (OG1) and support trench (OG2) but had not managed to get beyond and were now occupied in fighting off fierce German counter-attacks. They were also attempting to join up with the 12th Brigade on their left, by bombing the stubborn Württembergers still holding the centre part of the Line. This gap was to prove extremely serious for the 14th trying to make headway on the left.

On the left flank, D Company of the 14th Battalion soon found itself down to one officer, having already lost three of its famous commanders.

Captain Orr was wounded in front of the wire, carried to a shell hole for protection but was then killed by an artillery shell. Captain Stanton, leading five men over the parados of OG1, rushed a machine-gun that was firing from the wire in front of the support trench. He knocked out the gun but was shot through the heart. Captain Williamson was killed shortly after, attempting a similar assault on OG2.[32]

Fighting off continuing counter-attacks, the survivors of the 4th Brigade soon began to run out of bombs and ammunition. Not only had they exhausted their supply but, according to Lieutenant Rule, nearly one third of their bombs had arrived without detonators due to careless packing.[33] The only way they could be re-supplied was across the half mile of open re-entrant, constantly swept by enemy machine-gun fire from the flanks. Anyone who appeared above the parapet was soon shot down, sometimes horribly mutilated:

> Jim was violently sick. A headless man nearly falling on top of him . . . a fellow being with whom he was very friendly, drenching him from head to foot .[34]

Many of the runners taking news back to battalion HQs were hit by shrapnel as they darted from one shell hole to the next, but it was the enemy machine-guns firing from the flanks that really cut off the troops in OG1 and OG2.

Just after 7.00 am, one runner did manage to get back to the 13th HQ on the embankment, but found everyone dead or wounded after the sandbagged dugout had received a direct hit. Miraculously, the battalion commander, Colonel 'Dolly' Durrant was the only survivor and was promptly given the message from Captain Harry Murray – 'With artillery support we can keep the position till the cows come home'.[35]

Given that fresh ammunition could be supplied to the stranded Australians, artillery support would have held any German counter-attacks at bay and the day might have been saved. But the Anzac artillery command stubbornly resisted pressure to put down a barrage in front of or on the flanks, allowing groups of German stormtroopers to pour out of Hendecourt and Riencourt to launch counter-attacks. By 9.30 am, at Brand's 4th Brigade HQ, staff officers were losing their patience with the gunners and, after heated arguments, the matter of artillery support was passed to Birdwood. Unfortunately, he backed Colonel R. Rabett, the commander of the central artillery group in the Noreuil valley who declined this vital support on the grounds that he still believed Australian troops were beyond OG2 and also in Bullecourt.

In fact, even at Fifth Army level, credence was given to these false reports, for shortly after 9.30 am, Gough ordered the Indian Sialkot Cavalry Brigade to gallop through the Siegfried Line on the left sector and on to Fontaine and Chérisy. It was one more muddle in a day of calamities, when firstly a party of dismounted Indian wirecutters approached east of Bullecourt and were badly shot-up; then the cavalry, assembling in 'splendid formation' behind the embankment, were heavily shelled. Colonel Melvill (commanding 17th Lancers) saw more than 30 large calibre 5.9" rounds fall right in the middle of a squadron, pole-axing riders and horses alike.[36] When the smoke lifted, he expected to see a 'slaughter house', but miraculously there were few riders among the casualties. Relief at the few casualties was short-lived however, as those around witnessed the terrible suffering of the horses:

> A horse is struck by a large lump of shrapnel just under its withers and the poor brute trembles, but makes no sound. Almost the only time that horses scream – and the sound is horrible – is when they are dying. Then they shriek from sheer pain and fear. Strange as it seems, one is often more affected by seeing horses struck than when men are killed. They are so helpless.[37]

After this debacle, the brigade was swiftly withdrawn. It was a similar disaster to that which befell the wretched 8th Cavalry Brigade the day before at Monchy, and was proof that massed cavalry no longer had a role on the Western Front. [38]

Meanwhile on the left, Braithwaite's 62nd Division awaited confirmation that the Australians had gained a foothold in Bullecourt, before entering the battle.[39] Their exposed position near Ecoust meant they had already been shelled and a forward company of the 2/6 West Yorks lost a Lewis gun team together with thirty others, killed outright in their jumping off post. Confirmation that the Australians had entered the village came just after 8.00 am and Braithwaite ordered out patrols prior to launching a battalion assault. However, the patrols reported that the enemy still held Bullecourt in strength and the wire was still uncut. They hastily retired to the railway, suffering sixty-three casualties to hear that, after all, the 4th Division staff was now 'not at all certain that the Australians held the place'. With requests from the 12th Brigade to shell Bullecourt, Braithwaite stayed his hand. The 4th Brigade were outraged by the apparent inactivity of the 62nd Division, but Bean privately admitted that this Australian criticism 'was damnably unjust'.[40]

Between 9.00 and 11.00 am, SOS flares were repeatedly sent up by the beleaguered Australians. Battalion commands tried to help with carrying parties who were all shot down as they tried to cross the open re-entrant. The Anzac artillery still refused to answer with a protective barrage on Riencourt, allowing the Württembergers to crowd into the first floor rooms of houses fronting the village. From these vantage points they could pick off any head or bomb-throwing arm raised above the trench parapets. Worse still, the artillery also failed to bombard the garrison village of Cagnicourt, which lay only two and half miles to the rear of OG1 and was an important collecting point for the German reserves. It was here in the old château that the 53rd Brigade Commander, Oberst von der Osten, maintained his HQ and issued orders for local counter-attacks.[41]

Furthermore, many of the German artillery batteries were sited around Cagnicourt and, such was their impunity, that commanders were able to push individual pieces onto high ground to allow direct firing over open sights. These German *Abteilung* ('detachments') comprised three batteries of four Q/F Field guns each, which could fire shells over a range of four miles. To the German gunners, the crawling tanks on a white background were easily within range and must have been impossible to miss. In OG2 to the front of Riencourt, the survivors of the gallant 4th Brigade now faced a stark choice. They could either clamber out and attack Riencourt, advancing perhaps ten yards before being annihilated, or they could withdraw. Their supply of Mills bombs had finally run out and there was no more Lewis gun ammunition. They could see groups of Germans flanking them and bombing their way back into the trenches, bay by bay.

By 11.00 am, back at Holmes' 4th Division HQ, the true situation was finally grasped and orders were at last wired to the Heavy Artillery batteries to put down a protective barrage in front of Riencourt. But it was too late.

Out in the trenches, the call went up from the remaining Australian officers, 'Every man for himself.' Hearing the call, the remnants of the four battalions jumped the trench parapets and made off across the open ground back towards their lines. After surviving the attack and then the hours of holding the captured trenches, it was tragic that so many were killed as they escaped. For the Germans had most of the exits covered by machine-guns which cut right through the desperate groups of Australians. Others were felled by the Anzac artillery barrage which now dropped short onto parts of the line as they were escaping.[42]

By 11.45 am, the Germans re-entered and captured all of OG1 and OG2 and rolled bombs down the steps of any dugouts, killing some of the badly wounded left behind. Many of the Australians were captured by the enemy before they could get out of the trench sally-ports, but some of the 4th Brigade did manage to make it back to the sanctuary of the railway embankment.

Over to the left, in the 12th Brigade's sector, the Australians were in a similar critical state. Shortly after 11.00 am, the 46th Battalion holding OG1 were driven out by the Germans who were bombing along the trench from the right. This left the 48th Battalion, holding OG2 to the rear, completely cut off. When their commander, Captain Allan Leane, heard that OG1 had been lost, he at once set about launching a counter-attack to drive the Germans out again. With pitifully few resources, he launched bombing parties at them and managed to get a foothold in OG1, but in the attempt he was wounded in the thigh. Pitching into the front trench, he was horrified to hear incoming shells smashing into OG2 behind him. He soon realised that it was his own artillery acting on delayed orders to lay down a barrage.

Allan Leane sent a runner back to the railway with the curt message, 'Our artillery is making trench untenable,' and at 12.30 he ordered a withdrawal.[43] Leane struggled out of OG1 behind his men, with his intelligence officer Lieutenant Watson, who was promptly shot through the spine. Leane was last seen hopping towards the wire with the remnants of his men, shortly before being overpowered and captured. While some of the 48th did make it back to the railway, many were killed by the withering machine-gun fire as they picked their way through the wire.

The Germans soon caught up with the walking wounded and took them prisoner, giving them medical attention. Then they were seen moving among the badly wounded in the wire, shooting those with horrendous injuries and placing others outside their lines for Australian orderlies to collect. This went on until nightfall, when snow began to fall on the shoals of dead and wounded. From their lines, the Australians could hear the shadowy grey figures in the distance shouting, 'Finish-hospital'. The agony was over.

It had been an extraordinary battle. The Australians had shown tremendous bravery and daring and their breaking of the Siegfried Line unaided was an incredible feat. But the 4th Division, who had gone into the fight at the peak of their performance, had been decimated. Nearly 3,500 men had been lost, including 40 officers and 1,142 men captured, by far the largest number of Australian prisoners taken during any action in the Great War.[44] Brand's 4th Brigade had suffered the worst and was virtually destroyed, losing 2,339 out of 3,000 men engaged, while Robertson's 12th Brigade lost 950. To I ANZAC Corps, the loss was all the more cruel as it was now deprived of so many of its future young leaders.[45]

The Australian prisoners, many of them wounded, were marched away to the rear towards Hendecourt. On the way they were accidentally caught in the open by another late Anzac artillery barrage and also received a strafing by a passing British airman who mistook them for retreating Germans. Unfortunately, they were destined for the notorious prison, Fort Macdonald known as the 'Black Hole of Lille'. There, many of the wounded died in appalling conditions, exacerbated by the Germans because of a continuing argument with the British government over prisoners being kept near the battle front.[46] Conditions eventually improved but it was too late for Allan Leane. His brother Geoff wrote to their father, Colonel E.T. Leane with the news that now a fourth member of the family would never return:

> Oh Dad, it eased the pain a lot to hear how those boys spoke of Allan . . . I know I can never describe Bullecourt the way the boys did it and tell you of Allan's beautiful work. I wish it had been me Dad and not Allan as he is worth a dozen of me and I thank God that you are at home to buck them all up.[47]

After the battle, the COs of the battalions involved were hopping mad. Brand, Peck and Drake-Brockman went into the YMCA hut, bought up all the stores and proceeded to pelt the lot all around the shed.[48] Both commanders and men were bitter and sad and vented their anger on those they thought were responsible for the disaster – the tank crews.

Lieutenant-Colonel Ray Leane thought the 'tanks were of no assistance in the attack, in fact they proved a menace'. Bert Jacka, who was responsible for getting the tanks into position before the attack, felt 'the organisation seemed to be bad and no-one appeared to be in direct command of the show. Personal safety and comfort seemed their sole ambition'. While E.J. Rule jibed that he 'never saw a more windy lot of officers . . . it was not the tanks' fault, but the chicken hearts who manned them'. [49]

Jacka prepared a damning report on the tanks which Birdwood restricted and eventually a sanitised document was circulated, signed by Peck and Drake-Brockman but drawing on much of what Jacka alleged. His most acute observation was that, in future, tank crews and infantry should always be trained to cooperate in battle and that tanks should come under the direct orders of the infantry commander. [50]

However, the general hostility of the Australians was misdirected. The tanks did in fact draw some of the fire away from the infantry.[51] It was true that, as eye-witnesses, Jacka, Rule and the battalion commanders had observed poor conduct among some crews and there were some 'windy officers', all no doubt horrified to find themselves in training tanks shredded by armour-piercing rounds. Bean privately noted that these testimonies should be treated with caution and that they did not tell the full story. Eye-witness accounts, which Bean nevertheless heavily relied upon for his Official History, could give a narrow view of the battlefield. Bean privately refuted Leane's report that 'the 12th Brigade received no assistance from the tanks', commenting 'This was not the case. Leane speaks of what he saw but there was evidently much he didn't see.' [52] Bean was referring to an incident when a tank distracted the enemy, allowing the relieving 47th Battalion to come forward.

However, Bean was unlikely to defend the Heavy Branch against the

AIF and the animosity got out of control, further fuelled by 'Pompey' Elliott. As an Australian senator several years later, he outrageously alleged that some tank crews had poured sand into their engines.[53] It was part of his wider campaign to discredit the operations commanded by Birdwood and White and thereby revenge what he saw as their stifling of Jacka's promotion prospects. These accusations against the tank crews were therefore wide of the mark, for many showed great courage. No. 11 Company, 'D' Battalion Heavy Branch lost 52 officers and men out of 91 committed to the battle.[54] Their only consolation for years afterwards was that Clarkson and Davies were thought to have crossed the Siegfried Line and gone on to Riencourt and Hendecourt followed by a company of Australians, before being swamped by the Germans.[55] Captain Cyril Falls, in the British Official History, cites this incident as 'a veritable legend and one of the most curious of the War', as it was based only on the reports of an airman and several artillery FOOs.[56] The war diaries of 'D' Battalion and 1st Brigade Heavy Branch, the records of the Fifth Army and even the despatches of Field-Marshal Sir Douglas Haig all confirmed this as fact.[57] Even Bean filed a report in *The Times*, published on 18 April 1917, stating that 'one of the tanks entered the village of Hendecourt, 2000 yards beyond the Hindenburg Line'. Unbeknown to Bean and the authorities, three months after the battle, Jessie Harding-Roberts, fiancee of 2nd Lieutenant Harold Davies, received a telegram from a prisoner-of-war in Germany:

> We were in an attack on the morning of 11 April, when our tank was put out of action. Mr Davies was badly wounded and I and my comrades did all we could for him. Acting on his orders we tried to get back to our own lines to bring assistance but we were cut off by the Germans and taken prisoner. I am very sorry to tell you that unless he had proper treatment, I am afraid it will go hard with him.

In fact, Davies's tank had gone the farthest. When the initial advance of the tanks took place, Davies moved too far and went out of sight over the ridge towards the axis of the Siegfried Line and the Balcony Trench surrounding Quéant. His male tank moved up and down the front trenches, strafing the defenders and firing its 6 pdr guns. As dawn broke, it crossed the wire and traversed OG1, just within the German 123rd Regiment sector, where it received the undivided attention of every machine-gun, trench mortar and field gun in the vicinity.

With the front cab flaps open, Davies could see that his tank was crossing the Moulin Sans Souci-Quéant road towards the support trench. Suddenly the crew were horrified when a volley of bullets slashed through the tank cab, ricocheting around them. The driver and gearsmen wrestled to turn the tank away from the fusillade, but it was no use. One hundred and fifty yards away, Oberleutnant Schabel kept his machine-gun trained on the smoking tank. He fired some 1,200 armour-piercing rounds at the tank, which sliced through the 9mm boiler plate 'turning the tank into a colander'. The petrol tank soon ignited and, in the roaring furnace, the ammunition store went up. Miraculously, a sergeant and three of the crew staggered out onto the road with their clothes on fire, dragging with them the mortally wounded Davies. While most of the Germans were stunned by the sudden explosion in the tank, Grenadier Christoph Heinkel dashed forward and quickly captured the badly wounded survivors. [58]

The capture of Tank no. 799 was a coup for the 123rd Württemberg Regiment, for it was the first British tank that the Germans had ever captured and held onto. Together with Clarkson's wrecked female tank, lying 1,000 yards to the west, the Germans now had two Mark II's within their lines and from which they could draw detailed plans of the design and weapons systems. Leading German commanders and machine designers came to view the tanks when they were removed to Hendecourt, appreciating the full effect of 'K' bullets on the ex-training machines.[59]

As darkness fell on 11 April, the officers and men of the Württemberg 27th Division realised 'they had accomplished something extraordinary and had achieved a success that was rare for a division in defence'.[60] Divisional casualties totalled only 6 officers and 132 men killed, with a further 11 officers and 520 men wounded. The 124th Regiment, who took the brunt of the Australian attack, suffered losses of 434. It was a notable German victory in what had been a bad week elsewhere for the Sixth Army and its commander, Freiherr von Falkenhausen. He readily conferred the Pour le Mérite on General von Moser (Gruppe Quéant) and General von Maur (27th Division), passing on copious praise from the Kaiser. However von Falkenhausen did not last long as Sixth Army Commander. Blamed for the tactical errors at Vimy, he was removed on 22 April and made Governor-General of Belgium.

Australian unit histories and even Bean's Official History blamed the tanks as one of the main reasons for the disaster, but the tanks were really a side issue.[61] Gough's decision to attack in a re-entrant with deep objectives was a fundamental tactical error, which he himself conceded in correspondence with the British Official Historian, Sir James Edmonds. Inevitably, any narrow salient pushed forwards was always going to be easy for the enemy to flank and counter-attack.[62] But Gough was determined to get forward and attack quickly to cooperate with the main Third Army thrust and, in his favour, there is evidence to suggest that had he waited for more artillery to be brought up, the Germans could have made the Siegfried Line impregnable. Their unit histories all confirm that at the date of the attack, their positions, especially the concrete gun emplacements and dugouts, were only partially completed.

But once the Germans had closed the re-entrant, by sweeping the ground behind the Australians with machine-gun fire, a classic trap had been set up which succeeded in cutting off the attackers from their support and logistics. With no means of communication except by runner, flares or one-way pigeon, the magnificent achievement of the Australians in capturing part of the Siegfried Line was lost.

Gough also cites poor communication between the Third and Fifth Armies as a reason why he attacked without waiting for confirmation of a Third Army success on his left flank. It was within his brief to correct this deficiency but, as we have seen, his rivalry with Allenby and the personality of his Chief of Staff, Malcolm, probably scuppered any chance of useful contact between the neighbouring Armies. However, despite Gough's tactical failings at Bullecourt, he was right about the importance of communication.

It was the failure of communication in so many areas that really sealed the fate of the attack. The links between brigade and battalion were often weak, as in the case of Denham's 46th Battalion misinterpreting its starting time, with disastrous results. This could have been avoided if the 46th and 48th had collaborated by sharing battalion headquarters in the same way as the 14th and 16th.[63] At other times, important instructions were not conveyed, such as the firing of machine-guns to disguise the noise of the tanks or the discharge of smoke to cover Quéant. Poor staffwork by the 4th Division contributed to much of this breakdown, most notably in the 'buckshee battle' when the 62nd Division suffered needless casualties. It should be remembered that one handicap the AIF suffered was a shortage of staff officers. Most staff in the 4th Division were in fact British and, in certain cases, far from competent.[64] Major-General Holmes was also criticised for not using the five battalions he held in reserve, but false reports persuaded him to hold their deployment. Despite his ability, Holmes generated prejudice among 'regular' colleagues in both the AIF and British Army as he was a successful 'citizen', and therefore amateur, soldier.[65]

The Heavy Branch, still in its infancy, failed to appreciate the need for tanks to cooperate closely with the infantry, and surprisingly this glaring error was slow to be rectified in its subsequent training programme. It was not until the Battle of Hamel in 1918, that the Australians restored their confidence in the tanks and their crews. But at Bullecourt, the use of training tanks without armour plating must have alarmed the novice crews and contributed to panic in some quarters.[66] Essentially, these early slow moving tanks were always going to be fodder for the enemy artillery. For although they were originally designed to defeat the 'deadly trilogy' of trench, barbed wire and machine-gun, they could not defeat that most destructive element on the battlefield – the enemy artillery. As

1 General Sir Hubert Gough (centre), commander Fifth Army ('Goughie'), with the King of the Belgians.

2 Crown Prince Rupprecht (left) with the Kaiser.

3 Major-General W.P. Braithwaite (commanding 62nd (West Riding) Division) with his son Valentine.

4 I ANZAC Corps staff. Lieutenant-General Birdwood (seated centre), Major-General C.B. White (seated third left), Major Jack Churchill (Winston Churchill's brother) 'Winston's eyes and ears' (middle row, extreme right).

5 Lieutenant-Colonel Ray Leane. 'Exercised initiative and expected it in others'.

6 Major-General W. Holmes (commanding 4th Australian Division). 'The Citizen Soldier'.

7 Australian artillery observers registering hits on the Siegfried Line. 'Some day their R.A. will let them down terribly'.

8 'Tankers' at 1st Bullecourt. 2nd Lt. Bernstein, wounded (top left), 2nd Lt. Richards, wounded (centre top), unidentified (top right), Lt. Money, killed (middle left), unidentified (middle right), Lt. Swears, killed (centre front).

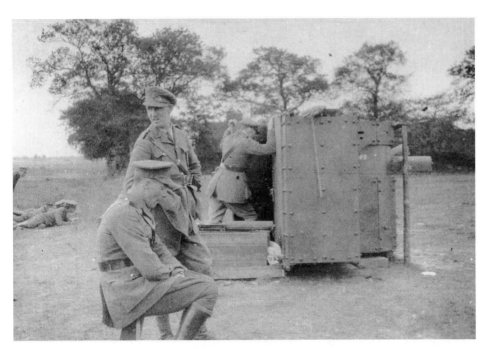

9 'Pantomime Tanks'.

10 Württembergers approach a crippled Mark II on the edge of Bullecourt.

11 'The Blood Tub' after 1st Bullecourt (south east). Birkett's tank tracks can be seen near Leane's HQ on railway.

12 AIF Battalion Commanders at 1st Bullecourt. From left: Lieutenant-Colonels Drake-Brockman, Durrant, McSharry, Peck.

13 Lt-General Sir William Birdwood presenting Captain Bert Jacka VC, MC, with a bar to his MC after 1st Bullecourt.

14 Tank No. 799. The first tank the Germans had captured and retained.

15 Riencourt 14 April 1917. 'Still needs to be bombarded'.

16 The Siegfried Line. Bullecourt was surrounded by wire up to four belts deep.

17 'The Red Patch' before bombardment. The dark lines to the front are belts of barbed wire.

18 2/6 West Yorkshires. 'Every officer who went into Bullecourt became a casualty'.

19 'The boys who hopped the bags'.

20 Brigadier-General John Gellibrand. 'The finest operational commander in the AIF'.

21 Major-General Shoubridge. 'The Dumas of the 7th Division'.

22 Private Roy Hankin. 'Given a blood soaked Deutschmark note'.

23 Roy Hankin, 101 years old. He still carries a bullet in his back.

24 'Lucky Combsy', 23rd Battalion AIF. He enlisted at age 15 years.

25 Robert Comb at age 95 years, holding the Bullecourt plaque. 'He came through without a scratch'.

26 Australian Gunners in Noreuil Valley. 'Give the bastards hell'.

27 'Possies' in the Siegfried Line.

28 Riencourt Catacombs. 'The damp and mildew of 400 years'.

29 'Low enough to see the Maltese Cross'.

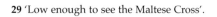

30 Rev. The Hon Maurice Peel (Chaplain 1/RWF) kia 14/5/17. 'Appeared like a guardian angel'.

31 Rev. Eric Milner-White (Senior Chaplain, 7th Division). He read the Collect for the Day over Peel's body.

32 The Diggers return, 1993.

long as their own heavy artillery failed to silence these guns, tanks would always be easy targets.[67]

Perhaps the most striking statistic was that only nine German artillerymen were killed on 11 April. Their battery positions were known to the Anzac Heavy artillery, so why were so few enemy batteries destroyed? Part of the reason was that as a preliminary barrage was dispensed with, the guns could not be ranged and registered before the infantry attack. Without refinements such as 'bearing pickets', when zero hour came the Anzac artillery were largely firing 'into the blue'. Flash Spotting and Sound Ranging, that would revolutionise the accuracy of artillery, were still in their infancy in the Spring of 1917 and the 'flash' and 'buzzer' boards, on which this new system depended, were not widely distributed[68] It was also true that ever since General Nivelle's directive to Sir Douglas Haig on 6 March 1917, the Anzac artillery had lost many of its heavy pieces to the 4th Army.[69]

However, for all this, its commanders still failed to put their available howitzers to effective use. Bean's prophesy that the ANZAC Corps artillery would let down the AIF became a reality at Bullecourt when a combination of poor 'forward observation' and staffwork allowed the German field guns to remain in action throughout. Furthermore, the artillery commanders showed remarkable inflexibility, even by Great War standards. As Norman Dixon has observed, 'War is primarily concerned with two sorts of activity – the delivering of energy and the communication of information. This communication collapses when a decision maker chooses to ignore it because it clashes with his pre-conceptions.' [70] This assertion, which has been more often than not levelled at Gough, is more applicable to the commanders of his artillery. Napier, as GOCRA, was ultimately responsible for the performance of the artillery. He controlled all divisional artillery and set the timings, allocated FOOs to divisional batteries, and issued coordinating maps and objectives.[71] However, Fraser as Commander of the Heavies and therefore in charge of counter-battery work, was more directly accountable. His subordinate, Colonel Rabbett, as commander of the central artillery group responsible for support, repeatedly turned down requests from the attacking battalions for protective barrages. Ignoring repeated SOS flares from the front line and pleading telephone calls from battalion and brigade HQs, he stubbornly refused to be swayed from believing the inaccurate reports of his FOOs.[72]

Despite the carnage at Bullecourt on 11 April, General Gough was determined to make another attack on the position as soon as possible. There had been successes by the British army on that day, most notably farther up the line at Monchy, and Gough was encouraged by this. But Brigadier-General de Falbe, commanding the British 185th Brigade in front of Bullecourt, despaired at such optimism, noting in his diary –

'After the battle, Army Command still convinced the German line was, or would be evacuated in a few hours. Patrols were sent out, with of course more casualties.' [73]

Gough was adamant that it would take just one more hammer-blow to crack the Siegfried Line.

NOTES

1   I ANZAC Corps Order no. 124, 10/4/17, WO95/982, PRO.
2   There are good portraits of many of I ANZAC staff in Baroness de la Grange's, *Open House in Flanders 1914-1918*.
3   Bean Diary p.24, AWM 38 3DRL/606 (113).
4   Bean Diary, AWM 3DRL 606/183, p. 44-45; T.H.E. Travers, 'Haig and GHQ 1916-18', *The Journal of Strategic Studies*, Vol 10, no.10 (Sept. 1987)
5   E.M.Andrews, *C. E. W. Bean & Bullecourt: Walking the battlefield and new findings* – Paper given to AWM History Conference, November 1991 .
6   Although the badge is often thought to represent the 'rising sun', it is derived from the badge worn by the first regiment to serve in the South African War. This was a trophy of swords and bayonets surrounding the crown.
7   Peck to Bean, 14 March 1923, Bean Diary AWM 38 3DRL/606 247.
8   Unfortunately, it was not until after the Arras battles that the improved Mark IV appeared on the battlefield. This model was a dramatic improvement on the Mark I and II. The fuel tanks were moved, gun barrels shortened and a proper exhaust system was fitted.
9   Fifth Army Intelligence Summaries 2 to 8 April 1917, WO 157/209, PRO; Maps of German Battery positions on Fifth Army front, 10 April 1917, WO 153/961, PRO.
10 Letter Otto Michaelis to author, 6/10/93; Richard Brechtle, *Die Ulmer Grenadier, p.* 93.
11 W. C. Groves Papers, AWM 2 DRL/0268.
12 According to captured soldiers from the 124th Regt. garrisoned in Riencourt, there was no sign of any infantry attack before 4.00 am, 14th Battalion, Precis of events, WO95/3494, PRO.
13 Groves Papers, AWM 2 DRL/0268.
14 According to Watson, this tank was destroyed shortly after evacuation, Watson, *A Company of Tanks* p. 62.
15 4th Division Order no. 54 WO 95/3443, PRO.
16 Major-General Birch (MGRA) to Falls 22/11/37, CAB 45/116, PRO.
17 William Oakes Papers, AWM MSS 0954. Although there were tracts of wire intact in this sector, the artillery had created some large gaps through which the 16th Bn. passed.
18 'The Death of Major Percy Black', *Journal of AWM*, Oct. 1989.
19 *Das Württemberg Kaiser-Regt. no. 120* , p. 65.
20 War Diary 14th Battalion, WO95/3494, PRO; *History of the 14th Battalion, p.* 192.
21 Ray Leane to Bean 27/7/37, AWM 38 3DRL 7953 Item 30. See also Bean's comments in the margin of his letter.
22 Interview with Private Bown's sister, Clara Hayles 10/11/93 (Michael Drakely); also *History of 124th Grenadier Regt.* p.66; Watson, *A Company of Tanks*, p.62.

23 Lieutenant Birkett to Charles Swears 11 Sept. 1917, Swears Papers, Anne Davison. Swears' body was later found and buried by the Australians on the battlefield. He, like virtually all the casualties at Bullecourt, had no known grave and was listed as 'missing in action'.

24 Letter Birkett to Charles Swears, Swears Papers; Haigh, *Life in a Tank*, p. 87; Watson, *A Company of Tanks*, p.63. Birkett spent the rest of the war in hospital.

25 Bean IV, p. 320.

26 Geoff Leane Papers, 25/4/17, AWM 1 DRL (0411).

27 In 1993 during excavations near Lieutenant Money's tank, Australian battlefield archaeologist, Terry Nixon, discovered a 'digger' sitting upright in OG1 surrounded by unused cases of British and German bombs. The unidentified remains were reburied by the CWG.

28 *Das Württemberg Kaiser-Reg. 120*, p. 66. The tank carcass was later used by the Germans as an observation post.

29 Haigh, *Life in a Tank*, p. 79-80.

30 Clarkson's tank is shown operating between OG1 and OG2 in James Scott's painting 'The Death of Major Percy Black'.

31 14th Battalion Precis 3, WO 95 /3494, PRO.

32 'Williamson, Stanton, Wadsworth and Orr', *Defence Force Journal* No. 52; Jacka to Stanton's brother, 15/4/17, AWM 2 DRL 155.

33 AWM 92 PR MSS 1380, E. J. Rule Diary (in effect the draft of *Jacka's Mob*), p. 173.

34 J. H. Case Papers, AWM MSS 1365.

35 *'Stand-To'* (Australian publication) Appreciation of Durrant, Sept/Oct 1963. Harry Murray went on to become the most decorated infantryman of all Empire troops.

36 Melville's report to Haig, Haig Papers, 9 May 1917, ACC3155/97/9, NLS.

37 Haigh, *Life in a Tank*, p.68-69. Great care was taken of animals in service and during the war over 2 million horses and mules were admitted to veterinary stations run by the Blue Cross.

38 For an account of the cavalry at Monchy, see Jonathan Nicholls, *Cheerful Sacrifice*, p. 144-146.

39 According to Operations Order No. 12.

40 Bean IV, p. 328; Wyrall, *History of 62nd Division, Vol I*, p. 43; WO95/3068, PRO; Bean to Gellibrand 19 May 1929, AWM 92 3DRL 6405.

41 Brechtle, *Die Ulmer Grenadier*, p. 94. Also *Württemberg Heer Im Weltkrieg* p. 58. Normally a Major-General rather than a Colonel (Oberst) would command a brigade. By 1917, the brigade comprised three regiments each of three battalions and a MG company.

42 Bean IV, p. 340.

43 Geoff. Leane Papers, AWM 1DRL (0411); Bean IV, p. 340.

44 *List of British Officers Taken prisoner in the various Theatres of War 1914-18*, Cox & Co.

45 Bean to Gellibrand, AWM 92 3DRL 6405 & 8040. The loss of so many officers of the 14th Battalion was keenly felt.

46 W. C. Groves Papers, AWM 2DRL 268. Groves recounted his experiences as one of these PoWs on Melbourne Radio during the 1930s. The story of the poor treatment of PoWs that Bean subsequently reported was taken up by General Monash and used to 'brace' his men prior to the Battle of Messines in June 1917, AWM 38 3DRL 6673 Item 71.

47 Lieutenant Geoff. Leane MC to Colonel E Leane, AWM 1 DRL (0411).

48 Rule, *Jacka's Mob* p. 184.

49   AWM 38 3DRL 7953 Item 30 (Leane); AWM 92 PR MSS 1380 (Rule). 14th Batt.
      Report on Tank Cooperation, WO95/3494, PRO.

50   The success of the Battle of Hamel in July 1918 would prove the necessity of
      careful planning, training and cooperation. However the rushed planning for
      the Battle of Amiens, a month later, would again result in high tank/infantry
      casualties, T.H.E. Travers, *How The War Was Won: Command and Technology in
      the British Army on the Western Front 1917-1918,*p.118-130.

51   Swinton predicted that this would be one of the advantages of using tanks in
      an attack, Harris, *Men, Ideas and Tanks*, p.48-49.

52   AWM 38 3DRL 7953 Item 30. The value of oral and eye-witness testimonies is
      examined by Peter Simkins in 'Everyman at War', p.292-294; Brian Bond (ed),
      The First World War and British Military History.

53   Commonwealth Parl. Debates Vol. XCV, p. 7826, National Library of
      Australia.

54   The figures include 4 officers and 12 OR killed, 3 officers and 25 OR wounded
      and 8 OR captured. Casualties compiled from '*Soldiers Died', Red Cross List of
      the Missing* and personal correspondence.

55   Even J.F.C. Fuller argued this was the case as late as 1934 in the *Royal Tank
      Corps Journal.* However, the publication of Bean's Official History Volume IV,
      together with the earlier *Die Ulmer Grenadiere an der Westfront* (123rd Regt.) by
      Richard Bechtle, put paid to this legend.

56   *Military Operations, 1917*, Vol. I p. 364. A clear instance of how unreliable even
      these 'original' sources can be.

57   Seven tank officers were killed or wounded which may explain why no
      individual tank 'action reports' exist for the battle. Major Fuller had made
      them compulsory for all engagements after 9 April 1917. Bean was careful to
      shield the identity of three tank commanders for fear of reprisals and
      similarly their names are also omitted from all battalion, brigade and Tank
      HQ records in public archives. The Press Bureau similarly censored Major
      Watson's account in his book *A Company of Tanks.* See Blackwood to Watson
      10/3/19, Blackwood Papers, NLS.

58   Nephew of the famous plane designer Ernst Heinkel; Otto Michaelis (son-in-
      law of Gren. Heinkel) to author, Sept. 1993; Bryan and Hugh Davies to
      author, June 1994; also Brechtle, *Die Ulmer Grenadiere an der Westfront*, p. 93.

59   When the improved Mark IV appeared with proper armour some months
      later, 'K' ammunition would not have the same impact. The Germans
      subsequently sent Davies's tank to No. 20 Bavarian Motor Park at Charleroi.
      There it was overhauled, painted with the Iron Cross and used as a supply
      tank near La Fere in the 1918 German Spring Offensive. Otto Michaelis to
      author, Sept. 1993. During 1917 and notably at Cambrai, the Germans
      captured many of the superior British Mark IV machines which they used as
      main battle tanks.

60   *Württemberg Heer Im Weltkrieg Die 27 Division*, p. 58.

61   Newton Wanliss to Bean, AWM 38 3 DRL 8040 Item 1.

62   Gough to Edmonds, 31 August 1930, AWM 3 DRL (7953 Item 34).

63   Wanliss to Bean 25 Aug. 1933, AWM 38 3DRL 8040 Item 1.

64   Elliott Diary Vol. III, AWM 2 DRL 513 Item 4.

65   McLynch to Birdwood 14 April 1917, AWM 3DRL 3376.

66   Examination by the author of many exhumed tank parts from the battlefield,
      revealed the tank cabs were peppered by armour-piercing rounds.

67   Robin Prior & Trevor Wilson, *Passchendaele: The Untold Story*, p.17.

68   John Innes, *Flash Spotters and Sound Rangers*, p.24 & 60-61.

69 Nivelle's 'Directive' 6 March 1917, 2/1/11 Spears Papers, KCL.
70 Norman Dixon, *On the Psychology of Military Incompetence*, p.30-31.
71 Griffith, *British Fighting Methods in the Great War*, p. 44-45.
72 The success of counter-battery work was the responsibility of the 'Heavies'. It was vital to any offensive, 'History of Royal Artillery', p. 118 Ref 1159/12. Anstey Papers, RAI.
73 De Falbe to Falls, 3/7/37, CAB 45/116, PRO.

CHAPTER VIII
The Guns at Lagnicourt

Undeterred by the disaster on 11 April, General Gough was determined to hit the enemy hard. Such resolute behaviour still found favour with Haig who was in turn being pushed by Nivelle, the French Commander-in-Chief, to keep as much pressure on the Germans as possible. At 9.00 pm on 11 April, even as some Anzac survivors were still crawling back to their lines in front of Bullecourt, Haig received an unexpected telegram from Nivelle. It referred to the imminent French offensive on the Chemin des Dames:

> Franchet will attack tomorrow, Micheler on the 15th and Pétain on the 16th; Advise you strengthen Gen. Gough and attack towards Quéant.[1]

So while Nivelle prepared for his ill-fated attack to the south-east, Gough called for a further full-scale assault on the Siegfried Line. Deadlines for the attack came and went over the following days, whilst the Anzac artillery pounded the strongholds of Bullecourt and Riencourt, razing most of the buildings to the ground.

On 13 April, the AIF 2nd Division under Major-General Nevill Smyth VC took over from the exhausted AIF 4th Division facing the Bullecourt re-entrant and prepared themselves for action. But while the Fifth Army were consumed with planning the forthcoming attack, their intelligence had failed to detect what was happening in the enemy camp. Tired of standing on the defence, the German XIV Corps commander, General Otto von Moser, decided to raise morale by a daring attack aimed at destroying the Anzac artillery, thus dashing Gough's hope of launching a new assault.[2] The main target of the Germans was the mass of artillery batteries bunched up in the shallow valleys between Noreuil and Lagnicourt.

As dawn approached on 15 April, Lieutenant John Wright, serving triple roles as the 17th Battalion Scout, Intelligence and Lewis Gun Officer, was writing up his latest intelligence report. Hearing a sudden eruption of gunfire outside his dugout, he rushed out to investigate. He was astonished to see large groups of Germans advancing up the valley towards him. He quickly ran the 100 yards to his forward battalion piquet posts to assess the extent of the German advance. All along the spurs and

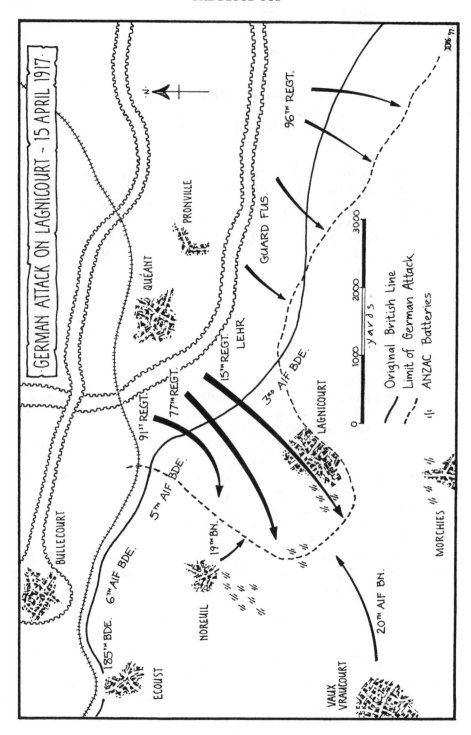

GERMAN ATTACK ON LAGNICOURT – 15 APRIL 1917.

96TH REGT.

GUARD FUS.

LEHR

15TH REGT.

77TH REGT.

91ST REGT.

3RD AIF BDE.

PRONVILLE

QUÉANT

5TH AIF BDE.

19TH BN.

BULLECOURT

6TH AIF BDE.

185TH BDE.

NOREUIL

ECOUST

LAGNICOURT

20TH AIF BN.

MORCHIES

VAUX VRAUCOURT

N

yards

3000

2000

1000

0

Original British Line
Limit of German Attack
ANZAC Batteries

ridges on his right flank Wright could see the smashed Australian outposts and realised that they were being rapidly surrounded by the enemy.

He tore back to warn his battalion, bursting into its HQ and surprising the CO, Lieutenant-Colonel Martin, who was totally unaware they were under attack. Martin swiftly dispatched Wright to tell the nearby AIF 5th Brigade HQ of the desperate situation, refusing to issue further orders until he heard back from his superiors. Meanwhile Brigadier-General Smith, GOC 5th Brigade, who did not possess Gellibrand's decisive nature, failed to organise a swift counter-attack and the moment was lost. When Birdwood later heard of this sluggish response, he was furious with Smith and his 5th Brigade staff.[3]

It was becoming clear that the Germans had achieved a swift break-through. They had attacked at 4.30 am without a preliminary artillery barrage and initially assaulted the thinly held sector of the AIF 1st Division. This division, commanded by Major-General 'Hooky' Walker, the British Pozières veteran, had been ordered to hold an absurdly wide front of over 12,000 yards to the right of the 2nd Division. The front which ran from Lagnicourt down to Hermies could only be defended by Walker by placing his 4,000 Australians staggered in depth behind a string of piquet posts. In order to disguise the piquets from enemy observation, all excavated earth was covered with grass and the usual protective barbed wire was dispensed with. In the event, this proved a tragic mistake.

It was certainly no punitive night raid as far as the Germans were concerned. The four attacking divisions comprised the 2nd and 3rd Guard, the 38th and the 4th Ersatz Divisions, in all some twenty-three battalions or 16,000 men. They included storm troop units and were equipped with the novel and terrifying *Flammenwerfer* ('flame throwers'). This equipment was always used to greater effect by the Germans, although few among the ranks were keen to carry it. Struggling into the attack with the heavy snail-like contraption on his back, the operative was a prime target for the first sniper's bullet.

As the Germans quickly encircled the piquets, the startled Australian sentries, who were without any defences, fought back for all they were worth and in some cases managed to halt the enemy attack. To the west of Lagnicourt, fierce fighting by the 3rd Brigade and heroic rearguard actions by men like Lieutenant Pope stemmed the enemy advance. Pope, a thirty-four-year-old ex-London policeman, found his piquet post was surrounded by the enemy and, leaping out of his trench, rallied his men and charged the attackers head-on. His body together with those of his men was later found among eighty enemy dead. For his gallantry, Lieutenant Charles Pope was awarded a posthumous Victoria Cross.

Most posts in front of the gun batteries in the important Lagnicourt/Noreuil valley were quickly overpowered. The survivors withdrew down the valley, unfortunately leaving the way wide open for the enemy to attack one of the principal field-gun groups. The guns were positioned less than a mile to the rear of the outposts so that they could easily range on the Siegfried Line but it had brought them perilously close to the enemy. According to Major-General Broad, the senior artillery officer of the Fifth Army, what followed next was a complete shambles.

> The Australian infantry and artillerymen streamed back through the British heavy and medium artillery [to the rear], suggesting that they had better remove their breech blocks and come too.[4]

These men, from the 1st Artillery Brigade in Colonel Rabett's artillery group, did not distinguish themselves, withdrawing in some panic and 'tumbling into the infantry bivouacs and artillery HQ in a manner which might have spread alarm'.[5] Their three batteries were now abandoned to the Germans who were in imminent danger of capturing a further fourteen batteries in the shallow valleys around Noreuil and Lagnicourt. What further hindered the Australian defence was that the field artillery commanders had failed to issue rifles to their men. These weapons had been left behind in the wagon lines and, without even a company of infantry to protect them, it was little wonder that the artillerymen beat a hasty retreat.[6]

When he heard that the Germans had broken into the Australian lines, Birdwood was as usual, markedly confident. 'Capital', he barked, 'we ought to scupper the whole lot of them before they can get back again'.[7] Surprisingly, he was not far wide of the mark for, even at that moment, companies of the AIF 9th and 12th Battalions were being rallied behind Lagnicourt for a counter-attack. The Germans, instead of blowing up their captured guns, were too busy looting dugouts for souvenirs. Their attack lost momentum and, under a sudden British artillery barrage, they started to fall back towards their own lines. Major Foot, a battery commander, recalled the sudden change in fortune:

> A dozen Australian gunners, two of them carrying 18 pdr breech blocks, joined us; they had been driven off their guns by the advancing Germans. And almost at the same moment, we could see a line of the enemy on an open crest to the south, coming on towards us. We pulled our two right howitzers out of their pits into the open, and for the first and only time in my career as a wartime field battery commander, I fired my guns over open sights. It was easy: The heavy 35lbs. shells, bursting on graze among them, made the line of German infantry disappear in a cloud of smoke.[8]

As dawn broke, the Anzac 'heavies' continued to pound Quéant to suppress any German artillery support and in this they were successful. So much so, that as the German survivors struggled through to their lines, they were already cursing their artillery units for the lack of covering fire.[9] Mayhem followed, as these retreating German infantry were caught in their own wire and swept by machine-gun fire from the closing Australians. By 8.30 am most of the front had been re-captured and a disaster had been narrowly averted. Only five artillery pieces were put out of action by the Germans but they still managed to inflict over 1,000 Australian casualties. Despite these losses, the men of Walker's 1st Division had given a good account of themselves and the heroism of men such as Captain James Newland and Sergeant John Whittle was recognised by Victoria Crosses. This was unique, as Newland and Whittle were the only pre-1914 Australian 'regulars' given this award. So, after a shaky start and having been allocated an impossible front to hold, the division had rallied and in their counter-attack added 2,300 men to the German casualty list.

Oblivious to the severity of the situation, Gough and Malcolm travelled up from Albert that same morning for a routine meeting with Fanshawe, the V Corps Commander. It was only as the commanders sat down to lunch at Fanshawe's HQ, that news was brought to Gough by his Fifth Army Staff indicating the severity of the situation. He was staggered by how close he had been to losing his guns and, with that, the ability to mount another attack. Lunch was promptly adjourned.[10]

Surprisingly, the news travelled faster to London where the audacity of the German attack had alarmed the British War Cabinet. At a meeting the following morning, the assembled Ministers received a short report:

> The recent counter-attack on our forces between Cambrai and St Quentin [Lagnicourt] had been made at 4.30 am and delivered with great determination. This event points to the conclusion that the Germans attach great importance to the southern end of the Drocourt-Quéant Line and would resist to the utmost any attempt to turn it. [11]

Lagnicourt had given the politicians or 'frock-coats', as Sir Henry Wilson delighted in calling them, a fright. Had the battle turned into a rout, it might well have forestalled further offensive action by the British which in turn would have let down the French. The War Cabinet did not want this delicate balancing act to be upset. This was a policy that all the members agreed with, though the fiery Welsh-born Prime Minister of Australia, W. M. Hughes, was not present. He was absent from meetings of the Imperial War Cabinet during April and May 1917 and, because of the risk of interception, Australia could only be sent short cables briefing her on military and Empire discussions.[12]

When the Arras offensive was first mooted at the Chantilly Conference in November 1916, France was still reeling from the sacrifices she had made at Verdun. 'Papa' Joffre, the French Commander-in-Chief, had pressed for his army to play a subsidiary role in 1917, with the big offensive on the Western Front being left for the British to pursue, and thereby draw the German reserves away from the exhausted French.

But Joffre was not the comfortable fixture he appeared to be and, in March 1917, he was toppled in favour of the dynamic General Robert Nivelle. Joffre was out and so was his cautious policy. From now on under Nivelle, the French were to play a far more vigorous role. 'We have the Formula,' he confidently predicted when explaining how he would swiftly defeat the Germans. His formula was based on the highly successful tactics he had employed when smashing through the German defences at Fort Douaumont during the Battle of Verdun. 'Violence, brutality and rapidity' were the three key elements which would stun the enemy and destroy them in a matter of days.

It all seemed like wishful thinking to the cynical French generals in the *Grand Quartier Général* (GQG) at Chantilly. Neither did Nivelle's scheme find favour with the British GHQ who were also busy fending off Lloyd George's overall plan to bring British troops under French control. This ploy was exposed at Calais in February 1917, when the British and French held a conference, purportedly to discuss transportation problems. The real agenda, which soon became clear, was planned by Lloyd George and elements of the French GQG to put British troops under Nivelle, as overall C-in-C. Nivelle would then employ Sir Henry Wilson as his Chief of Staff, to ensure his orders were carried out on the British side.[13] Wilson, Gough's old adversary, was extremely pro-French and had the manner of a dilettante which irritated many of his colleagues. His appointment would have been a disaster, but to Lloyd George, the whole shake-up seemed a logical step, given his high regard for Nivelle whom he thought something of a kindred spirit.[14] After all, there had been so few French generals who could converse in fluent English and argue their case so persuasively. Where had the years of Haig and Joffre's tortuous 'wearing down' policy got the Allies? It was time for unorthodox military tactics to be employed and Nivelle would certainly have the support of Lloyd George if it meant quick, tangible results.

The Frenchman had charmed his way through the British War Cabinet to such an extent that they could see few flaws in the scheme. In an effort to fight his corner, Haig displayed a map in front of the 'frock coats', showing Nivelle's plan for piercing the German front near the Chemin des Dames and advancing twenty-five miles within thirty-six hours. It was immediately apparent that there was a huge gulf between the military and political mind. Haig recalled:

They could not understand why it should not be possible to reach the objectives indicated and thought me very narrow in my views when I ridiculed the scheme.[15]

Of all the politicians, Lloyd George was the most extraordinary contrast to the generals. Lord Esher observed, 'it is amusing to see him among our stolid officers. It is like a fire burning away in the midst of a frozen world'.[16] Haig, of course, was no great communicator and 'Wully' Robertson's manner hardly helped the GHQ argument. As Tavish Davidson observed, 'he [Robertson] was very difficult – it was impossible to open one's mind to a man who was so impatient and rude – as you know, he used to bark at one.'[17] And Gough also realised that Robertson could be impossible, 'in some ways he never outgrew the Sergeant-Major'.

However, what ultimately prevented this loss of British military control was not the outrage of Haig and Robertson when they discovered the plan, but political expediency. Although Lloyd George enjoyed widespread support in France, where his speeches were regularly recorded in national newspapers, he soon realised the dangers of getting into bed with them. When the question of the safety of British troops arose, he realised it would be electoral suicide to place that responsibility in the hands of the French Government, so he backtracked and the new watered-down plan emerged.

The French were to carry out a full-scale offensive on the Chemin des Dames front while the British, now only temporarily under French direction, would attack on the Arras front. Meanwhile, Nivelle's attempts to repair his damaged relationship with Haig fell on stony ground after a series of staff blunders but, nonetheless, Haig complied with the spirit of the agreement to support the French.[18] If his long cherished plan for a Flanders offensive was to have any chance of success, he would need French cooperation to relieve British troops in the line. Consequently, any British advisers who chided the French received short shrift from Haig. Major-General Edward Spears, acting as Head of the British Military Mission, recalled:

I reported to D.H. on my return, that I was not impressed with the French preparations or with the general atmosphere among the lesser commanders. He was very abrupt with me and told me to keep my mouth shut. I rather expected that D.H. would do something to limit the scope of our operations but he did not do so. He subsequently told me that he was determined to do all he could to assist the French, failure or no failure. [19]

Haig was indeed anxious to be seen to be assisting the French offensive in any way possible and this underpinned his whole policy in allowing

Allenby and Gough to launch repeated assaults against the Siegfried Line. With an eye firmly fixed on Flanders, Haig confided to Edmonds:

In April 1917, <u>after</u> we had taken Vimy and Monchy le Preux, we had to go on attacking in order to prevent Nivelle & Co. from saying that 'the British had not held the German Reserves and so the French attack was not successful!' [20]

While Nivelle, his Chef de Cabinet d'Alençon and General Charles Mangin had no doubt that the offensive would be successful, optimism was not universal among the French commanders on the eve of the offensive. The Army Groups commanded by General Franchet-d'Esperey and General Pétain were lukewarm about the plan, but General Alfred Micheler, commander of the Group of Armies of the Reserve (GAR), who was charged with the responsibility for the main attack, was thoroughly disillusioned. He warned Nivelle that the depth of his objectives in the centre was impossible. Nivelle rebutted, 'You will go straight through, there are no Germans there'. It was clear that the Commander-in-Chief believed that the Germans would retire shortly before or under the weight of the attack, just like their recent withdrawal to the Siegfried Line. Such ignorance frightened Micheler, who branded his fellow 6th Army Commander Mangin 'a madman' for his unflinching support for the plan.[21] Despite his misgivings, Micheler would carry out his orders to attack, as would the 800,000 infantrymen in the fifty-three French Divisions, huddled in their jump-off trenches facing the Chemin des Dames.

This romantically named ridge was once a coach drive, laid down for the daughters of King Louis XV. Captured by the Germans early in the war, in 1915 its nature changed dramatically when its tactical value was realised and it was incorporated into the German lines. This front had been quiet for the next two and a half years of the war, in fact so quiet that it was known as the 'sanatorium' of the Western Front. Things were about to change in April, for now all along the forty-five mile front, the German defences bristled with machine-guns, mortars and gun emplacements, locked together by a network of bunkers and concrete pill-boxes. Deep down in the tunnels and caves, twenty-one German divisions waited for the French to come. These front line troops were confident of victory for they knew that behind them they had a further seventeen *Eingriff* divisions stacked to a depth of twenty miles, poised to counter-attack in line with the new system of 'elastic defence'. This system had not been a success at Vimy the week before but, as dawn broke on 16 April, they knew exactly where and when the French attack would fall. Although the outline of the French plans had been known to the Germans since early February (the French Official History fails to disclose how this happened), it was the discovery of detailed maps on 4 April that allowed the enemy to concentrate their defences. They found the maps in a forward trench, in a satchel belonging to a sergeant of 3rd Zouaves. Hardly believing his good luck, Crown Prince Wilhelm, directing the German defence, brought in von Below's First Army to stiffen the existing Third and Seventh Armies on the front. This latest Army had come down from the Somme and was placed in exactly the sector where the main French thrust was expected.

The French offensive was to be reinforced by the largest number of tanks yet to appear on a battlefield. The Schneider tank, which weighed over 13 tons, only carried a short 75mm gun and two Hotchkiss machine-guns. It was crewed by an officer and five men, but its top speed was unfortunately only half that of the British Mark II. It was, however, made available to Nivelle in such large numbers, that 132 tanks could be mustered on the first day, largely employed in General Micheler's central Army Group. Unlike the plan for 1st Bullecourt, the French tanks were only to come into action once the front two German trench systems were captured by the infantry. The enemy would be attempting to re-organise its defences and would be taken by surprise. The tanks would also provide cover as the French field batteries moved forward.

Well before dawn on 16 April, the French preliminary artillery barrage had commenced. It gave heart to the waiting troops, and when they finally clambered over the top at 6.00 am, they saw the reassuring sight of a rolling barrage moving forward towards the enemy lines. As the riflemen and bombers of the first waves staggered forward, they began to realise that the barrage was moving too fast. As it swiftly moved over and beyond the enemy fire and support trenches, the Germans were soon out of their bunkers and hauling their machine-guns back into position. As the dense mass of French infantry advanced towards their positions, the Germans opened fire.

The French infantry, attempting to cross the Craonne plateau, were slaughtered in their thousands. As the attack faltered, so the French reserves who had been pushed forward started to bunch up in their jump-off points. These units, trying to untangle themselves, were then swamped by panic-stricken, screaming Senegalese troops, fleeing the butchery on the plateau. The morale of the colonial troops had been shattered by the severe shelling and gunfire as well as the bitter weather, and now the yelling and the shrieking of their wounded was wrecking the nerves of those waiting to go over the top.

The French artillery, in an effort to correct their rolling barrage, brought it backwards. As successive waves of infantry moved forward, they were horrified to see their own barrage rolling back towards them. The shells fell on wave after wave of the attackers, soon crushing any hope of success in the centre. There was some ground gained on the wings of the attack, but fast German counter-attacks prevented any breakthrough.

Meanwhile, after dawn, the tanks had advanced under the command of Commandant Bossut who rashly decided to lead from the front in one of the Schneiders.[22] His officers were mostly from the cavalry or artillery, men with bags of spirit and dash but little concept of tank operations. Many had been wounded in the early battles of the war and had been out of action until the Nivelle offensive, so the power and range of the latest German artillery surprised and horrified them. Crawling towards the German lines in broad daylight, at less than walking pace, the tanks made easy targets for the enemy artillery. Because of their numbers, some reached the deeper German defences but most became bogged down or were dashed to pieces by close range fire. By the end, seventy-six tanks were lost together with 180 officers and men, the gallant Bossut burning to death in his leading tank.[23]

By early morning, the battlefield was littered with dead and wounded. It was also illuminated by the blazing wrecks of Bossut's tanks, which like the British tanks had promised so much, but in their first large action had delivered so little.

Nivelle, however, continued to press the attack during the next few days despite a rapid deterioration in the weather. Torrential rain and snow squalls added to the misery of the troops as artillery and supply columns stuck fast in traffic jams to the rear. Although Nivelle still refused to accept it, it was now clear that his concept was wrong and methods used successfully at Verdun could not be expanded to an offensive of this size. A further weakness bedevilled French military planning and it was a weakness that was similarly evident in the British camp. Although the French commanders had been given the latest in battlefield technology, they had neither the time nor the inclination to understand that all arms had to cooperate to make these new weapons effective. [24]

To the French reserves moving up to the front line, the spectacle was indeed depressing. Waiting on station platforms, train after train passed them, each packed with the wounded, their sad and hollow faces staring out from the railway carriages. These were the more fortunate wounded, for, farther up the line, thousands were left in the open to die of their injuries or drag their shattered limbs through the mud in a bid to find medical care. They searched in vain, as the French Medical Service was swamped with over 60,000 wounded in the first few days. In line with Nivelle's optimism, the Service had been organised to deal with a maximum of 15,000 casualties and this hopeless planning caused much grief and anger at the front and increasingly at home.

Equally, the German Army had little cause for celebration despite the trumpeting of the German Crown Prince. Certainly they had prevented a French breakthrough and allowed only one of their second positions to be overrun, but they too had paid a high price. Over 83,000 men had been lost and few German divisions remained which were not badly cut up and exhausted. Even if they had known of the impending French collapse, they would not have been in a position to capitalise on it with a counter-offensive.[25]

As for Nivelle, still notionally Commander-in-Chief, there remained some explaining to do. He tried to shift the blame onto Mangin and then rounded on Micheler who refused to accept responsibility for a plan he had warned would end in disaster. There followed an undignified 'slang-ing match' between the two generals in the GAR headquarters at Dormans, in the presence of many of their subordinates. The word quickly spread that not only was the offensive a disaster but the French command was falling apart amidst bitter recriminations. The Nivelle offensive had been one of the few occasions in the Great War when a supreme Commander had imposed his complete plan upon subordi-nates, rather than allowing them to work out the detailed tactics.[26] It was a disastrous plan and Nivelle was finished, but there were repercussions far beyond his own personal career.[27] It was the last straw for his demor-alised men. Worn out and stirred up by political agitators in the rear, ele-ments of the French Army started to mutiny on 29 April. The 2nd Battalion, 18th Regiment had suffered 400 casualties out of 600 engaged on 16 April and were broken and demoralised. The survivors were promised rest in Alsace but instead found themselves back in the front line. They mutinied and four of their leaders were promptly executed. It was a small incident but, nevertheless, it was an indication of what was about to happen in May and June.

The British, who did not know the full extent of the impending French collapse, now stood alone against the Germans on the Western Front. The French were unable to launch another major offensive and would probably hold tight and wait for America's appearance on the battlefield. Italy, and to a greater extent Russia, could no longer be counted on, so Haig, with 'that cold confidence of the Fifeshire Laird', left it to Allenby and Gough to occupy the Germans.[28]

The resources the British Commanders were given were quite simply not up to the job for, whenever Haig accumulated new reserves, the French demanded that they be used to take over even more of the line. At the same time the French 'implored, begged and insisted' on the British mounting offensive operations.[29]

While I ANZAC Corps accused Gough of pushing these offensive operations too hard, alarmingly, one man at GHQ thought he was not pushing hard enough. Brigadier-General John Charteris, Haig's Intelligence Chief and the 'eyes and ears' of GHQ, made a cursory entry in his diary for 18 April – 'I think Hubert should have been in Cambrai by now'.[30]

NOTES

1 Major-General Sir C. E. Callwell, *Field-Marshal Sir Henry Wilson – His Life and Diaries*, Vol I. p.337.

2 Von Moser, *Feldzugsaufzeichnungen*, p. 268-270.

3 Bean Diary, May 1917, AWM 38 3DRL 606.

4 Broad to Falls 14/11/27, CAB 45/116, PRO.

5 Bean IV, p. 379; AWM 38 3DRL (79).

6 General Sir Martin Farndale, *History of the Royal Regiment of Artillery*, p.176.

7 AWM 38 3DRL 606 Item 79.

8 IWM 86/57/1 Brigadier R. C. Foot.

9 Ellott Diary, Vol III, AWM 2DRL 513 Item 4.

10 Fanshawe to Falls 3 July 1937, CAB 45/116, PRO.

11 War Cabinet Minutes 16/4/17, 15/2/7, Liddell Hart Papers, KCL.

12 War Cabinet Minutes, 1365-142, 15/2/7, Liddell Hart Papers, KCL.

13 Colonel Herbillon, *Du General en Chef au Gouvernement*, Vol. II, p.27.

14 'Notes on Chantilly Conference & subsequent developments', VI/3, Kiggell Papers, KCL.

15 Haig to Edmonds 20 June 1924, II/4/34, Edmonds Papers, KCL.

16 Lord Esher to L.B. 21 April 1917, Oliver Esher, *Journals & Letters of Reginald Viscount Esher*, Vol IV.

17 Davidson to Spears, 19 March 1933, II/3/8, Spears Papers, KCL; Gough to Liddell Hart 9 April 1935, LH/1935/72, Liddell Hart Papers, KCL.

18 Diary of General Sir Sidney Clive, 13 April 1917, II/4 Clive Papers, KCL.

19 'Delay of the British Preparations', 2/3/8 Spears Papers, KCL. Spears gave a full and detailed account of the tensions in British/French relations in *Prelude to Victory*. For his account of the Chemin des Dames offensive and subsequent French mutinies, 4231/3, Sound Archives, IWM.

20 Haig to Edmonds 6 Aug. 1925, II/4/39 Edmonds Papers, KCL. Even though Haig offered help and encouragement to Edmonds, the Official Historian continued to gossip about Haig's personal life in private correspondence, Edmonds to Swinton 21 March 1950, II/5/18 Edmonds Papers, KCL.

21 Clive Diary 1917, p. 27, II/4 Clive Papers, KCL. Mangin claimed that the Nivelle offensive was successful in his *Comment finit la guerre* published in 1920.

22 Major-General Hugh Elles, GOC British Tanks Corps, went into action at Cambrai in a similar fashion. He had the sense to dismount from the tank 'Hilda' after the first objective was reached.

23 Captain Dutil, *Les Chars d'Assaut*, provides a full account of the tank actions during the Nivelle Offensive. See also Spears, *Prelude to Victory*, p. 485-514.

24 One of Pétain's first actions on assuming command was to tighten up liaison between senior officers of the infantry, artillery, aircraft and tanks. His Directive No.2 dated 20 June 1917 is damning of prevailing military attitudes, Correlli Barnett, *The Swordbearers – Studies in Supreme Command* p. 250.

25 *Military Operations* 1917 Vol. I, p.499.

26 John Terraine, *Douglas Haig: The Educated Soldier*, p. 140.

27 On 15 May, Nivelle was officially replaced by General Pétain as C-in-C.

28 Esher, 18 April 1917, *Journals of Viscount Esher*, Vol IV.

29 Edmonds to Bean re OH p.572, AWM 3DRL 7953.

30 Brigadier-General Charteris Diary 18 April 1917, Charteris Papers, KCL. Charteris has been criticised for his over optimism. However it was a maxim that subordinates who provided evidence that the C-in-C's plans were going wrong, were usually 'degummed'.

CHAPTER IX

Another Dress Rehearsal

Lieutenant C. A. Parker RFC and his observer, Lieutenant James Hesketh, took off from Bellevue Airfield on a routine reconnaissance operation over the Siegfried Line. It was early afternoon on 22 April and Parker had little trouble in cranking his obsolete FE2b up to 5,000 ft to join the five other planes on the mission. By 5.00 pm, Hesketh, out in the forward observer's cockpit, had taken his photographs of the German troop concentrations and they headed for home. Just as they crossed over the Siegfried Line near the Bullecourt sector, five hostile Albatros D IIIs of *Jagdstaffel II* ('fighter squadron 2'), swung onto the tail of the British patrol. The lead Albatros peeled off and closed on the sluggish FE2b, now stalling against the headwind. In a short machine-gun burst, Manfred Freiherr von Richthofen shredded the hapless British fighter, which spiralled down, crashing near Lagnicourt. Parker dragged the mortally wounded Hesketh clear of the wreckage, just as it received a direct hit from an artillery round and burst into flames.

The FE2b was the 'Red Baron's' 46th kill to date and the month had already been christened 'Bloody April' in response to the appalling losses suffered by the RFC. Air activity above the Siegfried Line was frantic, but the constant superiority of the enemy squadrons meant that British efforts to gather intelligence on the Drocourt-Quéant 'switch' were frequently hampered. New and sleeker British fighters, like the SE5a and Sopwith Pup, were only just starting to come through, and by the time Richthofen went on leave on 30 April, he had accounted for a further six kills in six days. Because of this German air superiority, British maps and intelligence reports were often incomplete. Worst of all, aerial spotting for the artillery suffered, making registration difficult.[1] This disastrous month in the skies, with so little RFC and artillery liaison, did little to help Haig's operations and thereby his plan to buoy up the French by further British attacks on the Arras front.[2] Nevertheless, on St George's Day, 23 April, Allenby's Third Army launched the 2nd Battle of the Scarpe in an effort to push the British line farther towards Gough's waiting Fifth Army. By the end of the day, Snow's VII Corps had advanced to the Chérisy-Croisilles road near Gough's left boundary, a distance of nearly a mile. It was a hard slog for this time there was no element of surprise and the exhausted British troops were pitched in against fresh German

Divisions. According to Bernard Montgomery (later Field-Marshal) it was the commanders, rather than the men who were tired:

> Snow of course was quite useless; he was an old man [fifty-nine at the time] and ought to have been sent home long before. He merely told his divisions to get on with it and there was no coordinated artillery plan. In many cases, failure is put down to tired troops. My experience is that it takes a lot to <u>really</u> tire the soldier. The more tired he is, the more it is necessary to ensure that he is given a good 'kick off'. So often this was not done. The real people who were tired were the commanders behind; Corps commanders were getting pretty old by 1917 and few of them knew what went on at the front. Snow was one of these.[3]

Allenby's other two Corps Commanders were Lieutenant-General Fergusson (XVII) aged fifty-two, and Lieutenant-General Haldane (VI) aged fifty-five. By comparison, Gough was appointed a Corps Commander at forty-four. However, despite any puffing and wheezing that went on at Corps HQ, the troops at the front line went in with great ferocity. Fergusson's XVII Corps in particular endured a hard slog against an enemy determined to hold onto Roeux and the Chemical Works. But gains were made only to be lost in muddle and confusion and German counter-attacks swiftly took advantage of the exhausted British battalions. At the end of St George's Day, the village of Guemappe was in British hands but Haig had little else to show for 10,000 casualties.

The relentless pressure was kept up. It had to be, for in April 1917 it looked as if the whole show might collapse altogether, leaving Germany with the spoils of war. At sea, U-boats continued to sink Allied ships at an alarming rate, accounting for a record 169 sunk and 100 damaged in April alone. And one fear that continued to dominate the allies was the risk of revolution at home before the defeat of the enemy.

The euphoria that greeted the Provisional government in Russia was quickly evaporating and, although the French mutinies did not become widespread until late May and June, Russian brigades in the French sector were already stoking up revolt. In England, Lord Esher observed that 'powerful social forces appear to be getting beyond control'.[4] This situation even worried military commanders on the Western Front as well as the politicians at home. Brudenell White, heavily involved in the planning for Gough's next Bullecourt push, feared that 'revolution was likely in England if it did not erupt first in Germany and end the war'.[5] To a man who valued Monarchy and Empire, White could see the imperative of keeping both tactical and strategic pressure on the Germans. He realised that before his I ANZAC Corps could assist, Allenby and Horne would have to push their armies closer to the Wotan Line.

So, before dawn on 28 April, the remnants of Allenby's 34th and 37th Divisions attacked in thick fog. A small gain was made east of Monchy, but the 34th in particular were subjected to heavy German counter-attacks – applications of von Lossberg's elastic defence which proved a success. The British misery was mitigated by the First Army's capture of Arleux to the north, but the operation as a whole did not meet Haig's early expectations. It was soon brought home to him by visiting commanders that tired officers and raw recruits were unlikely to win battles:

> Motored to Liquereuil [HQ 37th Division.] and saw Gen. Williams. I discussed with him his latest experiences in the fight. He had had bad luck with his battalion commanders, having lost five by chance shots. The men were very fit. Officers were very tired when relieved. With inexperienced troops, the Company officers are always on duty and so get little sleep when fighting. The Division was now being trained in musketry.[6]

Haig was convinced that, now Nivelle's offensive had failed, there was no alternative but to return to a policy of 'wearing down the enemy by vigorous operations'. That meant pushing every available man into the line. Even if the British could break through to Cambrai, there would be little point if the French could not come up from the right. So a plan evolved for the British to push forward to a good defensive line, running from Lens down to Riencourt. With his obligation to the French satisfied, and the Germans occupied on the British front, Haig could then turn all his attention to mounting the Flanders offensive.

On Monday 30 April, Gough, who had been making preparations for another crack at Bullecourt and Riencourt on 3 May, was out riding with Haig. Returning for lunch to Haig's dreary château just outside Montreuil, Haig surprised Gough by offering him the command of the main thrust in Flanders. It was of course still secret, but the choice of Gough must have been a surprise to both Rawlinson and Plumer (whose plans Haig had recently considered). Gough, however, was a man after Haig's heart, who would not 'bite and hold' territory but could be counted on to 'fix his gaze on distant objectives'.[7]

On the eve of 3 May, as Gough pored over his charts and intelligence reports on the Siegfried Line, he was aware that the dawn would bring his last real chance of claiming a success at Bullecourt. There would be no further delays or changes in the plan, for the logistics of mounting any offensive were massive and now everything was in place, it was almost impossible to cancel.[8] Gough was to attack in conjunction with Allenby's Third Army but this time, instead of exploiting a Third Army breakthrough, Gough's Fifth Army would be part of the actual breakthrough, carrying forward the right flank He had detailed Braithwaite's 62nd Division (V Corps) to attack the village of Bullecourt at the same time as the fresh Australian 2nd Division, under Major-General Nevill Smyth, assaulted the adjacent Siegfried Line. The V Corps Reserve comprised the British 7th Division and 2nd Line Territorial 58th Division, both waiting north-west of Bapaume, while I ANZAC Corps held the 1st AIF Division in reserve, south of Bapaume.

A few tanks were still available but would be used only with the British 62nd Division, as the Australians were still smarting over their last involvement with the machines. It would take until July 1918 to convince the Australians to work with tanks again, when the Battle of Hamel proved an outstanding success.[9] However, for the moment detailed preparation was to be the hallmark of this second attempt. Smyth, the highly regarded veteran of Gallipoli and Pozières, was a British regular who enjoyed the close support of the Australians under him. Brudenell White thought him, 'sphinx-like, silent and imperturbable' but nevertheless the man was a stickler for detail, even going to the extraordinary lengths of borrowing aircraft to do his own 'trench-spotting'. So, with planning more meticulous than even for the Gallipoli landing, Smyth instructed the men of the 5th and 6th Australian Brigades to rehearse their attacks, well behind the lines, with mock-ups of the Siegfried defences. It was estimated by General Ivor Maxse, that eighty per cent of the work in a particular battle should be carried out in training beforehand. Whether this would work at Bullecourt remained to be seen.

The Fifth Army Heavy Artillery had also been busy. Since the disaster of 11 April, there had been a transfusion of artillery pieces, so that V Corps now possessed twenty and ANZAC Corps, twenty-eight siege and heavy batteries. At divisional level, the 62nd had all their own artillery together with pieces from the 7th, 11th and 58th Divisions, all of which succeeded in pounding Bullecourt and the nearby Sugar Factory to smithereens. Meanwhile, the 2nd AIF Division artillery was similarly bolstered by the 1st and 4th Divisional artillery and Brigadier-General Johnston's guns made short work of smashing the belts of wire in front of the Siegfried Line and destroying much of the village of Riencourt to the rear of the German lines. But tragically, some artillery lessons of 11 April were ignored, most notably the importance of the enemy flank around Quéant, and this dangerous ridge remained largely untouched prior to the attack.

By 20 April, there was not a building left standing in the village. Despite this, the concrete bunkers inside the village and in the line to the west of the village (known as MEBUs) had largely survived and provided the desired cover for machine-gun crews. When the British attacked, these crews would scramble up on top of the bunker and fire from the exposed position, while the German riflemen would come up from honeycombed cellars and fire from behind the rubble. The defenders were masters at positioning machine-guns but the same could not be said of the attackers. For on the Anzac front, the distribution was poorly planned with too many machine-guns being placed in the centre and on the left, leaving the right flank dangerously unsupported.[10] Nevertheless, the sheer quantity of machine-guns (ninety-six Vickers) brought into the front line, raised the morale of the Australian infantry. Furthermore, the shortage of ammunition, which had proved fatal to the beleaguered troops at 1st Bullecourt, had now been remedied and each man in the eight waves of attackers would carry six bombs stuffed into his tunic.

There remained the problem of co-ordinating a zero hour between the Armies. On Wednesday 2 May, Haig convened a meeting for this purpose. Later that night, he recorded in his diary the difficulties in determining that hour. The decision he reached was to thwart Allenby's last chance of success:

> Bavincourt. 2 May 1917.
> Held conference at 11 am. with Gens. Gough and Allenby and fixed zero hour at 4.45 am for tomorrow's operations. The difficulty is that on Gough's right, the Australians must cross some ground in the dark – while on First Army front opposite Oppy, there is a wood which can only be passed conveniently by daylight. Allenby must conform to Horne. If Gough went in early and the others attacked later, it is almost certain that the enemy would become alarmed and barrage our front before the troops can get out of their trenches! So we must start to attack at same hour.[11]

Gough realised that the Australians would not stand for a repeat of 1st Bullecourt where the attack had been delayed until dawn, exposing waves of infantry as they crossed almost flat terrain. They had spent the last few weeks training for a night attack and Gough was going to make sure they had one, arguing for a 3.30 am start. Even at that hour, the first glimmer of dawn would appear and one hour later, recorded Bean, 'it was pretty well light'. The timing of zero hour was absolutely crucial but, under pressure from the Third Army, Gough had to concede a zero hour of 3.45 am. But Allenby and his commanders were still furious that Haig had again allowed Gough his way, at their expense. Few of the exhausted Third Army troops had any experience of night fighting and Major-General Deverell, commanding the 3rd Division, was one of many who felt bitter:

> I regarded the change to a night attack at such short notice, with dismay and anger and I did my utmost to get the decision changed. The ground over which the 3rd Div. had to operate was particularly

difficult for a night attack on a big scale and was in an area in front of Monchy in which the hostile fire was intense. Monchy used to be subjected to sudden bursts of intense fire at varying times and was one of the hottest places I ever had to visit. A more unfortunate place for an unprepared night attack on a big scale could not have been found.[12]

It was a view shared by all the other divisional and brigade commanders on the Third Army front, who wasted little time in haranguing Malcolm. 'The Third Army are disgusted,' they told Malcolm. 'Comes of having these Cavalrymen commanding infantry'.[13]

Fortunately for the Anzacs, Gough had his way and now their fighting brigades, the 5th under Brigadier-General Robert Smith and the 6th under Brigadier-General John Gellibrand, stood some chance of reaching their objectives on 3 May. On the eve of the battle, the brigade troops had moved up behind the railway embankment, ready to jump off from the same forward positions in the re-entrant that had been occupied on 11 April.

To their left lay the three British brigades, facing Bullecourt. The 185th, comprising the 2/5, 2/6, 2/7 West Yorkshire battalions, took up the same position it had occupied at 1st Bullecourt on the Australians' left flank.[14] Attempts had been made to shelter many of the men from enemy fire prior to their jump-off and the caves under Ecoust had been recently opened up. But as 2nd Lieutenant Charles Stewart noted in his diary, the conditions hardly helped to prepare a man for combat:

> The caves under the former church in Ecoust, which were opened up for the first time since 1560, could give shelter to 500 men. It was possible to get to Bullecourt by these passages. The place is foul – the damp and mildew of 400 years. It is a poisonous place to sleep in. One wakes up with heavy eyes and a sore throat that prevents speech for an hour.[15]

The 185th Brigade was charged with one of the toughest assignments, that of attacking and capturing the village together with part of the Siegfried Line to the north-east. In the centre, four battalions of the Duke of Wellington's formed up under the control of Brigadier-General F. F. Hill's 186th Brigade. Their task was to capture the enemy trenches around the south-west of Bullecourt and then to press on and capture Hendecourt, half a mile to the north.

A further problem for the British was that the Germans had organised another re-entrant on the west side of Bullecourt. The 500-yard front was defended with the familiar system of belts of wire with 'funnels' covered by machine-guns. 186th Brigade's only chance was for its flanks to be successfully screened by the advance of the 185th on its right and the

187th on its left. This latter brigade was made up of two battalions of the York and Lancs (Hallamshires) together with two battalions of the King's Own Yorkshire Light Infantry (KOYLI) and was to attack on a front of 750 yards.[16]

In order to achieve a successful link up with the Australians attacking on their right flank, there would need to be maximum cooperation between de Falbe's 185th Brigade and Gellibrand's 6th Brigade. After the mutual hostility over the events of 1st Bullecourt, this looked unlikely and the respective positions of brigade HQs hardly helped matters. The three British brigade HQs were housed in Nissen huts and dug into sunken roads some three miles back from the front line, while Gellibrand's HQ had recently moved forward to a dugout in the railway embankment. Despite the obvious danger, it was readily apparent which brigade staff could react most quickly to changes of fortune on the battlefield. Gellibrand also faced the same problem on his right flank, where the AIF 5th Brigade had placed their HQ back in the village of Noreuil.[17] Malcolm, to his credit, constantly tried to instil in his subordinates the importance of moving HQs forward. His memorandum, first issued in October 1916, was distributed to all divisions and brigades prior to major attacks:

> Whenever the country permits, it is essential that Brigadiers should select forward positions whence they can observe the fight from their original Battle Headquarters; then, even if communication fails they will be able to see what is going on. It is equally important that Divisional Headquarters should be well forward at the outset of an attack. It is a very serious error, almost an unpardonable one, when Brigadiers do not go forward as their command advances.[18]

Malcolm must have been aware of the siting of all divisional and brigade HQs before the battle commenced, but there is no evidence that Fifth Army Staff attempted to change these HQ positions. There was always the risk that Gellibrand's control could be totally lost by a direct hit on his HQ, but his close proximity to the front line meant that when communications failed, he could react quickly.

For the British troops facing Bullecourt, it was an extremely tough task to assign to second-line territorial battalions, drained of their best men and untried in battle. At least they were to have some support in the shape of Major 'Roc' Ward and eight tanks (with two in reserve) of no. 12 Company, 'D' Battalion Heavy Branch. Ward's company could boast some battle experience from Vimy Ridge and Ward himself was a more robust character than Watson. Known as 'Roc' after his initials and because of his solid athletic build, the thirty-six-year-old Canadian was in good shape, despite being wounded twice the previous year, while serving with the Buffs. As a renowned boxer and Cambridge blue, he was a formidable personality whose enormous voice could be heard from outside his sandbagged HQ, booming out orders and chivvying his young subalterns – there would be no 'windy officers' in his Company. All remembered the ghastly events of 1st Bullecourt and, out of superstition, all Ward's tank officers, who were going into action, shaved off their moustaches. They then led their tanks up from Mory Copse and were close at hand to accompany the infantry into Bullecourt at zero hour. Everyone now realised it was a mistake to base the whole timetable for an attack on the mechanically unreliable tanks and their role would revert to one of support and the crushing of strongpoints.[19]

Although the Australians would have nothing to do with the tanks, Charles Bean privately recognised the problems the Heavy Branch faced. As the Official Australian Historian, Bean was responsible for recording the achievements of I ANZAC Corps and tended to identify publicly with any grievances the diggers felt.[20] From his early days as a journalist covering the Australian wool trade, he held a lifelong admiration for the 'bushman' and, despite the fact that they were a minority in the AIF, he felt the bushman's qualities of self-reliance, loyalty to one's 'mates' and hardiness all typified the Australian in a hostile environment. Bean played an important role in reporting Australia's war and commemorating it afterwards yet, although he idolised the diggers, he was not one of them.[21] Nor did he always sit comfortably in the officers' mess, despite his honorary rank of captain and British public school education. On the one hand, he admired Brudenell White for his 'gentleman officer' qualities, yet on the other he castigated the British officer and class system, wishing a 'revolution would sweep it all away'. However, from his schooldays at Clifton before the war, Bean was certainly familiar with this world – even his housemaster 'Pup' Asquith, was a brother of the Prime Minister. He knew many of the British officers, or their families, who were involved in the Bullecourt operations and his contemporaries at Clifton included 'Roc' Ward and Hugh Elles of the tanks, Birdwood's younger brother Richard, and two of Neill Malcolm's brothers. Both General Birdwood and Field-Marshal Haig were also old Cliftonians but, although Bean spent time with 'Birdie' recalling school stories, he rarely complimented him in his private diaries.[22]

As Bean roamed the old battlegrounds to the rear, checking and verifying eyewitness stories, he could hear the British artillery pounding the Bullecourt sector. The neighbouring villages of Riencourt and Hendecourt were also subjected to fierce shelling and the original German trenches had been blasted out of all recognition. They were now a series of craters linked together. The veterans of 11 April, the Württemberg 27th Division, were still manning the myriad tunnels, catacombs and bomb-proof bunkers that riddled the villages. They were frantically trying to complete the Artillery Protection Line running behind Bullecourt, but the incessant rain of British shells kept the Württemberg Pioneers in their dugouts.[23]

Consequently, this increasing activity from the British artillery and aircraft during the last weeks of April had convinced the Germans a major attack was imminent, and a fresh unit, the 2nd Guard Reserve Division, was brought in to bolster the Quéant flank. In turn, the large concentrations of Australians observed to the rear of Bapaume had alarmed the enemy and their artillery had been pounding British assembly positions for days around Noreuil and Ecoust.

The half-hearted efforts by the British to disguise their forthcoming offensive by digging dummy trenches had not fooled the enemy. On 2 May, a German aircraft, flying too low over the British lines, was brought down by groundfire. The plane landed in the Anzac forward area and the two surviving German airmen were soon surrounded by excited Australians. Although one German was seriously wounded, the other looked up from his cockpit and staggered his captors by suddenly asking, 'What time is zero. When do you start?' [24]

As one officer observed, it was all rather like a production of the hit show 'Chu Chin Chow', playing at His Majesty's Theatre in London's West End. The cast had done their rehearsals, the props and lighting boys had set the scene and now the audience were getting restless for the show to begin. It was to be a terrible first night.

NOTES

1   H. A. Jones, *The War in the Air*, Vol. III, p. 357; Peter Kilduff (trans), *The Red Baron*.
2   Jones, *War in the Air*, Vol. III, Appendix IX.
3   Montgomery to Falls, 8 Oct. 1938, CAB 45/116, PRO.
4   Esher to Robertson, *Vicount Esher Journals Vol. IV*, 1917.
5   Bean Diary, AWM 38 3DRL 606 Item 94.
6   Haig Diary 11 May 1917, ACC3155/97/9, NLS.
7   Prior and Wilson, *Passchendaele: The Untold Story*, p.51. Rawlinson would be responsible for the coastal attack.
8   *Army Quarterly*, Oct. 1986, p.446.
9   Travers, *How the War was Won: Command and Technology in the British Army on the Western Front 1917-1918*, p.112-115.
10 *Army Quarterly*, April 1966, p.78.
11 Haig Diary, ACC3155/97/9 NLS; Malcolm to Falls 25 Sept. 1930, CAB 45/116, PRO. Strangely, Haig incorrectly recorded zero hour in his diary only eight hours after the meeting. Zero hour was in fact 3.45 am.
12 Deverell to Falls, 24 Nov. 1938, CAB 45/116, PRO.
13 Malcolm to Edmonds, 9 Sept. 1930, AWM 7953 Item 34. This common jibe was directed as much against their Chief, Allenby (also a cavalryman), as against Gough and Haig.
14 185th Brigade was commanded by Brigadier Vigant de Falbe, who was

present at 1st Bullecourt and had recently returned to the line after illness.

15 Diary of 2nd Lieutenant Charles Stewart, Devonshire Regiment Archives.

16 On 24 Feb. 1917, the same 2/4 York & Lancs. had covered 1000 yards towards Serre without confronting the enemy. It was Gough's first indication that the Germans were withdrawing.

17 Lieutenant-Colonel Wiltshire, 'Liaison with the British at Bullecourt', *Reveille* 1 May 1933.

18 AWM 3DRL 2600 Item 9.

19 WO95/110, PRO.

20 Bean narrowly beat Keith Murdoch to the post of Official War Correspondent. Murdoch, heavily involved in the Gallipoli controversy, joined Bean at 2nd Bullecourt.

21 The theme of Bean's part in the creation of the digger legend is discussed by Eric Andrews, *Bean and Bullecourt: Weaknesses and Strengths of the Official History of Australia in the First World War – Revue Internationale d'Histoire Militaire*, No. 72, 1990.

22 William Malcolm became ADC to Lord Curzon. Richard Birdwood was killed in 1914. Despite his ambivalent attitude to British traditions, the spirit of the school stayed with Bean all his life. He even named his house in Lindfield, NSW after Clifton.

23 Brechtle, *Die Ulmer Grenadiere* p. 94-96.

24 Bean IV, p. 429.

CHAPTER X

Into the Blood Tub – 3 May

Charles Bean, eager to witness the action for his Australian Official History, made his way up to the front line at Bullecourt on 2 May. Passing unbroken columns of the 5th and 6th Brigades moving with their support wagons along the sunken roads, he was surprised by how the landscape reminded him of home:

> Spring is at last coming fast. The trees during the last two days have been shooting and bright green grass is visible in patches on the half-shelled areas. It reminds one of the wind scorched area of the Western Plains in New South Wales – where the land has been damaged by sheep feeding and treading on it after a drought. There is the same shallow soup-plate depression, the same hard baked pink clay and scratchy ridges of grass – The same endless line of telegraph poles runs out across it.[1]

Some of those telegraph lines that remained intact carried back information for the artillery in the rear who were racking up their rate of fire. Watching the shells bursting on the enemy positions, Bean with his friend and fellow journalist, Keith Murdoch, knew that it was going to be hard to distinguish friend from foe when dawn broke, as the barrage was generating terrific dust clouds. When the sun went down, green and orange flares soon erupted on the skyline. Sporadic shots echoed across the re-entrant, as patrols from both sides skirmished.

In an Australian jump-off trench, seventeen-year-old Private Robert Comb of the 23rd Battalion, along with thousands of others, impatiently counted the minutes before zero. Waiting with his Lewis Gun team and looking towards the Siegfried Line, 'Combsy' swapped the familiar bravado with his friend Brown, an ammunition carrier, 'Well mate, I might see you there and I might not'. [2]

Meanwhile, farther back beyond the embankment, Bean scribbled frantically in his notebook as zero hour arrived:

> 3.44 am. More gun shots – The G's think they have seen a patrol
> 3.45 am. Everything perfectly quiet. – Barrage flare on left – Battery officer's voice.

3.46 am.   Barrage has started away on left – They're off – Red flare

3.50 am.   Flares along line – Figures of men going forward seen against gun flashes

3.53 am.   Brilliant flashes about Bullecourt.[3]

As Private Comb went forward into the re-entrant with the rest of the Australian advance, they were soon obscured by smoke and dust clouds. Comb lost sight of Brown and never saw him alive again. But over on the left, the British advance on Bullecourt could be seen more clearly.

Four companies of the 2/6 West Yorkshires, each comprising more than 100 men, were ordered to attack the south-east and east of the village, and rushed the 200 yards to the wire under a heavy enemy barrage. As the shells came down on the attacking waves, great holes were ripped in the ranks, but the officers and NCOs succeeded in steadying the men as the lines reached the first wire. Not only did they have to cope with enemy shells landing among them, but also their own supporting artillery barrage which lifted forwards, 100 yards every four minutes. This meant that they were only allowed seven minutes to get through the belts of wire in front of the fire trench surrounding the village. It was simply not enough time and, as their own barrage moved quickly ahead of them, the Yorkshiremen knew they would never catch up. As they staggered through the wire, they could just see the enemy in front emerging from their dugouts. At first, single shots from the German marksmen hit random men in the first wave, and then a stream of machine-gun bullets gashed the second wave. As men fell all around, an officer screamed for a runner. He frantically scribbled a message, folded it and gave it to twenty-one-year-old Private Bill Greaves, who with his friend Tom Illingworth, had answered the call. Greaves vividly remembered:

> The officer shouted, 'H.Q, quick'. Who he was I never knew, as he was filthy and quite unrecognisable, even though I knew them all. We dashed off, excitement dominating our fear of the bursting shells. Bullets buzzed around us like angry hornets. Soon we were out of range but not before one hit me. It felt as if someone had laid a red hot poker across the calf of my leg. After putting a field dressing on it, we carried on from shell-hole to shell-hole getting what brief respite we could. I was hit once more by a piece of shrapnel. It felt as if an elephant had kicked me – blood spurted all over my tunic. I was glad to have a pal. When I came round, there was Tom doing what he could for me. He refused to leave me and half carried me until we reached battalion H.Q.[4]

When the exhausted runners reached HQ, based in a ruined house in Longatte about half a mile behind the embankment, they found the staff

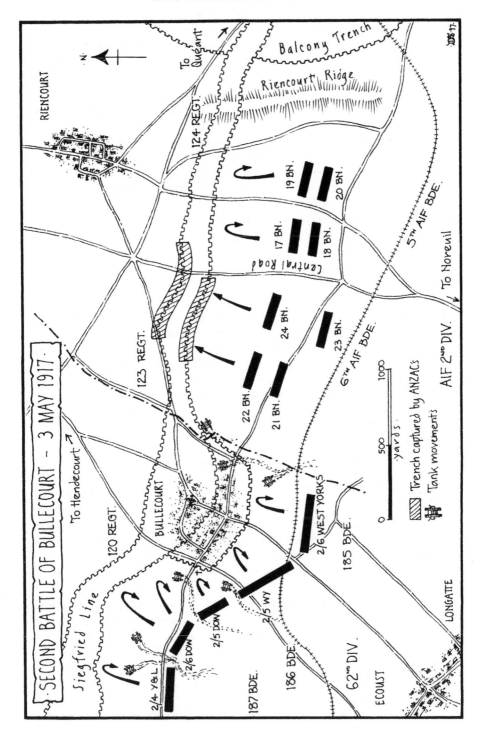

SECOND BATTLE OF BULLECOURT – 3 MAY 1917.

officers hungry for news. Their commander, Lieutenant-Colonel John Hastings, had heard little of his companies since they went into the attack. He knew that 'D' Company had made progress into the heart of the village, but to the left, 'C' Company under Lieutenant T. Armistead were held up in the first trench. Armistead sent a subaltern to muster help from a nearby tank but, by the time it arrived, he and most of his company had been wiped out. To the north-east of the village, where it joined the Siegfried Line, the supporting barrage would not sweep over the German positions until 4.15 am, so the Australians were kept at bay. Their three trench mortar batteries, which had been detailed to provide cover for the British right flank, had been destroyed and the 2/6 West Yorks were left exposed for a crucial half hour. Consequently, 'A' Company met withering fire from this stretch of the enemy line and they had not been heard of since. Now Hastings learnt that 'B' Company had been annihilated in the front trench just inside the wire.[5]

It was the same story all along the front, and the Germans had also forced back the attacks of the 186th and 187th Brigades in the re-entrant to the west of Bullecourt. Several tanks supported these brigades but, as at 1st Bullecourt, the chronic lack of cooperation between infantry and the tanks severely reduced their value to the operation. Often the two had problems meeting up as smoke and dust reduced the visibility of the tank driver to ten feet. Sometimes infantry subalterns or NCOs failed to exercise initiative. 2nd Lieutenant Herbert Chick, commanding his tank in action for the first time, was ordered to assist the 2/4 York & Lancs who had just been beaten back. Opening his cab flap, he was staggered by what he saw:

On entering the small dip, I saw about 600 or 700 men with one 2nd Lt. hanging about doing nothing. I enquired of the 2nd Lt. as to why he was not going forward and was informed that the wire and machine-guns at U.20.b 3.4 were holding them up. I arranged to go forward and attack this point with the infantry in support but after getting into it, found that no infantry were near. I returned and found that this large body of men had dwindled to about 200. The only man left in command to my knowledge was a Corporal.[6]

British NCOs rarely acted with the same initiative as their Australian counterparts. Neither were they trained to show the same enterprise as the German NCOs, as Lieutenant-Colonel Lord Stanhope observed:

The enemy NCOs would hold on grimly to a pill box or trench when units on either side of them had been knocked out, or they crept forward and made a determined attack, regaining positions of importance. If however our troops lost their officers, too often they retired, not because they had been beaten, but simply because they did not know what to do once they had lost touch. This was true of Arras.[7]

It was also true of Bullecourt, for in the chaos of the 62nd Division attack, the 'stragglers posts' of the Provost Marshal collected one officer and thirty men.[8] Now, with their officers dead or wounded, elements of the 2/4 Y&L had moved over to the left to find gaps in the wire but, in doing so, collided with the 2/5 KOYLI coming forward on the left flank. In an attempt to rally his confused troops, the commander of the 2/5th, Lieutenant-Colonel W. Watson, rushed forward with his adjutant but both were killed before they had gone fifty yards. Isolated pockets of men held out in shell holes but by noon most survivors were back where they had started from on the embankment. One cheerful note was the report that came in later in the day telling of 'D' Company, 2/6 West Yorks reaching the church, in the heart of Bullecourt. However, just as they touched with the 2/5 West Yorks on their left, the Company commander, Captain E.C. Gregory, was shot and wounded and the party were caught in a withering crossfire. The advance collapsed.[9]

Others were more lucky. Private William Hartley, who had been detailed to move forward with a captured Maxim machine-gun, recalled how fate intervened to save him:

> We were approaching a cross road and were waved up another road to let some wagons pass us. Then the sky went dark and the ground shook, tossing those same wagons and horses into the air.[10]

Some, like Corporal Billingham of 'D' Company, 2/6 West Yorks, managed to rally stragglers and hold isolated positions around the village but all hope was given up of taking the objectives that day.[11]

The three tanks designated to attack the village itself had all entered the ruins. The machines were still Mark II's and their unarmoured boiler plate offered no resistance to the enemy's AP rounds. All tanks suffered casualties but all managed to retire except for Lieutenant William McCoull's tank. He was given the unenviable task of clearing the east side of the village which in the early hours of the battle was untouched by the British artillery. He didn't get far. Two direct hits from a trench mortar knocked out the tank and McCoull and his crew started to evacuate. As they staggered out of the smoking wreck, the enemy machine-guns opened up on them. Then Feldwebel Rahn, a platoon leader from the 123rd Württembergers, thinking that all the crew had been accounted for, dashed forward and entered the tank. Inside, he found the tank NCO still clutching his basket of carrier pigeons who were none the worse for their ordeal.[12]

The Heavy Branch suffered thirty-three casualties out of sixty-four men engaged on 3 May, but some infantry battalions never recovered. The 2/6 West Yorks, who had attacked the village head on, had been virtually destroyed in their first real action. Every single officer who went into the attack became a casualty together with 287 out of the 393 men who had formed up at zero hour.

As the progress of the British battalions ebbed and flowed on the western part of the battlefield, so the news reaching the AIF 6th Brigade HQ became more confusing. Sadly, liaison was poor between the British 185th Brigade and their neighbours, the AIF 6th Brigade, and there was still mutual distrust between the respective staffs, going back to the events of 10/11 April. Nevertheless, there were many acts of kindness between individual Australian and British soldiers. 2nd Lieutenant David Pailthorpe RAMC was scouring the rear of the embankment looking for a secure dugout and a telephone line. He came across an Australian Company HQ, but the commander couldn't let him stay and use the telephone as it had to be kept open to the front line. Pailthorpe was left with no option but to go out to a hot spot in front of the embankment:

> I went out and we stayed in the same spot, building a sort of parados to stop back bursts. About an hour later, an Australian soldier deposited some fresh bread on my parados – said it was from his officer and volunteered no further explanation. I went down again to the Australian company commander – the appearance of bread here seemed uncanny. Outside his dug-out was a dead officer lying with a waterproof sheet covering his face and head. The company commander told me that soon after I left, his subaltern went outside for a minute and had been hit through the brain by a shrapnel bullet. He added, 'I thought you might as well have his rations'.[13]

Reports coming in to Brigadier-General Gellibrand, Commander of the AIF 6th Brigade, were not good. Despite conflicting reports from the British, he realised from his advanced position in the railway embankment, that the Germans had not been driven out of Bullecourt on the left. He had never liked the 62nd Division's commander, from his days at Staff College, and he was not prepared to take reports from Braithwaite's staff at face value. With news also coming in of an Australian collapse on the far right, he knew that the combined battle plan was in dire trouble.[14]

The battle had started well for the Australians, when four battalions of Gellibrand's 6th Brigade on the left captured the first and second trench objectives (OG1 and OG2) within half an hour. But when Captain Maxfield and his 24th Battalion pushed on towards Riencourt, they found they had no support on their right flank. Smith's 5th Brigade, who were supposed to be keeping up on the right, were nowhere to be seen. Even the HQ staff of the leading 17th Battalion had no idea what had happened to their men. So their commander, needing a man who knew the ground, sent for the battalion Intelligence Officer, Lieutenant John Wright, to investigate.

Wright immediately guessed what had happened to the 5th Brigade. Before the attack, he had argued that the 'balcony' trench, running out of sight behind the Quéant ridge, posed a real threat. It had been ignored before 1st Bullecourt with disastrous results and Wright had recently seen that it was still bristling with machine-gun nests ready to enfilade any assault. He appealed at the time to his superiors that, as it became light, the diggers charging across the skyline towards Riencourt would present a superb target for the enemy. He was promptly told by his superiors, 'shut-up – the artillery will keep your nest of machine-guns quiet'.[15]

But Fraser's 'Heavies' failed to silence them. Following the same hopeless plan as they had on 11 April, they continued to ignore Quéant's balcony trench and the enemy batteries around Cagnicourt.

Wright knew that he was going into an inferno. He picked a corporal and disappeared at once into the clouds of dust and shell-smoke to search for the missing battalions. His corporal was soon shot but Wright carried on towards OG1, keeping the deadly Quéant ridge to his right. He did not get far, as he later recalled:

It was daylight and I had ample opportunity to see the [enemy] machine-gun barrage which was perfect. I had to screw myself up and plunge into it. After a few steps I was hit, the bullet entering my abdomen and passing out of the left side.[16]

Wright was so badly wounded that, at the time, he could not report what he had seen. He was cut up by the same machine-gun barrage which had routed the 5th Brigade some hours earlier. However, when he later recovered, he repeated his criticisms of his commanders and outlined the reasons for the rout in a letter to Charles Bean. When Bean was compiling his Official History, he largely dismissed Wright's allegations, merely undertaking to include his points in a later edition.[17]

When the survivors from the rout came back, more details of the defeat emerged. They reported that when the front waves of the 17th and 19th Battalions had advanced, they veered off course to the right, moving up the ridge towards Quéant, and therefore provided excellent silhouettes, just as Wright had warned. Most of the officers to the front of the charge were felled within the first 200 yards and, as the deluge of shrapnel shells burst, often at head height among the waves, the Australian attack collapsed. Men dropped into the nearest shellholes, some of which could have accommodated double-decker buses, and the intense enfilade fire kept their heads down. Private E. G. King, attacking in the leading wave of the 19th Battalion, was an early casualty:

> There was considerable confusion, the shells falling so thickly that it was impossible to see where you were going through the smoke. I went about 30 yards and fell into a huge shell hole and was immediately wounded in the face, right arm and chest. I lay stunned for a while until our chaps retreated when I found that I could walk and struggled out.[18]

Attempts by the surviving NCOs to rally the men for a dash to the wire failed, and one of the few officers left lost his head and shouted 'Retire'. The word quickly spread among the remnants of the brigade who fled. The Germans were then quickly up onto their trench parapets and loosed off volleys into the retreating Australians.[19]

So one hour into the battle, virtually all officers and over 300 men in each of the front battalions of the 5th Brigade were casualties. For the Australians, it was the worst incident of its type in the war but it was one that could have been mitigated. Brigadier-General Robert Smith, the tall, florid ex-wool merchant had placed his HQ in the ruined village of Noreuil, over one mile behind the front line. It was an extra distance for the runners to cover and it was an old beef of Gellibrand's that the 5th Brigade HQ always hung back from the action. And as 2nd Bullecourt was fast developing into a 'brigade battle', with attacking parties made up from different battalions, a Brigadier's grip on the fighting became even more critical. However, the ultimate responsibility for the performance of, and liaison between brigades rested with the divisional commander. With this in mind, Gellibrand had based himself near Lieutenant-Colonel Leane's old sandbagged dugout in the railway embankment.[20]

Gellibrand could see the advantage gained by his 6th Brigade slipping away for want of support. He had to act quickly to save the situation on the 5th Brigade front. He therefore summoned one officer he knew well, Captain Walter Gilchrist, and ordered him to take a company of the 26th Battalion and assault that part of the line that had defeated the 5th Brigade. Gilchrist and the brigade signals officer, Lieutenant Dougal Rentoul, rushed the enemy, picking up remnants from the 5th Brigade on the way. Rentoul was hit twice and killed. Most of the others in the party fell, but Gilchrist made it to the first trench and, with the few survivors, set about bombing up the line. Shedding his coat and helmet in the blistering heat, he continued to exhort his men for a further hour until, mounting the parapet, he too was shot and killed.[21]

By this time there was a steady stream of casualties hobbling or crawling towards the rear. Many, like Captain Maxfield, tumbled wounded into shell holes, never to be seen again. Others did make it back to the

Casualty Clearing Stations, where the overworked field surgeons could only attend to those with a chance of surviving. For the men with terrible wounds, the only comfort was a cigarette and brave words but they remained unflinching to the end. Captain Savige, adjutant of the 24th, recalled:

> One man's entrails were showing through a gash in his abdomen but he lay smoking a cigarette. 'Stick it out lad', I encouraged and the man responded with bravado, 'Don't worry about me, give the bastards hell'. Shortly afterwards he put a rifle between his feet and shot himself.[22]

One comfort for the wounded was the help and support frequently given to them by the Army Chaplains. Their role covered not only the spiritual side of conducting battalion services, communion and the burial of the dead, but extended to the mortal welfare of the men. The Rev. J. A. Cue, Senior Chaplain to the AIF 2nd Division, remembered setting up a chapel in a bell tent using his portable Cowley Altar, and then getting down to work in the Dressing Station outside Noreuil. By midday on 3 May, the wounded 'diggers' were streaming in and, despite their agonies, Cue was moved by their extraordinary humility:

> Time after time I received apologies because they thought me writing home for them must be a trouble. They were very sensitive indeed about being a bother, because they could not walk and had to be carried on a stretcher. They were all highly grateful for anything done for them; for a drink; for a smoke; for taking off their boots; for whispering a prayer. I found a man in one of the tents with his head badly knocked about, his face (what could be seen of it) covered with blood, his eyes covered. His jaw was smashed and so he was unable to speak. He was vomiting blood badly at the time and I went to see if I could help him. He made signs with his hand as if he were writing and so I got his paybook from his pocket, found his next-of-kin and wrote it down in my book. It did not satisfy him for he propped himself up and made the sign of writing again, so I put my pencil and book in his hand. I still have the bloodstained page with his words 'Tell him I am so sorry I was sick.'
>
> How a man suffering as he must have been, could have been so thoughtful and unable to rest until he had apologised for being sick on the ground next to a wounded comrade, is beyond my comprehension.[23]

Meanwhile, one mile to the north of Cue's Dressing Station, the battle for possession of the Siegfried Line had settled down to a grim bomb, bayonet and knife fight. The survivors of Maxfield's 24th Battalion advancing towards Riencourt had been halted by their own Anzac artillery shells dropping short. With the gallant Gilchrist dead, the remnants of Gellibrand's 6th Brigade were now surrounded on all sides.

By noon on 3 May, the 6th Brigade held about 400 yards of both trenches to the west of the 'central road', but the Germans still held the 500 yards of trenches coming out of Bullecourt to the west, as well as their positions to the east of the road. To try and take this latter position, Major-General Smyth put the 28th battalion at the disposal of Brigadier-General Smith to redeem the fortunes of his 5th Brigade. At 3.45 pm, Major Arnold Brown, a hero of Pozières Ridge, was commanding the 28th in the trenches and made every effort to extend the Australian line. He found the enemy were not his only problem, when he tried to marshal the remnants of the 5th Brigade to help his bombing attacks:

> The men of the 5th Brigade were under the impression that we had come to relieve them. I could not find any officer of the brigade in the trenches or along the Road U29. Before I could stop it, all the 5th Brigade men had left in the direction of the railway. I do not know whether any liquor had been issued to these men of the 5th but numbers of them appeared to be under the influence of same.[24]

Rum rations were liberally dispensed during the day among both the Australian and British troops. Sergeant William Bradley of 2/HAC recalled that when his company moved up to the line, they 'found that the battalion which had just left, had not moved their rum dump. It was served out to us in mugfulls with disastrous results'.[25]

Major Brown repeatedly requested more men and bombs from 5th Brigade HQ. Brown asked for help no fewer than six times, but each time he was promised them and told to keep attacking in the meantime, with whatever resources he had.[26] Finally at dusk, much to Brown's relief, a carrying party arrived bearing crates of bombs. Tearing at the lids, in the trench, the exhausted men of the 28th were horrified to find that most of the bombs were not primed. Brown demanded that the 5th Brigade carrying party stay to help him to sort out the detonators:

> I first saw three 5th Brigade officers whom I at once asked to detail me some men for examining bombs. They replied that their men were laid out and that they would not ask them to work. I at once detailed a 5th Brigade Sergeant and 15 or 20 men who started work. Shortly after, the party had dwindled until there were none left. [27]

Fed up with the attitude of the 5th Brigade, Brown had to use the wounded and shaken men from his 28th Battalion and eventually sought help elsewhere. Grimly, he and his little band fought on through the evening.

Reports reaching Gough's HQ during the day were yet again conflicting but it was apparent that the 62nd Division attack against the village of Bullecourt had failed. However the AIF 6th Brigade had lodged themselves in the centre of the Siegfried Line, a position they were determined to hold. Gough was getting impatient, for word had come through that Chérisy, in the Third Army sector, had been captured. Lying three miles to the north of the Fifth Army attack, Chérisy was one of the main Third Army objectives that had to be taken before Allenby could sweep across and be joined by Gough coming up from the south.

However, this success, one of the few on the Third Army front on 3 May, was short-lived. The 18th Division, commanded by Major-General Richard Lee (Gough's ex Chief Engineer), was comparatively fresh and had captured Chérisy soon after zero but his men were soon driven back to their starting point by ferocious enemy counter-attacks. A promising advance by the 54th Brigade soon turned into a headlong retreat, when a tank supporting a neighbouring division suddenly careered across their front. The tank commander was lost and his machine lumbered through the advancing waves causing confusion and panic. A cry of 'Retire' was heard and it was enough to make many of the nervous youngsters turn and run. The 54th Brigade had, until recently, been commanded by Thomas 'Harry Tate' Shoubridge, who now as Major-General, commanded the 7th Division. He was, no doubt, relieved not to have been associated with this disaster.

The only other division with any fresh brigades was the 21st, commanded by Major-General David 'The Soarer' Campbell, on Gough's immediate left flank.[28] Campbell had been allocated the only three tanks available to the Third Army, but they all broke down or were knocked out by mortars.

Battalions only trained for daylight fighting floundered around in the dark. Chaos reigned all along the front. Major-General Deverell, commanding the 3rd Division, recalled that 'such was the confusion, that British troops from a division on our left captured the trench from which troops of the 3rd Division had just started'. When Deverell was next out of the line, he told Allenby what he thought of the disastrous 3 May plan. The 'Bull' was unmoved and according to Deverell, 'very pious'. He said 'It was General Gough's fault'.[29]

Gough of course was blamed for pushing for a night attack but he personally felt the blame lay elsewhere – among certain commanders in the Third Army. Whilst he had time for Lee and Campbell, he thought others like Major-General Victor Couper, 'were useless'. And Gough went on, 'Why he had not been got rid of long before, except for his connections, was a mystery'. Gough's opinion was later confirmed when, in the German Spring 1918 Offensive, 'Couper's division was driven back and staff officers later found Couper crying in a ditch'.[30] But, for the moment, Couper's 14th Division, which had been in the line since 25 April, was badly cut up by enfilade machine-gun fire before it had got anywhere near Vis-en-Artois. Rallying the men was a hopeless task, especially when they saw the 18th Division in retreat and so soon followed suit.

The Germans had stemmed and crushed the British Third Army attack by a combination of accurate and devastating artillery fire as well as cunning tactics. In many instances, the Germans had let their forward positions be overrun fairly easily, and did not allow the bewildered British units time to consolidate, before they hit them with violent counter-attacks. The whole sorry story became officially known as the Third Battle of the Scarpe and the struggle for Bullecourt might well have ended at the same time had it not been for Gellibrand's successful hold on a section of the Siegfried Line.

As Gough hurried forward to a hastily convened conference near St Léger, Fanshawe (V Corps) ordered the 7th Division to come in and take Bullecourt. This division, once commanded by Gough, was now under Major-General Thomas Shoubridge. It was a crack unit which, despite not having existed before the outbreak of war, originally contained regular battalions. These battalions had been out in France since the beginning of the war, and had since been supplemented by a number of Service and Territorial battalions. Gough had sacked the previous commander, Major-General Barrow, over his failure to show sufficient 'offensive spirit' when attacking Bucquoy and Croisilles, but Shoubridge was made of sterner stuff.

The situation was critical in all sectors. By 11.00 pm Gellibrand's 6th Brigade were well and truly on their own in the line and surrounded by the enemy. Major Brown's band from the 28th Battalion, who had been supporting Gellibrand, despaired at the lack of help from 5th Brigade HQ. In fear of being cut off by the enemy, they acted rashly. They had heard rumours that the 6th Brigade were retiring and, seeing a group of men cutting across in front (which they took to be a German 'pincer movement'), they decided to pull out. Only one of their officers, Captain Jack Roydhouse, refused to believe the 6th Brigade would retire, and he made for Lloyd's beleaguered post, to carry on the fight. But the retirement of the rest of the 28th was a disastrous event. The 6th Brigade had no intention of retiring and, unfortunately, these men seen crossing in front were not Germans at all, but men from the 5th Brigade who had been in shell holes, waiting for a chance to get back to their lines.[31]

Captain J. Lloyd, commanding the 6th in OG2 was fuming and his brigadier was aghast that they should be left on their own. Gellibrand later recalled that 'the hardest blow that day was the defection of the

28th'.[32] His concern was that, since the 28th had retired, no-one was guarding the central road – the vital artery for supplies and ammunition to his men.

Gellibrand's men could not be expected to hold on for much longer, with the 123rd Württembergers closing in on the Australians from the east and the 124th Regiment, from the west. More ominously, lorries were spotted delivering units of *Stosstruppen* ('stormtroops') to the head of 'Ostrich Avenue', the main trench leading from Riencourt to OG2.[33] The use of motor transport, which was rare in the German Army, enabled these elite assault detachments to reach the front line quickly, carry out their raids, and be rushed back to their bases. The German Commander, General Otto von Moser, was raising the stakes.

NOTES

1 Bean Diary, May 1917. AWM 38 3DRL606 Item 77.
2 Interview with Robert Comb M.M., Canberra November 1994. Comb came through the war without a scratch.
3 Bean Diary, AWM 38 3DRL 606 Item 77.
4 W. Greaves Papers, 2/6th West Yorkshire Regt. IWM 1457.
5 Hastings to Falls 8/1/39, CAB 45/116, PRO.
6 'Tank No. 785 Battle Report', WO95/91, PRO. Despite its apparent inactivity, this tank fired 42 rounds from its 6 pdr guns at enemy strongpoints.
7 Stanhope to Falls, 27/11/38, CAB 45/116, PRO.
8 They were impounded in the divisional pen at Ervillers, WO154/72, PRO.
9 WO95/3082, PRO.
10 W. Hartley, 212th. Machine-Gun Company, 62nd Division, IWM 1457.
11 Corporal R.F. Billingham met a relieving party from the 7th Division later that night and went back into the battle again. He was awarded the DCM.
12 Brechtle, *Die Ulmer Grenadiere* p.97.
13 Memoir of Major D. W. Pailthorpe MC, Gordon Highlanders Museum.
14 Gellibrand to Bean, 23/1/31, AWM 3DRL 606 Item 271. Gellibrand reserved his only praise for the Scotsmen of the 7th Division.
15 Wright to Bean, AWM 38 3DRL 606 Item 271.
16 Wright to Bean 14/9/37, AWM 38 3DRL 606 Item 271.
17 Ibid.
18 AWM PR83/018. King was sent to Rouen and then Birmingham, England to recover.
19 Lieutenant-Colonel Mackenzie, *17th Battalion AIF*, p.177; Bean IV, p.435-437. The battalion War Diary merely states – 'attack unsuccessful', WO95/3314, PRO.
20 Gellibrand to Bean, AWM 38 3DRL 606 Item 260. Gellibrand was scathing in his criticism of the 5th Brigade in the approach to the Siegfried Line.
21 *Reveille*, 28 Feb. 1931. Gilchrist had been awarded the MC at Pozières the year before. In 1918 his brother Lieutenant A. Gilchrist was killed at Mont St Quentin.
22 Bean IV, p.484.
23 AWM 1DRL/0625.
24 Hand written report by Major Brown. Also '28th Battalion HQ, Report on

Operations- 3 May', Item 345, WO95/3343, PRO. The problems of drink affected some units and Lieutenant-Colonel Davidson was later sent home for ignoring the problem in his 22nd Battalion.

25   Sergeant W.J. Bradley Memoir, Liddle Collection.

26   Battalion HQ telephone log, Appendix 4/5, WO95/3343, PRO.

27   Item 345, WO95/3343, PRO.

28   Named after the horse on which he had won the Grand National before the war.

29   Deverell to Falls, 24 Nov. 1938, CAB 45/116, PRO.

30   Liddell Hart in conversation with Gough & Lloyd George, 27/1/36, 1936/31, Liddell Hart Papers, KCL.

31   Bean Diary, May 1917, AWM 38 3DRL 606 item 78.

32   Gellibrand to Bean, AWM 38 3DRL 606 (271).

33   The idea of Stormtroopers, famous in World War II, gradually evolved after 1915. The name *Stosstruppen* was conceived by Major Hermann Reddemann, who also designed tactics for the flame-thrower, Ian Drury, *German Stormtrooper 1914-18*, p. 6.

CHAPTER XI
'The Red Patch'

During the afternoon of 3 May, in a small tin shack at the side of the Ervillers-St Léger road, Gough hammered out the next stage of the battle plan with his commanders, Fanshawe of V Corps and Shoubridge of the 7th Division. As the gunfire rumbled outside, Malcolm stood by, curtly issuing further details to his subordinate staff officers. It was a scene Haig would have approved of, with an Army commander taking close responsibility for the preparation of a battle. Haig had after all made quite clear in the past what he considered were the duties of an Army commander:

> In actual execution of plans, when control by higher Commanders is impossible, subordinates on the spot must act on their own initiative, and they must be trained to do so. In preparation for battle, close supervision by higher commanders is not only possible but is their duty.[1]

These duties were, of course, in addition to the normal brief of co-ordinating Corps activities and distributing reserves. But it was the planning of operations that really stimulated Gough. He now decided that, in order to secure the gains made by the Australians in the Siegfried Line, the British 22nd Brigade (which had now taken over the front of the shattered 185th Brigade), would attack Bullecourt without delay. The remaining brigades of the 62nd Division would protect their left flank.

The job fell to the 2nd Battalion HAC and the 1st Battalion Royal Welsh Fusiliers. The former battalion belonged to the Honourable Artillery Company, the oldest territorial formation in the army.[2] Although this particular battalion had been formed at the outbreak of war, it had stayed in England to train and provide experienced men for the 1st Battalion, and only arrived in France in October 1916. By comparison, the regular 1/RWF had seen action in some of the earliest battles of the war. Despite the fact that the battles of the Marne, 1st Ypres and Somme had claimed most of the old veterans, and the 'regular' battalions now barely had more 'regular' officers than the Territorial or New Army units, the battalion's famous and illustrious reputation was carried on. Captain Siegfried Sassoon had only left the 1/RWF in March but still continued to feel it was 'his spiritual home'.[3]

On receiving their orders, the company commanders cantered forward on horseback, dismounting short of the railway embankment. Through their field glasses they could just make out their objectives, 'Tower Trench' to the front of Bullecourt and somewhere beyond through a cloud of black shell smoke and red brick dust, a second trench running through the middle of the ruins. Directly in front of them lay the grim prospect of a 300-yard dash across ground of pockmarked earth as flat as a tennis court and littered with bodies of the West Yorkshires. When this reconnaissance had been carried out, it was agreed to delay the attack until the battalions could be properly prepared at 10.30 pm.

At this hour, the 1/RWF, still sporting their famous 'black flash' on the backs of their collars, attacked on the left of the Ecoust-Bullecourt road. The HAC followed up afterwards on the right of the road. Both battalions managed to force their way into Tower Trench and in hand-to-hand fighting, captured fifty prisoners. They pressed on into the ruins of the village where they were met by a deluge of machine-gun fire with enemy snipers picking off the leading officers. At 1.00 am on 4 May, 'C' Company 2/HAC, who were dug in near Tower Trench, managed to get a message back to Brigadier-General J. Steele at 22nd Brigade HQ that they were desperate for more bombs. Their call went unanswered. Staff at the brigade HQ, which had been moved forward from Mory to Ecoust, discovered that the ammunition boxes in their store were empty and there could be no further help for the encircled men. At best, the standard of bomb priming was erratic and even if there were properly primed supplies, they often went missing – 'borrowed' by other units. It was a problem that the Australians were also experiencing to their cost.[4] The 2/HAC were then hit by a German counter-attack sweeping down through the east of the village, a part so far untouched by the British plan. This part of the village, together with several hundred yards of trench to the east, was not subject to the attack, as the British and Australians were to 'bomb towards each other'. They were heavily mauled by the enemy and by 2.30 am had to withdraw to Ecoust, having lost eleven of their officers and over 200 men. Meanwhile to the left, pockets of Welshmen had dug in to the front of Tower Trench hoping to be relieved. But 22nd Brigade had already decided to push in its two other battalions in a final attempt to break into the village.

At 3.10 am, the 1/RWF were ordered to withdraw in preparation for a bombardment and the 2/Royal Warwicks and 20/Manchesters began to form up on the railway embankment. By the time the order to retire had passed around the pockets of 1/RWF, they had no hope of getting back before their own artillery bombardment started. At 3.40 am, just as groups of 1/RWF began scrambling back across no man's land, the V Corps artillery bombardment fell on them with terrible accuracy.[5]

With the knowledge that the enemy gunners had now ranged on the embankment, it seems incredible that the two fresh battalions should have formed up there. Not so, the 2/HAC, who, despite having less experience than their sister battalions, insisted on forming up to the rear of the embankment. Needless to say, the German gunners could not believe their luck and just minutes later, companies of Manchester 'Pals' and Warwicks, standing and checking their kit, were suddenly ripped apart. The effect of high explosive on human flesh was terrible. A survivor remembered the death of one of his friends:

> I saw a shell hit him. It either knocked him right into the earth or blew him into fragments. I was next man to him and was knocked unconscious for half an hour. When I came to my senses, where the poor fellow stood, was a large hole; nothing was ever seen of him again. I was talking to him minutes before he was hit. He was talking about his baby.[6]

In the dark, there was absolute chaos and when eventually after 4.00 am, the companies were regrouped and led into the attack, the shaken troops could make little impact on the stubborn German resistance. The British were thrown back out of Tower Trench. Private A.P. Burke of the 20/Manchesters was still distressed by the experience some days later:

> I've seen some fighting this last 18 months but never so terrible as we went into last Friday. We went up to the front line where we learnt the previous attack had been a complete washout – not surprised at that division. [reference to 62nd Division] At 4.00 am we advanced but owing to the other battalions retiring and coming towards us, we were hopeless and could not get thro' the enemy barrage. We had terrible casualties. Out of the other 4 servants, I'm the only one to come thro' untouched – 2 missing (most likely dead) and the other 2 seriously wounded. Our company went in 104 strong and came out 44.[7]

As dawn broke on 4 May in no man's land, a small party of RWF without officers or NCOs, peered out of their shell crater. Directly in front, they could see Tower Trench unoccupied but littered with British and German dead. One hundred yards to their left, they could see the stump of an old crucifix standing proud at the junction of two sunken roads to the west of the village. Beneath it, the German helmets of a *Grabenpatouille* ('trench patrol') bobbed about. Otherwise there was little movement among the smouldering ruins. Deep under those ruins, platoons of the 123rd Württembergers lined the steps of their deep dugouts, standing to arms and waiting for their sentries to bellow out the alarm that heralded a dawn attack. They were as exhausted and fearful as their enemy, and without food save for scraps they had rifled from the British dead.

Hauptmann Richard Bechtle of the 123rd, told of a brutal and bloody night.

> The English seemed willing to pay any price to gain Bullecourt and the battle raged with relentless bitterness. It was a battle of life and death and no pardon was given, as was found when one officer and eight men of No. 1 Company who had been taken prisoner, were immediately taken outside and shot on top of the tunnel they had been defending. This nightfighting had torn terrible gaps in the combat units. Our losses in No. 1 Company amounted to 90% – of officers, only the Company commander survived.[8]

The killing of prisoners on either side was not such a rare occurance. Ernst Jünger, in his memoir, *Storm of Steel*, recalls an orderly calmly dispatching a dozen British prisoners with a 32 shot repeater, while Bean confirmed that in some Australian attacks, 'no prisoners were taken'.[9] Sergeant Clive McKenzie, a machine-gunner with the Victorian Scottish Rifles, remembered that, even if German prisoners had survived their own artillery barrage, their captors gave them short shrift in the battle area. In one incident, several Australians, having just lost a lot of mates, captured a group of Germans and removed them to a nearby shell-hole. One German constantly hassled his captors and was summarily shot.[10]

The fighting had been just as bloody during the night in OG1 and OG2, where the German 124th Regiment had been trying to evict the AIF 6th Brigade from their captured positions. The Germans were using their *Eierhandgranate* ('egg grenade') to deadly effect. Weighing only 11 oz. and about the size of a hen's egg, it could be thrown fifty yards but more often was lobbed by the handful over traverses or barricades. Despite getting through vast quantities of these egg bombs, the Germans had failed to recapture any trenches west of the Central Road, and the Australians retaliated with their own 'leapfrog bombing'. In small teams consisting of two bombers, two carriers, two bayonet men and an observer, they forced their way along, lobbing Mills grenades into traverse after traverse. Before the smoke had cleared, the men would charge round the corner and bayonet the survivors. The officers, blasting anything that moved with their revolvers, would rip the grenade pins out with their teeth and lob showers of bombs into the next traverse.[11] Often it would not go smoothly and the bayonet men would charge blindly in, to be shot by unwounded enemy soldiers or even blown up by a mate's badly timed grenade.This grim sport went on through the night.

The Australians had to contend not only with enemy bombs and trench mortars but counter-attacks employing the *Flammenwerfer*. Sergeant P. Kinchington, commanding a flank post, vividly remembered one such encounter:

I saw about 150 Germans coming down the road. I got all the men to stand to, and said, 'Don't fire till I tell you'. I got alongside the machine-guns. When the Germans were about 40 yards away I saw a fellow shoot a jet of flame into the bank. It was the first flammenwerfer I had seen. I fired and shot the carrier through the belly; my machine-guns let them have it hot and strong; my bullet went through the flammenwerfer and it caught fire at his back. You could hardly see for smoke. There was a hole in the road; the man fell into it, and about a dozen men on top of him – they all appeared to catch fire. Bombs fell thick and heavy – this was where the egg-bombs came in. The nearest German reached five yards from the post; my platoon killed over 80 in the road alone – we counted them.[12]

Gellibrand's men had hung on, and before dawn on 4 May they were rewarded with the sight of columns of the 1st and 3rd Battalions (AIF 1st Brigade) making their way up Pioneer Trench to relieve them. This support trench had been dug by the 2nd Division's Pioneer Battalion and ran adjacent to the old 'Central Road', right up to OG1. It was a fine achievement under the most difficult conditions and the battalion paid dearly in lives.

The relief of the 6th Brigade also meant that Gellibrand's control of the front would now be relinquished. From his wretched dugout in the embankment, he and his small brigade HQ continued to monitor and direct the Australian front, until the evening of 4 May, when he handed over to Lieutenant-Colonel Iven Mackay's 1st Brigade. Brigadier-General Smith (5th Brigade) was relieved a day later.

It had been a great personal triumph for Gellibrand. He had shown great initiative and quick wit, qualities that were rare indeed among commanders on 3 May, and his brilliant achievement in capturing and holding part of the Line against all the odds would be unsurpassed in AIF lore. At times his eccentricity, refreshing though it was, had alarmed those he came into contact with. At Bullecourt, a British staff officer stumbled into Gellibrand's cramped dugout:

He was confronted with a figure lying rolled in a blanket on a small table and asked 'Where shall I find the brigadier?' 'I am he', said the figure turning round, 'What do you want?' 'I beg your pardon sir, I wanted to speak with your brigade-major. Could you tell me where he is?' 'I keep him under here', said Gellibrand, pointing under the table, between whose legs Major Plant was curled up on the ground, snatching a rest.[13]

The physical appearance of 'Jellybean', as White affectionately called him, belied his sharp and critical intellect. Unlike his Corps Commander, he was not bothered about sartorial elegance and failed to see any link between appearance and military competence. As he walked out of his dugout on 4 May, he looked just the same as he had in 1914, when Brudenell White had persuaded him to rejoin the army. 'Exactly as he had left his orchard – baggy old trousers, soft white collar – or rather collar which had once been white; and a gleam in his old eye.' [14]

Gellibrand was exhausted mentally and physically by the stress of Bullecourt. Ironically, at exactly the same time, seventy-five miles away in Paris, his superior commander, General Sir William Robertson CIGS, found himself in an exhausted state. But it was not brought on by battle fatigue. The occasion was a conference at General Pétain's offices, to enable both British and French to display their 'offensive spirit' and to satisfy each other that they were both shouldering the burden. When it was rounded off by an agreeable lunch, Robertson had to decline the offer of an afternoon stroll with Lloyd George. Haig wryly noted:

> It was very hot. 'Wully' [Robertson] however found the combination of new breeches, riding boots, a big lunch and the hot sun too much for him to face a walk! So he got into a car after walking a few yards and went direct to the hotel.[15]

Despite Robertson's temporary incapacity, he made sure that he 'collared' Lloyd George later on. The Prime Minister had for some time been toying with the option of an Italian campaign at the expense of a Flanders offensive. While Robertson had severe reservations about Flanders, he was still a die-hard Western Front man and would back Haig's plan if it meant seeing off the far-fetched Italian idea. Anyway, the ultimate responsibility for any Flanders campaign was political and, therefore, had to have the support of the Prime Minister.[16] There was also the position of the French to be considered. Although Lloyd George's unbridled confidence in his French allies had been shaken by the Nivelle disaster, both he and Haig still needed their support for any new offensive. In this they were united, and if nothing else, the meeting was remarkable for the thaw in their relationship. In his diary entry of 4 May, Haig is fulsome in his praise of Lloyd George. Similarly, Lloyd George's attitude was more conciliatory towards Haig, now that he realised the sense of the Field-Marshal's caution before the Nivelle Offensive. So the British required French operations to continue because, as Haig wrote in his diary – 'if the French do not act vigorously, the enemy will be free to transfer his reserves to oppose our attack in the north'.[17] In turn, the French would back the Haig plan as long as they were satisfied that the British were keeping German reserves occupied on the Arras front. Although Pétain did not spell out the French slide into mutiny to the British party, Lloyd George was perceptive enough to have realised the severity of their position.[18] Continued action at Bullecourt would be used as a token show and, as Haig repeatedly noted in his diary, it was becoming the main display of British 'offensive spirit' on the Western Front. In fact, Haig set great store by the fighting at Bullecourt and his diary entries during May detail the ebb and flow of the battle.[19] Once the attacks of the Third and First Armies had petered out on 3 May, all eyes were on 'Gough's show'.

But Gough had now failed twice to capture Bullecourt. Haig could have intervened to put pressure on his Army Commander to change his plans, as he had done with Rawlinson over the attacks at Guillemont on the Somme.[20] However, Haig was happy for the Germans to be continually engaged at Bullecourt, at least for two further weeks. Gough no doubt had his own reputation to consider and, with competition from Rawlinson and Plumer, wanted to move onto his important command in Flanders, with a success at Bullecourt under his belt.

Gough was therefore eager to 'put some stick about' and put the pressure on his V Corps Commander, Fanshawe, to get some results. This meant replacing the 22nd Brigade (7th Division) which had been badly mauled. By the time the brigade pulled out of the 'Blood Tub', as it had become known by the troops, on the evening of 4 May, they had lost thirty-two officers and 747 men killed, wounded or missing.

Shoubridge decided to put in his 20th Brigade for the next attack planned for 8 May, which allowed three days for proper preparation. Just as he was discussing the plan of attack with Brigadier-General H. C. R. Green on the evening of 5 May, he was summoned to the telephone. It was Fanshawe ordering him to attack Bullecourt before dawn on 7 May, barely thirty hours away. The 7th Division Staff were dumbfounded, and angry that the V Corps commander did not stand up to Gough and demand more time.[21] Despite Shoubridge's protests, Fanshawe told him that a delay of three days was a luxury they could not afford. The British were to attack the south-east of the village only, leaving the troublesome south-west (the 'Red Patch' in operations orders) to be dealt with later.

The object was to link up with the Australians still isolated in the centre section of the Siegfried Line. The AIF 1st Brigade were to bomb down the line westwards towards Bullecourt and thereby protect the right flank of the British attack. That, of course, was assuming that the Australians could hold their position until 7 May. They were finding it extremely difficult to contain the German attacks, especially those from the east.

As the enemy fire intensified, so the work of the stretcher bearers became more hectic and dangerous. Private E. C. Munro of the 5th Australian Field Ambulance found himself running the gauntlet between the Australian lines and OG1, to bring back the wounded:

The shelling was terrific and it is a marvel how anyone escaped. It was particularly severe on the railway embankment and also around an old tank out of action. We dreaded approaching these points as 4 big H.E. shells would burst at a time and big chunks of iron would hit the track. The MO put on a rough dressing on the casualties and we proceeded to carry the stretcher cases back to the next dressing station in the sunken road at Noreuil, about 1½ miles back. Fritz seemed to have a special grudge against the stretcher bearers for he shelled the track from one end to the other. He also played a machine-gun along it and our first casualty among the bearers was caused by a bullet in the back. Geddes died after being evacuated to England. [22]

As well as strong nerves, the bearers possessed extraordinary stamina and carted wounded men on heavy field stretchers, sometimes at the double, across craters and through collapsed trenches. Unlike the attacking infantry who faced their enemy, the bearers normally had their backs to them and could never see trouble looming. Private Munro continued his hazardous mission:

We were carrying a man back on the stretcher, shoulder high. About 20 yards further back another squad was following us with a case. Near where the road was sunken, a high explosive shell burst with a terrific report. It wounded two of the rear squad and also hit our patient. We hurried on as these shells usually come in 3's or 4's. We tried to get assistance to bring in the wounded bearers but there was no-one available. I later heard that 22 bearers had been killed and 22 wounded.[23]

On the eve of the combined British/Australian attack, the AIF 1st Battalion holding the forward posts near the Central Road, were hit by another German counter-attack from the east. Inspired by the heroism of Corporal G. J. Howell, a twenty-four-year-old former builder, the Australians halted the attack and even succeeded in pushing the enemy farther back along OG1. Howell leapt up onto the parapet, in full view of the enemy snipers, and ran along the top of the German held trenches, hurling bombs down at a startled enemy. At the same time Lieutenant T. Richards, the well known international footballer, charged forward along the floor of the trench, firing bursts from his Lewis Gun into the stumbling groups of Württembergers. It was not long before Howell fell wounded into the trench but his example spurred on his comrades and the Germans broke and retreated to the junction of the Noreuil-Riencourt road. For this action, Corporal George Howell was awarded the Victoria Cross.

The last few days had utterly exhausted the units of the German 27th Division which were gradually relieved and, by the eve of 7 May, the whole division had been replaced by the 3rd Guard Division. These were the troops who had taken part in the attack near Lagnicourt the previous month, and comprised the Guard Fusilier, Landwehr and 9th Grenadier Regiments. The 9th Grenadiers were a particularly tough unit who had lost over half their men at Thiepval the previous year. Now rested and reinforced, they took up positions in the ruins on the west side of Bullecourt and awaited the British onslaught.[24]

Barely 200 yards away from the German Grenadiers, the 'Jocks' of the 2nd Battalion Gordon Highlanders were forming up together with two companies of the 9/Devons, ready for zero hour. They were two very different units. The 2/Gordons had been raised as long ago as 1794 and were steeped in battle honours, whereas the 9/Devons were one of the first 'Service' or 'New Army' battalions in their regiment. Since being led out beyond the embankment by their scouts, both battalions held steady under the full moon as the enemy shells rained down on them.

Captain Arthur Acland realised that the Germans were throwing a particularly nasty 'triple protective barrage of 5.9's, Pip-squeaks and Machine-guns', at them. Owing to the short notice given to the 20th Brigade, Acland's men were having to lay down 'jump-off tapes' under a barrage and in darkness. It was therefore by no means certain that the Gordons would charge in the right direction.[25]

Then at 3.45 am they were off, with the Gordons in the leading waves followed by companies of the Devons. The 'Jocks', whose young platoon commanders managed to keep the attack on course, went in hard with the bomb and bayonet and were soon on top of the Germans, taking the first objective of Tower Trench. 2nd Lieutenant David Pailthorpe RAMC, attached to the 2/Gordons, was detailed to set up a Regimental Aid Post, just behind the attack. This post, which was actually a shell-hole, was the first stop for the wounded coming out of the battle. It was manned by Pailthorpe, together with thirty bandsmen who were acting as stretcher bearers. And, as each casualty arrived, Pailthorpe applied a dressing, gave them a shot of morphia and they were labelled and hastily despatched to an Advanced Dressing Station in the rear. Despite the relief offered by the drug, the Regimental Aid Post was no place to loiter, as Pailthorpe confirmed in his diary:

The attack went off before 4.00 am and as usual we soon had the first stream of fairly lightly wounded men who said it was bloody murder in front. Two men stopped at our spot, lightly wounded – they both had first field dressings on but thought they would like more attention. I advised them in the vernacular to get back as soon as possible as the embankment was no quiet resort but they waited a few minutes puffing cigarettes – then the disaster happened – there was a direct hit, a high velocity shell – both the wounded men were killed instantly.

One had a bit of shell through his chest but I found no fresh wound on the other so I think they were actually done in by the force of the explosion. Kerr, my dresser, got a small bit in his neck, not for the first time but it was quite useless to him as a wound. I was hurled to the ground. Rather shaken, I gave some neat whisky from my flask to Kerr and swallowed some myself. [26]

Meanwhile, inside the village, the Gordons went on to capture their second objective and were soon within reach of the Australians, valiantly bombing their way down OG1 towards the village. At 5.15 am, Captain Maitland Gordon, a former Civil Engineer, was seen on top of the trench parapet, signalling the Highlanders' success, as the Devons came in behind to mop up the remaining resistance. Shortly afterwards, Gordon jumped down to join a party of Queenslanders, consolidating the link. An enemy machine-gun opened up and shot them all.[27]

At last the British had broken into Bullecourt and, although they had only captured the south-east corner of the village, they had established that vital link with the stranded Australians. They were also amazed to find in the ruins a party of the 2/HAC who had been left behind on 3 May. The twelve men under Corporal R. Billingham had held out for four days without food and water and had seen off countless enemy assaults.

With their job done, the Jocks retired leaving the Devons to dig in. It was the first British tactical success but it cost the Gordons 186 casualties and the Devons 130 killed, wounded or missing. When the frantic hand-to-hand fighting was over and the adrenaline had stopped pumping, officers and men alike reflected on lost friends. While the next duty or battle would concentrate the mind, periods of inactivity would bring back the haunting images of the dead. 2nd Lieutenant Charles Stewart of the 9th Devons grieved for his fellow subalterns, particularly Montague Sandoe, a lively twenty-one-year-old medical student who was hit before he had even got to the embankment:

I am very sorry poor Sandoe is dead – killed by a shell before the advance began. He was a very cheery and well liked fellow in my old D Company. Morse of D Company who was with me at Bournemouth, has been badly wounded and had not been brought in up to 11 pm last night.

I have been thinking a good deal of Morse and Sandoe. They were two of the very best. The last time I was with Morse was when he and I set out about 1.30 am, the night before we were in the line by Bullecourt. He and I went from Gommiecourt across country to Ervillers to find a camp for the battalion.

The last time I saw Sandoe[28] was at Mory. I was just setting out for that railway embankment of evil memory, to build a Battalion HQ as best I could with half a dozen snipers. I went up in the afternoon – the battalion followed later and Sandoe was killed that same night. I can vividly recall how he stepped into my tent just before I left – 'What do you think of this stunt..St..St. . . . Stewart?' he asked (he always stuttered the devil). 'Not much', said I. 'From what I've seen of the arrangements, you're going over with D Coy., aren't you?'

'Yes, I think it will be something of a box-up', and he smiled in that attractive way of his. 'All these stunts seem like that at the beginning. Anyhow, I'll have to be off. – Hard luck old man,' he laughed. A few hours later he was dead. I wonder if the British and Bosch continue the fight up aloft? [29]

Even if the scrap was not continued in the heavens, it was certainly pursued in the skies above Bullecourt. 7 May had seen a ferocious aerial combat between ten SE5s patrolling with six Spads and a group of enemy Albatros fighters. As the duelling continued towards Lens, Captain Albert Ball, the famous ace with forty-one 'kills' to his credit, was shot down, probably by enemy anti-aircraft fire.[30] However, despite the loss of one of the RFC's most gifted pilots, the British fighters were now in the ascendant and exploding many of the enemy observation balloons to the rear of Riencourt, which were artillery spotting. The RFC even took to flying low over Bullecourt at a height of 100 feet, to strafe the Guard Fusiliers darting for cover among the ruins. Some days later, one such RFC plane caught the attention of Oberleutnant Lothar von Richthofen, who was circling above. Lothar was the brother of 'the Red Baron' who was on leave, and was destined himself to become Germany's ninth highest fighter ace. The temporary commander of Jagdstaffel 11 lifted his plane over in a long descending curve and, riding back the throttle, engaged his gun gear for what he thought was going to be an easy kill. Suddenly, out of the clouds above him appeared an SE5 which went into a humming dive and, in two short bursts, crippled the German fighter. Lothar von Richthofen, although seriously wounded, managed to crash land his plane near Vimy.[31]

The aerial dogfights above the battlefield continued to fascinate those on the ground, and a British victory always boosted morale. 2nd Lieutenant Charles Stewart watched one combat directly above Bullecourt:

A squadron of 5 Bosch planes was above us, low enough to be able to distinguish the Maltese Cross on the wings and the characteristic flat fish like tail. A short while later, a vast round of cheering broke out. We turned in amazement and looking up, rejoiced to see one of the planes falling in flames. We plainly saw both the pilot and observer fall and drop to earth – the first time I have ever seen the occupants fall out of a plane. The plane appeared to fall near Hendecourt, behind the German lines.[32]

So with temporary air supremacy and a foothold in the south-east of Bullecourt linked to the Australians, the British had to act quickly to secure the rest of the village. A communication trench had been dug, at great cost to the pioneers of the Manchesters, between the embankment and Bullecourt and this enabled bombs and ammunition to be supplied to the front-line troops. So from the British position in the south-east, the 8th Devons were ordered to attack the 'Red Patch', that south-west part of the village still stubbornly held by the enemy.

As dawn broke on 8 May, the blistering heat and sunshine had given way to heavy drizzle and the hard-baked trenches turned to rivers of mud. At 11.00 am, two companies of the 8th Devons trampled and slithered along Tower Trench, clambered over the barricades and disappeared into the ruins. The bombers went first, followed by alternate sections of rifle-grenade men and Lewis gunners, the whole attack being supported by trench mortars. They managed to flush out large numbers of Germans onto open ground south of the village where they were caught by machine-gun fire from the embankment and a British artillery barrage. Stewart spent most of the day crawling the half mile backwards and forwards between his battalion HQ and the neighbouring Australian HQ. He was then suddenly detailed to guide twenty Lewis Gunners up to the front line to cover the flank of the attack. He soon realised that fear could grip any man, regardless of rank:

I set off along the most direct route – a road running direct from Ecoust to Bullecourt – hardly recognisable of course owing to shell holes and debris. The Bosch dropped some heavy stuff along the road and I'm afraid the men became demoralised, chiefly owing to the despicable cowardice of the Sergeant S**** I fancy his name was. Many of the men had taken cover in the shell-holes or behind banks. I had him before Col. Morris later.[33]

Mercifully, with few such exceptions, the leadership of the officers and NCOs was sound but this fear was not always present in the actual bitter hand-to-hand fighting that typified Bullecourt. Chaplain to the Devons, The Rev. Ernest Crosse remembered:

All agreed that there was no apparent connection between the actual extent of the danger and the amount one felt afraid. A few stray bullets in moments of enforced inaction were often more terrifying than walking through hell's own barrage. The worst agonies were endured when one was due for leave in the near future. [34]

Furthermore, to keep up morale at Bullecourt, few officers or men would publicly admit to feelings of terror. Privately though, the toughest of men would concede to such feelings. 2nd Lieutenant D. W. Pailthorpe, still manning his Regimental Aid Post, certainly had forebodings:

> We stood some 300 yards from the railway embankment for what seemed to be hours and was probably about 5 minutes. The sweat dropped off me and I would have given much to have doubled off with my staff to the embankment where we should be more or less under cover but this would not have helped the morale of our reserve company so we stood fast.[35]

Courage and morale, however, were sometimes not enough to win the day. By the evening of 9 May, the Devons had been driven back out of the Red Patch and found themselves within 100 yards of their starting point. This south-west part of the village, which was about the length of Pall Mall and only a little wider, had cost the 8th Devons eleven officers and 241 men. Their Chaplain, Rev. Ernest Crosse, reflected afterwards:

> It is an awful fact that before a particular action which offered little or no chance of success, I remarked 'whoever else doesn't come through this game, I'll lay my bottom dollar that Private *** (who had twice been court-martialled for desertion) will'. – And of the tiny remnant of the battalion which crawled back the following night, Private ****** was the first to reach camp. We all probably know of exceptions but the broad fact remains that on the whole it was the best and not the worst who were killed.[36]

Crosse knew that was true of the enemy as well as his own army. He recognised bravery regardless of whether it was shown by British or Germans and this invariably got him into trouble. He had been reprimanded after he insisted on giving a Christian burial to 'a very plucky German stormtrooper' who had displayed great courage when leading his men on a raid. The unlucky soldier shouted out one of the few English phrases he knew – 'Still going strong like Johnnie Walker' just before he was shot.[37]

The fate of Crosse's Devon battalion was shared by the 20th Brigade as a whole. In fact, the 20th suffered as badly as the 22nd Brigade it had replaced, losing a total of thirty-six officers and 725 men. The only remedy to this gruelling slogging match seemed to be to put more and more brigades into the 'Blood Tub'.

All the brigades of the 1st and 2nd Australian Divisions had now been used and Gough decided to employ the AIF 5th Division. They were to have gone north to prepare for the Flanders offensive, but Gough wanted

Major-General Hobbs to take over command of the Australian sector from Smyth, who had been in the line since the Battle of Lagnicourt on 14 April.

So Hobbs took over on 10 May, just as Brigadier-General Cumming's 91st Brigade, in front of Bullecourt, prepared for a combined attack on 12 May. This time, Cumming knew he had one last chance to prove himself to Gough.

NOTES

1 Prior & Wilson, *Command on the Western Front*, p. 223.
2 The exact status of the HAC has always been in dispute as it was formed much earlier than the territorial force of which it was part.
3 'A Subaltern's Service in Camp and in Action', S. Sassoon, *The War the Infantry Knew 1914-1919*, Capt. J.C. Dunn.
4 Major Goold Walker, *The HAC in the Great War*, p.310.
5 War Diary RWF, WO95/1665, PRO. For an analysis of the consequences of 'friendly fire', see Lieutenant-Colonel C. Shrader, 'Amicide – the Problem of Friendly Fire in Modern War', *Combat Studies Inst. Research Survey No.1* (1982), U.S. Army Staff College, Fort Leavenworth, Kansas.
6 Phillips, *Rutland and the Great War*, p. 82.
7 Pte. A.P. Burke Papers, 6/5/17, IWM.
8 Brechtle, *Die Ulmer Grenadiere an der Westfront*, p.99; Ernst Jünger, *Storm of Steel*, p.262.
9 Bean Diary, AWM38 3DRL 606 Item 78 p.52.
10 Interview with Clive McKenzie, November 1994, Caulfield, Victoria.
11 For a detailed account of these techniques, see Journal of Private Harry Old, Liddle Collection.
12 Kinchington to Bean, Bean IV, p. 493.
13 Bean IV, p. 483.
14 Bean Diary, AWM 38 3DRL/606 43.
15 Haig Diary 4/6/17, Acc3155/97/9, NLS; Wilson, *The Myriad Faces of War*, p. 457.
16 Prior and Wilson, *Passchendaele: The Untold Story*, p. 35-41.
17 Haig Diary, 3 May 1917, Acc3155/97/9, NLS.
18 Graham & Bidwell, *Coalitions, Politicians and Generals: Some Aspects of Command in Two World Wars*, p.99.
19 Haig Diary, May 1917, Acc3155/97/9, NLS.
20 Prior & Wilson, *Command on the Western Front: The Military Career of Sir Henry Rawlinson 1914-18*, p.221. 'The repeated failures to capture Guillemont have convinced the C-in-C that the method of attack adopted, requires careful and full reconsideration.'
21 Colonel H. J. Brooks Diary, Liddle Collection.
22 Private E. C. Munro Diary, AWM 1DRL/0526.
23 AWM 1DRL/0526.
24 Doc. 905, United States War Office, *Histories of Two Hundred and Fifty-One Divisions of the German Army*.
25 Acland to Falls, CAB 45/116, PRO.
26 Memoir of Major D. Pailthorpe, Gordon Highlanders Museum.
27 WO95/1656, PRO.

28   Barely a year later, Montague's father, who was the village doctor in Broadclyst, Devon, received news that his younger son Captain Charles Sandoe MC had also been killed in action, Honiton Museum Archives.

29   2nd Lieutenant Charles Stewart Diary, May 1917, Devonshire Regiment Archives.

30   Jones, *The War in the Air Vol. III*, p. 376-377.

31   Lothar scored forty victories in his career. He was eventually killed in a flying accident in 1922.

32   2nd Lieutenant Charles Stewart Diary, Devonshire Regiment Archives.

33   ibid.

34   Canon E. Crosse, DSO, MC, Essay on *The Work of the Chaplains,* Crosse Papers, IWM.

35   Memoir of Major D.W. Pailthorpe MC, Gordon Highlanders Museum. For a study of the role of morale in a Scottish Regiment, John Baynes, *Morale – A Study of Men and Courage.*

36   Canon Crosse Papers, IWM.

37   ibid.

CHAPTER XII
Fight for the Crucifix

Brigadier-General Hanney Robert Cumming was unusual among brigade commanders. Although a career soldier since the Boer War, he had no hesitation in putting his job on the line if he felt orders were foolhardy. He had already fallen out with Gough over the attack on Bucquoy two months earlier, and subsequently wrote a scathing report on the failure of Divisional Command to allow sufficient time for planning. At Croisilles in April, his brigade was given another suicidal task – that of crossing a mile of flat open country before assailing a heavily fortified position, and again Cumming made his feelings plain in a clear and concise report.[1] Now he was ordered by Shoubridge to take Bullecourt, without delay, when all other attempts had failed.

Mindful of what had happened recently to his predecessor, Barrow, Major-General Shoubridge, the 7th Division Commander, realised the heat was on him. Gough, who was simultaneously planning for Flanders, was becoming impatient over the slow progress at Bullecourt and wanted an end to it. The pressure on Shoubridge was mounting and his normally suave appearance, which he maintained even in the squalor of the Western Front, was deteriorating. Often compared to one of Dumas' Musketeers, who had 'the legitimate, generous swagger of the soldier who believes in the pomp of war', Shoubridge was losing his composure and was desparate for Cumming to get results.

Cumming had little time to prepare his 91st Brigade. The attack was to be made at 3.40 am on 12 May. This time, the 2/Queen's (Royal West Surrey Regiment) and 1/South Staffordshires were to capture the whole of Bullecourt. The 15th AIF Brigade was to attack westwards along OG2 and join hands with the British, north of the village. Meanwhile the hapless 185th Brigade (62nd Division) would be given another chance to capture the Crucifix, on the western edge of Bullecourt.

Cumming's brigade had been out of the line since support duties on 4 May. But 'out of the line' never meant complete rest, and units of a committed division would always be employed in bringing supplies forward. The 91st had already lost over fifty men that week in carrying and recce. duties. But although they were tired, the 2/Queen's, attacking on the left, and the 1/South Staffs on the right got off to a good start. The 2/Queen's advanced quickly to get in under the German barrage and were soon reported to have reached the ruins of the church, near the north-east boundary of the village. Known as 'The Lambs', after the emblem on their badge, they belonged to the second oldest line regiment in the army, but they were no longer a battalion of professionals – they had been wiped out long ago at 1st Ypres. Nevertheless their 'Kitchener' successors proved they were made of the same metal.

The Queen's even managed to establish contact on the right, with the Australians who had bombed along OG2 to meet them. However, the Australian advance had flagged and someone was needed to inspire the men. Lieutenant Richard Moon of the 58th Battalion, a shy, former bank clerk, suddenly charged forward. Despite being hit in the face, he turned and shouted back to his men 'Come on boys, don't turn me down', and pursued the German bombers who were taking refuge in distant dugouts. He winkled them out and, directing Lewis guns to cover his flank, went on down the line, bursting into shelters and emptying his rifle into groups of stunned Germans. For his gallantry and leadership, he was awarded the Victoria Cross.

Meanwhile, the British progress on the left sector also became bogged down.[2] The 2/7 West Yorks had failed to capture the Crucifix and therefore left intact the German lifeline to the 'Red Patch'. The Germans proceeded to pour men into this stronghold, who then lined up behind the rubble barricades and unleashed volley after volley into the groups of 1/South Staffs attempting to advance through the centre of the village. The British presented easy targets as they hopped and clambered over the smashed walls, rarely being more than fifty yards from the end of the German rifles.[3]

The British were now in an extraordinary position. They controlled virtually all the village except for the 'Red Patch' in the south-west, which the Germans stubbornly refused to give up. Cumming ordered the 22/Manchesters forward to deal with this tactical nightmare. Such was the intensity of the enemy fire that Lieutenant-Colonel Beaumann, commanding the British troops in the ruins, couldn't deploy his men in daylight.[4]

As usual, the situation at brigade and divisional HQ was far from clear. The 7th Division staff 'ranted and raved' that they were not kept informed by their brigade, but the truth was that their brigade hardly knew what was going on. It was that old problem of communication. Prior to the attack, it seemed as if Signals had provided ample equipment for the job. The staff had laid telephone lines in duplicate, complete with power buzzer and backed up by a complete field telephone system. Some of the infantry had struggled into battle with baskets of carrier pigeons and there were also plenty of runners to carry back messages. However, in the end, all these methods were rendered useless, as Brigadier-General Cumming recalled:

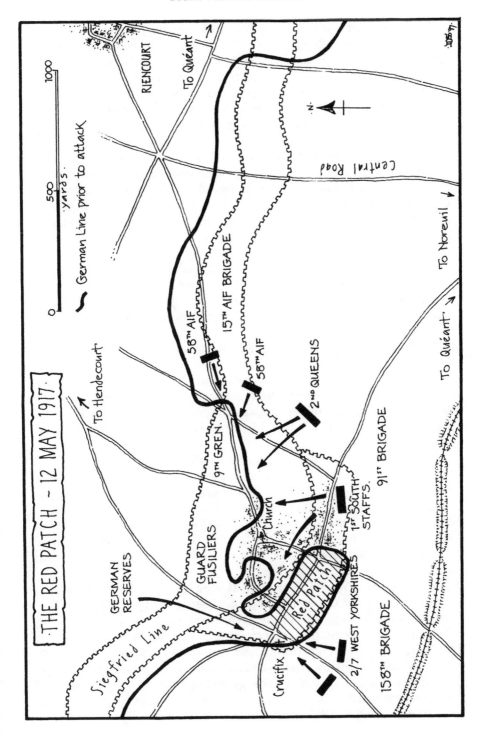

THE RED PATCH – 12 MAY 1917.

The enemy put down a heavy H.E. and shrapnel barrage, which in a few minutes cut both telephone wires, smashed the power buzzer and the wireless apparatus. The telephone lines remained useless for the rest of the day; as soon as they were renewed, they were cut again and again. All communication therefore devolved on the hard worked 'runners', many of whom became casualties. The pigeons were also a failure for they refused to fly through a heavy barrage.[5]

As the troops in the ruins were exhausted, scattered and still pinned down by the enemy, Cumming decided to surprise the Germans with a fresh attack the following morning, assaulting the Red Patch from the east and without a prolonged artillery barrage. That evening, he telephoned Major-General Shoubridge and, with his customary vigour, put his plans to the Divisional Commander. Cumming was shocked by the response.

Shoubridge, who was normally the last word in courtesy and elegance, screamed down the telephone, telling Cumming his last attack had been a complete failure and his new plan was hopeless. Furthermore, no troops were to be relieved until further orders came from 7th Division HQ. The phone line went dead.

In the dank caves below Ecoust, where Cumming had set up his brigade HQ, the staff officers stood in silence knowing what was coming next. A few minutes later, the telephone rang. It was handed to Cumming. Shoubridge calmly told him he was 'too tired to cope with the situation and that his judgement was warped'. Cumming protested and was instantly dismissed and told to hand over command to the next senior officer.[6]

As Cumming collected his personal effects together for the long journey home, Shoubridge hastily prepared his own plan of attack to commence at 3.40 am on 13 May. That night there were other changes made in the line, but this time they were welcomed by the shattered troops. So, during the night of 12/13 May, the AIF 58th Battalion were at last relieved by the British 173rd Brigade. This left the 54th Battalion, defending the 400 yards east of the Central Road, as the only Australian unit remaining at the front.

Ever since the AIF 5th Division had been brought into the line, their commander, Major-General Hobbs, had been lobbying 'Birdie' to allow the Australians some rest. During April and May, the four active AIF divisions had some of the toughest fighting they would ever experience, with little respite. So when they heard constant stories of other British units being relieved, they were understandably fed up and their letters home reflected this.[7] The mood was getting ugly and both Birdwood and White were worried that, if these grievances were aired in Australia, recruitment to the AIF would suffer. The normally diplomatic White became incensed when he heard that this problem was not being conveyed to Haig (although Kiggell had ample evidence of the problem). He told Malcolm that unless there was an Australian put on Haig's staff, to ensure the Chief heard the AIF case, he would never sanction an Australian overseas force again. This was heady stuff and Malcolm lost no time in passing the message right to the top. It had the desired effect for, on 12 May, Bean had some good news to report:

> White tells me that the [Fifth] Army has given way about our 1st Division. After a really hot fight – I don't know what Birdie threatened – they are to be allowed their holiday. They were to have gone in again today or tomorrow, but just as they were going in, it was countermanded. The 5th Division is also to be relieved after 13 May.[8]

The 5th Division, together with the exhausted 2nd and 1st Divisions were to be sent north to rest in the area of the old Somme battlefield, which the undergrowth was slowly reclaiming. But for the men of the 4th Division, who had fought so bravely at 1st Bullecourt, there was no such rest. Bean heard that they too were to be moved north, but this time to prepare for the imminent Battle of Messines:

> I met some of the 4th Div. and the old 13th Bn. going to the Baths at Amiens. They said to me – these three officers, 'Have you heard of our move. Isn't it a bastard?'[9]

In what was the last Australian attack at Bullecourt, the 58th Battalion managed to link up the two trenches of the Siegfried Line to the British-held portion of the village. This was achieved at great cost to the battalion which suffered the loss of sixteen officers and over 300 men. It did however round off and secure the earlier Anzac gains.

Shoubridge was still commanding the British operations, although the 7th Division had been severely worn down. For his next attack, he proposed that the 2/Royal Warwicks assault the Red Patch from the south at the same time as the 22 Manchesters attacked it from the north-east. Meanwhile, the 2/7 Duke of Wellington's (186th Brigade) would again assault the Crucifix to cut off the German lifeline. The artillery plan was extraordinarily complicated because the gunners had to lob their shells into the Red Patch just as the British closed on the stronghold from both sides. Lieutenant William Oaks realised that, when the flares started going off, chaos was going to be the likely outcome:

> The men saw a party of Germans coming towards them across open ground and fired their SOS signal for a protective barrage. It came down but green lights now went up all along the front line and the

German artillery as well as the Australian and British opened up a tremendous bombardment into the same area.[10]

The practice of letting off SOS flares was becoming so commonplace that, not only were large quantities of shells wasted, but no-one knew what was going on. As jumpy forward guards let off more and more flares, the dawn sky erupted in a brilliant firework display and shells fell indiscriminately.[11]

The Warwicks and Manchesters, ordered to go in with the bayonet, fought ferociously, but then the British barrage fell short. It came down first on the Warwicks, then lifted onto the Manchesters, causing heavy casualties to both. The British barrage never touched the enemy positions and the attack collapsed. Most field artillery fire was done 'off the map' and area shooting proved to be the order of the day, with the inevitable consequences. Over on the left, the Duke of Wellington's suffered heavy casualties among their officers and again failed to take the Crucifix. Shoubridge's plan, in the words of one of his own staff officers, 'was the most appalling failure', and he now decided to go back to Cumming's original idea of attacking the infernal Red Patch from the east.[12] The Royal Welsh Fusiliers would take it.

So at 2.10 am. the following day (14 May), 'B' and 'D' Companies, 1/RWF went into 'the Blood Tub'. They were repulsed but attacked again two hours later, to be pushed back by the enemy for a second time. Two fresh companies were brought forward and went in at 6.15 am, under a Stokes mortar bombardment.[13] They too failed to break up the extraordinarily tough German defence, which not only hung onto the Patch, but also made life unbearable out among the ruins in the rest of the village. Any British soldier who stood up was liable to be shot by enemy snipers. So by the time a fourth attack was mounted, the 1/RWF were worn-out; their wounded and dying lay scattered among the ruins all the way back to the church. Through the dust and heat haze, one familiar figure could be seen, constantly crawling and scrambling over the rubble to give succour to the living and prayers for the dead – the Chaplain to the 1/RWF never gave up.

Born into an illustrious family (his father was Speaker of the House of Commons and his grandfather the statesman Sir Robert Peel), The Rev. The Hon. Maurice Peel had taken the traditional route for a younger son – into the church. He had been Vicar of Tamworth and St Paul's, Beckenham before the war and he carried his ministry effortlessly into the trenches. He was wounded at Festubert in 1915, after insisting on 'going over the top' with his men, walking stick in hand. He later returned to his old battalion the 1/RWF.

Peel kept up his constant visiting. He would appear, sometimes in the dark, sometimes in a mist, like a kind of guardian angel. As he never spoke about what he did, a great deal must remain unrecorded but it should not be forgotten how, after being three days cut off and surrounded by the enemy, he met his death in the very forefront of some of the hardest fighting in the war – in May 1917, in the reeking ruins of Bullecourt. So heavy was the fighting in that village that it was true to say that the parapet was in part composed of dead bodies. So keen were the enemy to retake Bullecourt, that they sent in one of their finest battalions, the 'Cockchafers of the Prussian Guard'. Huge great fellows they were and fine soldiers too, who reckoned an order like that to be an honour. For something like a week, the infantry fought it out mainly with bombs, whilst all around the ceaseless barrage fell. At the end of that time, the village remained in our hands and at the furthest point of all, just in front of the church, lay the mortal remains of Maurice Peel. Though he had had opportunities of getting back, he refused to do so until the last of the wounded should have been cleared. Getting up in broad daylight to bring in a wounded man, he had been shot through the stomach and had bled to death.

A day or two later, Ascension Day as it happened, which had been Peel's favourite day, the senior Chaplain of the 7th Division, Eric Milner White, crawled out and read over his body, the beautiful Collect for the day. Those who think that Peel threw his life away should by the same argument say that Jesus squandered his.[14]

When Gough heard of Peel's death, he was deeply moved. They had known and respected each other from the days of Festubert and, even after Peel's death, Gough insisted that Chaplains should be allowed to go where they liked, a practice which was gradually adopted by all the other Armies. The Chaplain of the 8th Devons, Ernest Crosse, knew only too well the importance of this practice:

Padres, unless they visited the front lines, couldn't offer men the kind of message which they needed, because the whole setting of men's lives was so totally different from times of peace.[15]

During the evening of 14 May, despite the sacrifices made by Maurice Peel and the men of the I/RWF, the 91st Brigade were adamant that the attacks would continue. At 6.30 pm the 1/RWF survivors were told that they were not to be relieved and that they were to mount a fifth assault that night. This was too much for their Commanding Officer, Lieutenant-Colonel W. Holmes who told brigade HQ flatly that until the Crucifix to the west of the village had been captured, there would be no more attacks.[16] Brigade backed down and cancelled the attack, ordering the

1/RWF to remain in the village and await support from companies of the 2/HAC, 20th and 21st Manchesters, who were now filing up the communication trenches towards the ruins.

To the east of Bullecourt, the old Australian positions in the Siegfried Line were being consolidated by the newly arrived British 173rd Brigade, part of the 58th Division. The Line had been pounded continuously and the entrances to many of the deep dugouts had now caved in. The German artillery had never let up since their troops had finally lost the 1,000 yards of trench and were making the 2/3rd and 2/4th Battalions (City of London) London Regiment suffer for their occupation.

Like the 62nd Division, these men from the 58th Division were territorials and had only landed in France four months before. They were even lower down the pecking order than the Yorkshiremen, having been originally 'third line'; they were only raised to 'second line' in June 1916. Nevertheless, they had great pride in their brigade and confidence in their brigadier. Private Walter King, writing home to his brother, was full of admiration:

> Our brigadier has a VC and bar, an MM and a DSO and 5 gold bars on his arm. He's only 28 and is always up the front line. The youngest brigadier in the army and a very brave chap too.[17]

There was no doubt about the bravery and reputation of Brigadier-General Bernard Freyberg. One of the small band of friends who had buried Rupert Brooke on Skyros, he had won acclaim at Gallipoli by swimming ashore and lighting landing flares under the noses of the Turks, and more recently, in November 1916, had been awarded the VC for his valour at Beaucourt-sur-Ancre.[18] Consequently, Gough ensured that he was one of the first New Army officers to be promoted to Brigadier-General.

However, 2nd Bullecourt was becoming a severe test of nerve for any commander, whatever his credentials. The Operations Report of 173rd Brigade HQ is testimony to the acute problems facing a brigadier trying to command his men in battle:

> Very heavy shelling of front and support lines with H.E. on the night of the 13th was followed by heavy bombardment of our front lines and incessant searching with shrapnel and H.E. throughout the whole day of the 14th. All Signal communications were broken off by a direct hit on the signal dug-out which killed the personnel and destroyed all instruments. After a short time the power buzzer also gave out and all communications had to be made by runner.[19]

There were long anxious waits for commanders and staff officers after the troops had gone into the attack and before any news came back. Often the biggest concern was when to order forward the Reserve – the timing of this was of vital importance and could easily change the fortunes of a battle. Major R. Laverton, who was on the staff of the 58th Division, well remembered these difficult hours but was young enough to realise that problems were just as great at the sharp end. 'I well remember as a Platoon and Company Commander, trying to get information back to Battalion HQ and usually being quite unable to do so'.[20]

This 'static' or 'fog', that often wrecked the flow of information from one unit to another, went right to the top of the chain of command. At GHQ, Sir Douglas Haig was having great problems trying to find out what on earth was happening in the camp of his French allies. Although he allowed Gough to keep Bullecourt on the boil to demonstrate British tenacity, he had no idea whether French policy was about to change and possibly abandon support for his Flanders offensive. After hours listening to the theatrical Sir Henry Wilson, recently arrived from the French GQG, Haig was none the wiser. Wearily, he wrote in his diary, late at night on 14 May:

> On Thursday last, it was all agreed that Pétain should be C In C, with Foch C.G.S – But next day all was changed and Nivelle was left as C In C with Pétain in Paris as C.G.S. The sad fact is that there is no-one in a position to direct and give orders. The result is that I have not received a reply to a letter I wrote on 5th May to the C In C French Armies. This letter was sent in accordance with decisions arrived at, at the Paris Conference on 3rd May. I had arranged at Nivelle's request to meet him in Amiens tomorrow morning but at dinner time I received a telephone message from him to cancel the engagement because the whole position of affairs seemed so obscure. In fact I gather that he is unable to answer my letter and really say what the French Army can and will do.[21]

Haig was not aware of it, but the French army was flickering into mutiny. Although serious outbreaks would not occur for some weeks, there had been disturbances and many infantrymen, or *poilus* ('hairy ones'), were boiling with anger. They were stoked up by Russian soldiers within their lines and pacifists at home. The seditious *Bonnet Rouge* journal inflamed their grievances and soon the government would have few divisions it could rely on. The situation was becoming critical and yet, remarkably, the British remained ignorant of the troubles until early June.[22] The Germans knew trouble was brewing in the French lines, but according to Major A. Martin (serving in the German 7th Army on the Aisne), they had no spare troops to capitalise on the situation.[23]

So whilst the Allied strategic policy hung in limbo during these weeks,

Generals Allenby and Gough were left to slog it out with a determined enemy. Bullecourt sucked in and spat out brigade after brigade from Gough's Army, while Allenby's Third Army were still battling to hold onto their gains around Arras. The ill-fated Chemical Works and the village of Roeux had at last fallen to the exhausted Third Army on 11 May after a terrific struggle, but became the subject of repeated enemy counter-attacks in the days afterwards. Still, a defensive line envisaged by Haig in the absence of a breakthrough, was taking shape. At terrible cost to the British, thirty-six German divisions had been occupied and the pressure kept off the French. As Allenby was unlikely to advance farther, there was no point in Gough aiming to 'roll up' the Wotan Line – he would have to be content with sealing the line around Bullecourt.

Otto von Moser, the enemy commander, showed no sign of wilting under the relentless Fifth Army pressure, but Gough had no new ideas. He had used up not only the crack Australian divisions but also the 7th Division, one of the best in the British Army, and none of these had succeeded in finishing the job. Now that the I ANZAC Corps were only represented in the line by their 54th Battalion, it fell to Sir Edward Fanshawe and his V Corps to command the whole Bullecourt operation. Gradually, the battalions of the 7th Division were being replaced by those of the 58th which brought Sir Edward's brother, Hew, into the sector.

This gave rise to the most extraordinary disposition of commands, for there were now three Fanshawe brothers controlling adjacent parts of the front. Edward and Hew were now joined on their right flank by their younger brother, Major-General Robert Fanshawe, commanding the 48th South Midland Division. This family affair may not have been to Gough's liking but there was no friction between these commanders and it looked as if they might swiftly wrap up the operation.

A report, received by 173rd Brigade Headquarters early in the morning of 15 May, soon put paid to this hope.

NOTES

1   WO95/1667, PRO.
2   WO95/1670, PRO.
3   ibid.
4   WO95/1632, PRO; Cumming, *A Brigadier in France* p.77-80.
5   ibid., p.76
6   WO95/1632, PRO; Cumming, *A Brigadier in France,* p.83-84.
7   Interview with Rex Willcox, AIF 6th Bn., Nov. 1994.
8   Bean Diary, May 1917, AWM 38 3DRL 606 Item 78.
9   ibid.
10 AWM MSS/0954; Griffith, *British Fighting Methods in the Great War*, p.41-44. The practice was finally stopped in 1918.
11 Vickery to Falls, 11/2/39, CAB 45/116, PRO.
12 Colonel H.J. Brooks, Liddle Collection.

13   WO95/1665, PRO.
14   Canon E. Crosse, 'The Work of the Chaplains', Crosse Papers, IWM . Milner-White destroyed virtually all his wartime correspondence but a short revealing series of letters survives, Milner-White Papers, Kings College Cambridge. See also Very Revd. Robert Holtby, 'Milner-White Letters from the Western Front', York Minster Library.
15   Crosse Papers, IWM.
16   WO95/1665, WO95/1667, PRO.
17   Private W. T. King Papers, 89/7/1, IWM.
18   During the Second World War, Freyberg became Lieutenant-General and GOC New Zealand EF, subsequently becoming Governor-General of New Zealand.
19   WO95/2999, PRO.
20   R. Laverton to Falls, CAB 45/116, PRO.
21   Haig Papers, 14 May 1917, Acc3155/97/9, NLS.
22   Richard Watt, *Dare Call it Treason*, p.166-168; John Williams, *Mutiny 1917*, p.155-8. The first mention of mutiny occurs in Haig's Papers on 2 June 1917. Sir Henry Wilson refers to it on 5 June 1917, Callwell, *F-M Sir Henry Wilson.*
23   Martin to Spears, 24 Dec. 1931, 2/3/71, Spears Papers, KCL.

CHAPTER XIII

The London Lads

At 6.36 am on 15 May, a message marked 'urgent' arrived by runner at the British 173rd Brigade Headquarters:

> Major Miller, 2/2nd Bn. London Regt., Battalion in support, reports from the front line that the Germans are massing for an attack, to the right of the Australian battalion on our right flank. Request that Artillery should be put on them.[1]

Miller rushed forward with a support company to assist the 2/3 Londons who were defending the right flank of the line with the AIF 54th Battalion. Such was the ferocity of the German barrage that Miller's party was destroyed within minutes. He managed to send back a last message:

> We have lost about 12 of our Lewis Guns, buried and destroyed. Also almost all the reserve SAA and bombs in the front line system have been buried or blown to pieces. The cartage of rations, water, SAA etc. is impossible.[2]

All across the sector, battalion and brigade HQs were in a state of alarm. A flood of reports were coming in that the enemy, after pushing forward probing patrols, were now mounting a massive counter-attack on all parts of the line – 'Operation Potsdam', as the Germans called it, was under way.

From a church tower in the distant village of Oisy, General von Moser watched as 60,000 HE and gas shells were fired by his artillery into the British infantry and gun positions. The bombardment heralded an attempt by the *Lehr* ('Training') Regiment to retake Bullecourt and the mile of Siegfried Line they had previously lost. It was also a chance for the new German Sixth Army Commander, General Otto von Below, to stamp his authority on the sector and put his subordinate von Moser in his place. Von Below had just arrived from the Macedonian front and, although he would become famous later in the year for his victory at Caporetto, he was still very much in the shadow of his brother, Fritz, one of the authors of the new defensive doctrine.[3]

Von Moser had been worn down by the persistent British and

Australian attacks and now believed that Bullecourt was becoming a lost cause – he felt strongly that too many of his specially trained stormtroopers were being killed in futile attacks. He had wished to launch this main German attack a week before when the 3rd Guard Division was fresh, but he had been ordered to wait while sufficient ammunition was stockpiled for a massive preliminary bombardment.

On the British side, this delay had benefited the young Londoners who had been able to fortify their defences. However, when the attack eventually came, Private Walter King, like his comrades in the 2/2 London Regiment, was still unprepared for the terror that lay ahead:

It was real hell. Fritz put a bombardment over our trenches that the boys will never forget. For hours we lay in the bottom of the trenches awaiting our end. Here and there our trenches were going up and our poor boys blown to pieces. I could not have stuck it much longer. My nerves were beginning to give way and officers and men were continually going out with shell shock. I shall never forget the ghastly sights of it all and the stench of the dead.[4]

Private King managed to keep his sanity only to be killed a month later in a raid on the German lines outside Bullecourt. He did not exaggerate the horror of the place as other men of the London Regiment would soon find out. Private James Moddrel, from Upton Park, London, had joined up under age and, until recently, had been confined to playing the bugle. Now as an eighteen-year-old, officer's 'servant', he was on his way up to Bullecourt just before the massive German attack:

We heard lots of stories from the men who had come out of the line as to the terrible nature of the fighting going on around the place. Bullecourt had been given the gruesome nickname 'The Blood Tub'. This was to be the battalion's first real battle in its history. We moved up from Mory to Ecoust – constant flashing and noise of the guns, the continuous moving to the side of the road to allow artillery wagons to go by, the difficulty of keeping up with one's own party in the growing darkness.

At Ecoust, there were three odours mixed in the air, first the smell of cordite, second the several kinds of gas, third and worst of all, the smell of dead horses and men. We were going up Bullecourt Avenue. It is impossible to give anything like an adequate description of the piece of ground – there was only one place I ever saw in France that was worse.

The ground was literally covered with dead, most of them being the HAC men that we had come up to relieve and we heard afterwards that although the HAC went into the line about 600 strong, only about 80 of them got out again. At night the German Very lights served to keep us from going into the line. They also served another purpose which was to show us that wherever we went, the ground was still covered with dead.

For cover, I climbed into a hole beneath an upturned railway truck. I heard orders being issued to my platoon to take part in an attack and I had a very strong temptation to stay where I was until the platoon had gone. Nobody knew where I was so I could have done. I got over my attack of funk and got out of my shelter to find the platoon sergeant. I heard in the morning that a shell had dropped on the shelter I had occupied and killed 2 men.

The platoon was already leaving – the other fellows climbed the bank and disappeared towards the tape line in NML. This NML was like the popular conception of a battlefield, every inch of the place had been shelled and a good many inches were covered with things that had once been human bodies but which were now unrecognisable among the mud and litter. Once we had to stop when a shell burst and I looked down to find myself nearly treading on a poor fellow who had had his legs and the lower part of his body blown right away. At the time this did not affect me but I have many times remembered his white face and sightless eyes and wished fervently that I could forget them.[5]

The remnants of the HAC, which Moddrel's battalion were going up to relieve, were still defending the western part of the village, together with companies of the 20th and 21st Manchesters. They faced a pincer movement from two battalions of the German Guard Fusiliers, one battalion pouring out of the 'Red Patch' from the south-west and the other battalion attacking the western outskirts of the village.

The first defenders to come into contact with the enemy were a Lewis Gun party of the 21/Manchesters, posted near the Crucifix. This unit, under the direction of 2nd Lieutenant S. R. Smith, continued to fire into the mass of enemy infantry until their Lewis guns jammed. They were then swiftly surrounded and slaughtered, except for 2nd Lieutenant Smith who, seriously wounded, was hauled out of the dugout and taken away by the enemy for questioning.[6]

Two hundred yards away, the enemy had got in amongst scattered pockets of HAC men and it was now impossible to tell friend from foe, as L/Corporal William Bradley found out:

Confusion reigned. When it got a bit lighter we saw a movement on the road in front and everyone had a crack. It was not until we saw the man's tin hat go into the air that we realised that he was one of our own men. Nothing happened for a bit and suddenly a swarm of unmistakable Germans climbed out of a trench and raced across our front at about 150 yards. Everyone then opened up on them.

Later I came across a very young RWF boy, badly hit. He wanted me to stay with him, which I did for a few minutes. Half an hour later, when I crawled out with a stretcher bearer, he was dead. Cheetham, our runner, was also in a very bad way and kept calling to me for water. Being hit in the lung, we were told not to give him any water but I kept moistening his lips.[7]

Such was the force of the enemy counter-attack that the HAC and Manchesters were thrown out of the Western part of the village, only managing to stem the German advance at the Longatte road, now unrecognisable but running through the middle of the ruins. A counter-attack by the 20/Manchesters later in the day, recaptured some of this western sector but the enemy had worn down the remnants of the 91st Brigade so much that the British unit had to be finally withdrawn that evening.

Out to the east, in OG1 and OG2, the 2/3rd London Regiment and the AIF 54th Battalion stoutly defended their positions, but the German bombardment had ripped great holes in their ranks, the British losing 300 and the Australians 400 men. For their part, the German II and III Battalions, Lehr Regiment, suffered badly and although they had made some gains in the village, they only managed to chip away at the British positions and were finally seen off by an accurate Anzac artillery barrage.

As the heavy guns began to slacken off during the evening of 15 May, columns of British reinforcements for the 58th Division were already on their way up to the front line. The 174th London Brigade came up to relieve the 91st Brigade in Bullecourt itself, and fresh companies of the 173rd Brigade had set off to reinforce the line to the right of the village. Private H. Hobbs of the 2/3rd London Regiment recalled his journey to the front, a journey that started in an atmosphere reminiscent of 1914:

The band started up. Water bottles filled to brim, bully beef stew and rice still sizzling in our insides. The brave old Sgt. Major (who always led until you got within a dangerous distance) put on his finest military stride and the Colonel and Adjutant rode in front. The whole procession was in artillery formation (50 yards between platoons). Jerry's balloons were quite visible.

The first halt, I was hot and thirsty but I dare not drink. The fellows flung down their equipment, said a few words about blighty, lay on their backs, pulled their caps over their eyes and rested. Off again, uphill and the plucky little band was still stepping out the music. They didn't have packs but to blow a cornet on a hot day, running up a hill, must be an ordeal.

After one day, the band was left behind, so nobody was whistling

'Tipperary'. We had now left the long roads of poplars behind and were in the land of sunken roads. Now one or two shells were coming over. It was a nightmare and the stunted trees on the top of the banks looked ghastly – shell torn and twisted.

Then it was into the trenches. Shells now came thick and fast. We progressed up the line in a succession of tumbles and falls – something like walking the plank. There was also telephone cable which served as an excellent trip wire. [8]

When the 'London Lads' finally struggled into the smashed British front line, they found a bewildering array of underground cellars and dugouts, which had survived the relentless shelling. Many had been occupied by the retiring British 91st Brigade, but there were so many vaults that new discoveries were being made all the time. Private Moddrel, who as a 'servant' to Lieutenant Herbert Wilkinson, was expected to follow him wherever he went, found himself in a newly occupied trench:

We occupied a trench and a machine-gun team at once got their gun into position in case of a counter-attack. We started to throw all the dead Bosch out of the trench. When we moved one particular fellow, we found he was very much alive. He objected to us touching him and finding his ruse, so he started to make trouble with a dagger.

We found in one German dugout, bundles of British clothing and equipment and there is little doubt that some of it had been used for the purpose of dressing Bosch soldiers as British troops.

In another dugout, halfway down the stairs a German soldier had been fastened with his face to the wall by a semi-circular piece of iron, clamped tight to the wall on both sides. The iron was around his waist and his arms were inside so that he could not possibly move them. He had obviously committed some crime – this was his punishment. He was quite dead having a large wound in his head made with a chopper. [9]

The German artillery continued to shell the British as they carried out their relief programme. At 10.00 am on 16 May, Major-General Hew Fanshawe, the spry cavalryman, rode up to Mory and formally took over the front from Major-General Shoubridge.

Hew Fanshawe's career was still on hold. He had been shabbily treated by Haig and Gough in the past when he was removed as V Corps commander on the eve of the Somme – he refused to allow Aylmer Haldane to take the 'can' for the fiasco at St Eloi Craters and so put his own head on the block. [10] He was subsequently given the 58th Division to train in England and had now brought them out to France. So far at Bullecourt, the division was acquitting itself well but Gough was keeping a close eye on Fanshawe, whom he knew to be still close to an old enemy, Viscount French.[11]

Having been briefed on the current position, the 58th Division Commander walked up the aptly named *L'Homme Mort* ('Dead Man') road to 174th Brigade HQ at Ecoust, to discuss with Brigadier-General Charles Higgins how to clear the Red Patch. Higgins had only been made up to Brigadier three weeks before, so the forthcoming attack would be a baptism for the commander as well as his battalions of London Rifles and Post Office Rifles. These battalions were unusual in that they hung onto their old titles from the days when they had been Volunteer battalions of the Regulars. Because the Territorial London Regiment was only formed in 1908, and therefore had no traditions, it was the battalions who kindled spirit and pride.

The first task to be tackled was the support trench to the north of the village, which had to be secured to prevent the enemy from reinforcing his troops in the Red Patch. This mission was entrusted to Freyberg's 173rd Brigade, who had endured frequent enemy counter-attacks, the most recent one occurring at dawn that day. Private H. Hobbs had welcomed the chance to hit back at the enemy:

I got up beside the Lewis Gun chaps and lay on my face with rifle ready. Bullets whistled through the air with a continual 'sloh-e-or' and background shrapnel like the wind in telegraph wires.

I enjoyed myself. I felt quite cool and callous and fired as if I was tapping a typewriter. We could see the field-grey uniforms gradually getting more definite in the morning half-light. Slowly they appeared to come, hesitating, stopping every now and then to take shelter.

The thunder of our guns was terrific while sections of enemy trench seemed to vanish in smoke with objects too grim to describe, flung in mid-air – so accurate was our artillery fire that we could imagine nothing getting through. The battle continued for three hours. All we had to do was fire and fetch new ammo as required.It was getting hot and sweltering and we had to go through a labyrinth of trenches blown to pieces, with a heavy box of 303 ammo. Anyone who has ever carried a box of 303 cartridges, will realise what a game it is with Lewis Gun ammo over one shoulder, a rifle and all the other attachments.

Soon as it died down, Jerries were strewn over NML in hundreds. One man was shot dead as he was kneeling to take aim and remained in that position. Several continued to fire at this object thinking it was still alive.[12]

At 6.30 pm that day, the 173rd Brigade at last went into the attack. The 2/1st (City of London) advanced in two waves and captured Bovis Trench, running east to west to the rear of the village and suffered surprisingly few casualties. To Hew Fanshawe, it looked as if the end was now in sight, for the intelligence from captured Germans indicated that there were few fresh enemy units coming forward. Unbeknown to Fanshawe, when the last great German counter-attack had failed on 15 May, von Moser was finally able to convince his Army Commander, von Below, that it was too costly to hang onto Bullecourt. During the evening of 16 May, as Fanshawe and Higgins were planning a final thrust into the Red Patch, the German 3rd Guard Division started to pull out and sent in its pioneers to blow up its old Company HQ dugouts.

At 2.00 am on 17 May, following a violent two-minute bombardment, the 2/5 Londons (London Rifle Brigade) attacked the Red Patch from the south. They knocked out the remaining enemy positions, but even at this late hour, resistance was stiff and the battalion lost four officers and forty-four men.[13] However, the last officer casualty of the 2/5th LRB avoided enemy fire only to fall headlong into a garden well. The 2/8th Londons (Post Office Rifles) then passed through the Red Patch and swept up the rest of the village, catching many of the enemy pioneers in the middle of their demolition job.

Finally, as dawn broke on 17 May, the forward posts of the 186th Brigade (62nd West Riding Division) could at last make out friendly troops surrounding the mound of the Crucifix. The Yorkshiremen had tried repeatedly to capture this position and their dead lay in heaps around it. The Red Patch, now so utterly pulverised that it was impossible to see the village boundary, yielded wounded German Fusiliers for days afterwards. There was still the job of exploring and making safe the vast complex of underground dugouts the Germans had left behind, while to the east beyond the Central Road, tunnelling companies of the AIF 54th Battalion were burrowing down to set up listening posts, in this newest of front lines.

Above ground, the trenches were being heavily wired, especially those in front of Riencourt, that second objective on 3 May, that was never taken. Hendecourt, the third objective, also remained in German hands. 17 May marked the end of the Second Battle of Bullecourt and effectively the end of the Arras offensive, although Fanshawe's 58th Division would lose hundreds of men in the last two weeks of May, consolidating the front.

The dead lay everywhere. In fact, when Major-General Hew Fanshawe walked the battlefield several days later, he made special note in his diary of the large numbers that lay unburied. The exposed nature of the battle-field and the commanding ridge held by the enemy had meant it was sui-cidal to retrieve those who were killed and so hundreds of Australians and British, including those killed in April, still hung on the wire, bleached by the fierce sun. Thousands of others lay out in no man's land continually buried, unearthed and reburied by incessant bombardments.

Still more dead lay in the trenches and deep dugouts of the Siegfried Line and heaped among the rubble of the village, often embracing their last enemy.

L/Corporal Bradley of the 2/HAC recalled that 'the dead were everywhere – mostly men of the 62nd Division killed on the 3 May and a lot of Germans from the Guard Division'. All that was left of Bradley's battalion were four officers and ninety-four men. After the battle, the exhausted soldiers rested at Mory, three miles to the rear where 'the awful stench of the dead came down on the wind from the front'. There, in a Nissen hut, oblivious to all the terrific noise and smoke, a swallow had built its nest in the cross stays. The soldiers placed a box beneath the nest and a long queue formed up to watch the chicks being fed.[14]

The Germans also left behind thousands of their own dead and wounded in trench dugouts and in the ruins and cellars of Bullecourt. Although there remain no accurate German casualty figures for 2nd Bullecourt, it is estimated that the Württemberg 27th Division lost over 2,500 men, while the 3rd Guard Division lost over 2,000 men. In addition to these two main divisions employed, troops from a further five divisions were used during the two weeks, with estimated losses of over 1,000. And, as with all German casualty figures, these estimates do not include lightly wounded men. These brave Württembergers and fearless 'Potsdam Giants' had taken part in fighting which they and their Corps Commander admitted was 'more bitter than the Somme'. But they had inflicted the most terrible casualties among the British and Australians in the two weeks of 2nd Bullecourt and although they had lost the village, they held on to Riencourt and with it the vital junction of the Drocourt-Quéant 'switch'.

The 62nd West Riding Division lost 191 officers and 4,042 men – a devastating introduction to the Western front, in this their first real test in battle. If the purpose had been to 'bloody' them, then it had succeeded, but their inexperience and at times irresolute attacks had been mercilessly punished by a tough, professional enemy. But what hope could there be for this second-line territorial division, when even a crack division like the 7th could not shift the enemy from Bullecourt? In their costly and stubborn assaults, Shoubridge's 7th Division lost a total of 134 officers and 2,588 men, killed, wounded or missing. And even that other territorial unit, the 58th Division, coming in towards the end of the operation, fared little better, suffering casualties of eighty-five officers and 1,853 men.[15]

To these British losses of over 400 officers and 8,500 men at 2nd Bullecourt must be added the terrible sacrifices of the Australian I ANZAC Corps. Of the 2nd, 1st and 5th Divisions, 292 officers and 7,190 men were killed, missing or wounded. During the fourteen days of 2nd Bullecourt, this amounted to a combined casualty rate of 1,000 men a day.

If the 3,300 casualties from 1st Bullecourt are added to the AIF tally, then the daily losses at Bullecourt exceeded any other Australian action in the war.[16] Incredibly, these appalling losses for so few tactical gains baffled even those conducting the war. At the end of 1917, Sir Henry Wilson tackled 'Wully' Robertson on his performance as Chief of the Imperial General Staff:

> After dinner I had a long talk with Robertson. I asked him if, looking back over two years, he was satisfied with the conduct of the war, and whether he would act in the same way again. He replied in the affirmative to both questions. Since he has been C.I.G.S., we have lost Rumania, Russia and Italy, and we have gained Bullecourt, Messines and Passchendaele. [17]

NOTES

1   WO95/2999, PRO.
2   Operations Report 15 May, WO95/2999, PRO.
3   Von Moser, *Feldzugsaufzeichnungen,* p. 173-175 and p.277. Otto von Below replaced von Falkenhausen as Commander Sixth Army on 23 April 1917. Otto is often confused with his brother Fritz who commanded an Army on the Somme and in April 1917 was sent down with his First Army to oppose the Nivelle offensive.
4   Private W. King Papers, 89/7/11, IWM.
5   Private J.F.R. Moddrel Diary, Liddle Collection.
6   He was released a month after the war ended.
7   L/Corporal W.T. Bradley Papers, 316.319, IWM. In the 1920s, when Bradley was playing hockey for the Regiment, he was surprised and delighted when Pte. Cheetham appeared, 'looking the picture of health'.
8   Private H. Hobbs Diary, Liddle Collection.
9   Private J.F.R. Moddrel Diary, Liddle Collection.
10 MS20249, Haldane Papers, NLS. Neither Haig, Gough nor Plumer came out of the incident with any credit. Birdwood was the only senior commander who stood by Fanshawe, recognising that many of the problems lay with the Canadian Command, Fanshawe Papers, PFC.
11 Gough and Haig knew that Fanshawe was 'the eyes and ears' for Viscount French, who, despite new honours, was still simmering back at home, Brooke Mocket to AF, Fanshawe Papers, PFC.
12 Private H. Hobbs Diary, Liddle Collection.
13 Donald Gristwood of 2/5th LRB was encouraged by his mentor, H.G. Wells, to recount his experiences with the battalion. His double novel, *The Somme* and *The Coward* was published in 1927. For a review of his work see Hugh Cecil, *The Flower of Battle.*
14 L/Corporal W.T. Bradley Papers, 316.319, IWM.
15 WO95/519, PRO. Divisional Histories and V Corps casualty returns.
16 The AIF suffered 23,000 casualties over six weeks at Pozières and Mouquet Farm.
17 Callwell, *Sir Henry Wilson – His Life and Diaries,* 5 November 1917 .

CHAPTER XIV
Epilogue

To Major-General Brudenell White, Bullecourt crushed the spirit and dashed the camaraderie of I ANZAC Command. Three weeks after the main fighting ended, the normally composed White wrote:

> I have felt my fellow man hard to live with, my Chief [Birdwood], a man of no quality and the majority of the staff, a set of gibbering idiots . . . I could have wept with anger. I vented my anger in rudeness to my chief . . . I was fed up and the sooner I was allowed out of this, the better.[1]

White was frustrated. The appalling loss of life for a heap of brick dust of little tactical value did not seem a fair exchange. After the agonies of Pozières and Mouquet Farm, Bullecourt was the final straw and relations among the Australian commanders were at breaking point. White had always maintained a good working relationship with his chief, Birdwood – far better than Gough and Malcolm – but neither was prepared to tackle the weak points in the Anzac plan for Bullecourt. White, one of the best administrators in the army, never showed the tactical flair he had demonstrated at the Gallipoli evacuation and the competence of other elements in I ANZAC Corps were similarly patchy. It needed John Gellibrand to point that out.

He drew up a critique of what had gone wrong at Bullecourt and confronted Major-General Nevill Smyth, GOC 2nd Division, who had commanded the front for most of 2nd Bullecourt. Gellibrand deplored the fact that constant demands were made on his resources of men and weapons by the 5th and 1st Brigades. He soon found out that either the weapons were not used properly or the men were not needed and 'few points created such ill-feeling as the use or abuse of borrowed units'. He also singled out the staff of the 2nd Division for not verifying reports or checking out the constant SOS flares erupting from the Siegfried Line, before they issued floods of orders. These orders, he alleged, resulted in needless loss of life.

He was particularly incensed by the actions on 3 May of the 5th Brigade and its Commander, Brigadier-General Robert Smith. Gellibrand felt he was constantly bailing Smith out of trouble and he conveyed his annoyance together with suggestions as to how the 2nd Division staff might improve.[2] Predictably, the divisional commander bristled at these suggestions from a subordinate and a falling-out followed. Gellibrand, blessed with one of the most powerful intellects in the AIF, was now at odds with it. On 3 June 1917, he wrote to White:

> Dear General,
> I regret that the insight gained during the last fortnight has fully satisfied me that I have served long enough with the 6th Brigade and I hasten to make way for an officer who will give you better service than lay in my power.[3]

The stress of Bullecourt had proved too much for him and an old nervous condition returned. Birdwood, who had often found Gellibrand difficult to handle, nevertheless found him a training command in England, until he was able to return to active command in November 1917.[4]

Other tensions simmering within the AIF leadership came to a head in 1918. In May of that year, the Fifth Army was re-established and Birdwood was put in command. Before he left I ANZAC Corps with Brudenell White, Birdwood set about replacing the British-born Bullecourt veterans Smyth, Hobbs and Walker. The policy was to create one combined ANZAC Corps with only Australians holding the senior commands. To this end, the sharp and articulate General Monash was appointed to command the new Corps, while Birdwood found Australian replacements for the divisional commands. However, Birdie's old adversary, 'Pompey' Elliott, was passed over in the promotion scramble and consequently never forgave him. Elliott then embarked on a vitriolic campaign in the press against Birdwood and White which drew to a climax in the Australian Senate after the war. Elliott, who had been elected to the Senate, attacked the system of promotion in the AIF, dragging in its most famous frontline soldier, Bert Jacka, as a prime example of wasted talent. Elliott railed against the conduct of the British at Bullecourt and attacked the further promotion of Gellibrand. His bitterness had sadly obscured his brilliance as a commander and he died in 1931, a disillusioned man. An inquest returned a verdict of suicide.[5]

Elliott's adversaries enjoyed a more comfortable peace. The genial 'Birdie' was made Commander-in-Chief in India and created a Field-Marshal. The honours flowed and he passed the inter-war years ennobled and ensconced as Master of Peterhouse, Cambridge. He would have welcomed the Governor-Generalship of Australia but it was not to be. He died at Hampton Court Palace in 1951.

Brudenell White came home to Australia after the war, the most celebrated soldier after Monash. As Chief of the General Staff of the Australian Army, he set about building a new citizen army that could both defend Australia in the Pacific and contribute to the defence of the Empire. It was his lasting legacy and such was his reputation that, in 1940, when Australia found herself without a CGS at a critical stage in the Second World War, White was recalled at the age of sixty-three. For five months he steered his country's defence policy but, on 13 August 1940, travelling to a cabinet meeting, he was tragically killed when his plane crashed near Canberra. So ended the life of 'the most scholarly and technically talented soldier in Australian history'.[6]

About a quarter of the AIF men who fought at Bullecourt had been born in Britain, but it was to Australia that most of them returned after the war. They still thought themselves part of the British race but increasingly they identified themselves with Australia rather than the 'mother country'. After master-minding the recapture of Villers-Bretonneux in 1918, British-born Joseph Hobbs, who had commanded the 5th Division, was one of the few commanders to end the Great War with his reputation enhanced. He eventually settled in Australia. He was joined by another 'Britisher', Nevill Smyth, who had led the 2nd Division throughout the long days of the second battle and who said that he regarded Australians as the finest troops with whom he had ever served, and he wanted to live among them in their country.

Two Australian commanders from 1st Bullecourt never returned. Major-General William Holmes, the 'citizen-soldier' who had commanded the 4th Division during 1st Bullecourt, was killed by a chance shell near Messines two months later. Lieutenant-Colonel Terence 'Jockey Jim' McSharry, who had commanded his 15th Battalion for an unusually long two years, was killed on the Somme in August 1918, his 'lucky' small-brimmed helmet having failed to save him.

To the British, Bullecourt seemed never-ending. For nine months after the second battle ended, they garrisoned this front line, until a misty morning on 21 March 1918.

It was the first day of the 'Kaiser's Battle' and General Otto von Below was back at Bullecourt. With all the British heavy guns already removed from the salient, von Below's Seventeenth Army drenched the British lines in gas, and then swept through Bullecourt, Ecoust and Mory and within a week had taken Albert, Gough's old HQ, fifteen miles to the rear. The Germans held onto their gains during the summer of 1918, but as the British and Canadians fought back, Bullecourt finally fell to the London Scottish Regiment on 31 August 1918 after two days of bitter fighting.

The stronghold of Bullecourt was thus one of the most contested pieces of ground on the Arras front. Of the troops who fought there, two British territorial divisions had been blooded. Unlike the Australian divisions who regularly fought under the same Corps, the British divisions could not 'pool' their experiences and mistakes in the same way. Braithwaite and his 62nd West Riding Division stayed under a cloud for some time after their poor showing at Bullecourt. Like the Australians, they had been given the unenviable task of attacking in a re-entrant and it proved too much for them. There was continued ill feeling between the division and the Australians over 1st Bullecourt for many years afterwards. When Cyril Falls was compiling the Official British History for 1917, he investigated the loss of over 150 Yorkshiremen on 10 April during 'the buckshee battle'. Falls, who had served with the 62nd Division, pursued Braithwaite over the incident but, to his credit, Braithwaite replied, 'the failure caused a great deal of heart-burning at the time and as you can imagine, the Anzacs were not very popular with the 62nd Division. But that is all past history and you have smoothed the whole thing over very nicely.' [7] For their part, the AIF 4th Brigade felt they had a grievance against the 62nd Division for not attacking at the same time on 11 April, but as Bean privately admitted, 'the 4th Brigade is still damnably unjust to the 62nd Division for not doing something it was never supposed to do and for which its officers ought to have been shot if they had done it.' [8] It was not long before the 62nd West Riding emblem, a pelican with a raised foot, gave rise to the common jibe, 'By the time t'pelican puts his foot down, t'war will be over.' However, by November 1917, the Yorkshiremen had proved their worth at Cambrai and again at Bucquoy in March 1918 where they stemmed part of the German Spring Offensive. They finished the war as one of the finest Divisions in France. Braithwaite, an old friend of Haig's, was given a Corps command in 1918 and eventually repaid his old Chief by organising his funeral in 1928.

That other underrated territorial division, the 58th London, also went from strength to strength afterwards, fighting bravely at 2nd Passchendaele and in 1918 during the final advance in Flanders. However, by this time, the 2/5 LRB, who had finally taken Bullecourt on 17 May, had been disbanded. The same could not be said of its commander, Hew Fanshawe, who became one of the last casualties of the Haig-French feud. He fell out with Ivor Maxse, the XVIII Corps Commander at the end of Passchendaele despite having given a creditable performance. It gave Haig the ammunition he needed and on 3 October 1917, he 'degummed' Fanshawe for a second time. Brooke Mockett, a staff officer who observed the spectacle wrote;

> The only conclusion I can come to is that a certain person is filled with spite against Lord French and is venting it on dear old Hew who he knows received his appointment from Lord F. This is the certain person's way of getting his knife into Lord F. [9]

However, like Allenby, Hew Fanshawe was to prove his ability in the Middle East when he was sent out to command the 18th Indian Division in Mesopotamia. 'Fanshawe's Column' attacked and defeated the Turks in Fatha Gorge and pushed on to achieve the capture of Mosul. Meanwhile his older brother Edward, who had commanded V Corps during Bullecourt, remained on the Western Front. He continued to command the Corps throughout 1917 but his reputation as a 'safe pair of hands' was put to the test in 1918, when a gap between V Corps and VII Corps was exploited by the Germans in their Spring Offensive. Nevertheless, he retained a Corps command, swapping to the XXIII Corps at the end of the war.

The 7th Division went off to the Italian front with Major-General Shoubridge in November 1917. Its senior Chaplain, The Rev. Eric Milner-White, was no longer with them. The aesthetic padre, who had bravely crawled out across the battlefield as snipers' bullets cracked around him, to read Maurice Peel's favourite Collect over his dead body, was no longer welcome in the army. Shortly after Bullecourt, he fell foul of the evangelical Chaplain-General and was sent back to base – his crime was that when all the officers in his unit had been killed in an attack, at the request of his men he assumed temporary command, thereby becoming a combatant. After the war, he became a celebrated Dean of York and instigator of the King's College Carol Service.[10]

The energy and élan of the 7th Division had been depleted by Bullecourt and even three of its battalion commanders had been sent home with shell shock. The Divisional Commander's reputation had suffered and when the war finally ended, Haig dumped the elegant Shoubridge in Folkestone and told him to sort out the job of demobilisation – it would be hard to imagine a more depressing task. However, the urbane general's fortunes later revived and he was made Commandant of the RMC but sadly did not live to enjoy it, dying in office in 1923, at the age of fifty-two.[11] His protagonist at Bullecourt, Brigadier-General Hanney Cumming, did not survive him.

After being 'degummed' during 2nd Bullecourt on 12 May, Cumming was sent home to look after the Machine-Gun Training Centre. In 1918 his ability was acknowledged and he came back to active command of the 110th Brigade. In 1920, he was commanding the Kerry Infantry Brigade in Ireland and was appointed Military Governor of Kerry under martial law. On 7 March 1921, while travelling in a convoy across North County Cork, his car was ambushed and Cumming was shot dead by Irish rebels. A year later in London, a similar fate befell Gough's old adversary, Sir Henry Wilson.

For the survivors of 'D' Battalion Heavy Branch, 1917 was an extraordinary year. The two battles of Bullecourt had been a ghastly experiment along the road of tank development, or as Liddell Hart would call them, 'the growing pains of the tank'.[12] In June, the Heavy Branch became known as the Tank Corps but no increase in numbers or tank efficiency would help them in the quagmire of Passchendaele. Later in the year, came the success at Cambrai. Using the same 'Bullecourt concept', tanks were used en masse and on a much larger scale.The British employed over 400 machines (mostly Mark IV tanks) with speed and surprise and even some of the old 2nd Bullecourt Mark II's took part, having been pressed into service as supply tanks.

Their old commander, Major Watson, would never again devolve a plan that would be adopted by an Army Commander. For whilst Hardress Lloyd was subsequently promoted and praised for his part in the Cambrai victory, Watson's career dipped after the 1st Bullecourt disaster and he spent the last year of the war organising supply tanks. However, in 1919, his account of the tanks at Bullecourt was serialised in *Blackwoods Magazine* and a year later, the story was published as *A Company of Tanks* but, by then, war-weariness had set in amongst the public and it was not a success.[13] His scholastic ability was better applied in the 1920s when he became a high-flier in the Civil Service. He died suddenly in 1932, at the age of 41 while Assistant Secretary at the Ministry of Labour. He never saw Bean's Official History for 1918, in which his erstwhile Australian critics heaped eulogies on the tanks.

Watson's fellow company commander, the energetic 'Roc' Ward who directed the tanks at 2nd Bullecourt, never saw out 1917. Imbued with bags of 'offensive spirit', he had insisted on going forward with his tanks and was shot dead by a sniper at Trescaut in November. Captain Richard Haigh, Watson's no. 2, was sent on a tour of Canada and America in 1918. He travelled around the cities in an old Mark IV tank to boost the U.S. Liberty Loan.

And what of the Frenchman, for whom Bullecourt had been continued for so long? On the Chemin des Dames, Nivelle had failed to achieve what he had led the French army to expect. Mutiny followed and was not dampened down until October 1917, when Pétain, the new Commander-in-Chief, finally restored order. Nivelle had meanwhile been whitewashed of blame for the military disaster by a court of enquiry. He was subsequently sent to command the French forces in North Africa, a good posting in the circumstances, and he died in 1924 without writing his memoirs.

Whilst 1st Bullecourt had been an attempt to assist the Third Army in a breakthrough that would eventually reach Cambrai, the reason behind 2nd Bullecourt had been entirely different. At first, the attack on 3 May was to see the Fifth Army forming the right flank of a breakthrough but, when this faltered, priorities changed. Haig was happy to leave Gough slogging away at the Bullecourt sector, if it convinced the Germans that the Arras offensive was not being broken off in favour of a Flanders push.

It is debatable whether this ploy worked and Haig did little to beef up Gough's troops and artillery to a level which looked anything like the continuation of a major offensive.

However, immediately after the large attacks by Allenby and Gough on 3 May, there was some indication that the Germans were taking the bait. For on 4 May, General Ilse, Chief of Staff of the German Fourth Army, declared that 'there was unlikely to be an imminent attack on Messines'. And as the struggle at Bullecourt continued until 17 May, Crown Prince Rupprecht waited until 29 May to despatch three divisions and six heavy gun batteries north to reinforce the German Fourth Army. A week later, with the British about to launch their attack at Messines, he belatedly transferred two more divisions and fifty-one gun batteries. So the savage fighting around Bullecourt had some effect. But overall, the British feint on the Arras front after 3 May was simply not strong enough to fool the Germans. It was no fault of the Third Army troops involved. Because of the French collapse, Pétain failed to send enough troops to relieve British units on the Somme, with the result that there were no fresh units available for Allenby's attacks around Arras.

The struggle at Bullecourt had consumed the Fifth Army for nearly two vital months. Since Haig had appointed Gough for the Flanders offensive on 30 April, Gough and his staff had therefore spent three weeks on 2nd Bullecourt which could have been better utilised in planning for Flanders.[14] It was extraordinary that, even by the time the stronghold finally fell on 17 May, the Fifth Army were no closer to understanding German intentions.

Malcolm, in his last Operations Report to GHQ on 19 May, thought it likely that the 'enemy was thinning his line, preparatory to a further withdrawal'.[15] If the Germans had retreated to defensive lines farther back, with Gough's Army moving north, the British would have been hard pressed to capitalise on the retreat.

To the Germans, the stoic defence of Bullecourt was the finest achievement of the 27th Württemberg Reserve Division, even dwarfing its achievements on the Somme – it was probably the toughest division the Australians ever faced. After the Württembergers' heavy losses in April and May, one complete infantry regiment was dissolved to provide its replacements and it was still in the line at the Armistice, commanded by General von Maur and a staff of dwindling Württemberg nobility. Another division attached to General von Moser's Corps, the 3rd Guards, was already a crack Prussian unit before Bullecourt and the battle enhanced the reputation of its new stormtroop units. They showed they were masters of 'fire and movement' and their deployment in this role, in small NCO-led groups, was a concept the British could not match.

The XIV Corps Commander, General Otto von Moser, used his Bullecourt experience with tanks to good effect, when he next found himself opposite the British at Cambrai. Finishing the war as a Lieutenant-General, he later published his diary *Feldzugsaufzeichnungen* ('Campaign Memoirs') and was one of the few German Commanders who took to the lecture circuit after the war. He was keen to point out that 'in 1917, it was the British who were militarily the most obstinate and most dangerous of Germany's enemies'.[16] He also readily conceded that, at the time of Bullecourt, no more German reserves could be taken from the Russian front and the physical specimens that arrived to replace the lost officers and men were poor substitutes – in short Haig's policy of 'wearing down' was bloody but successful. As for the famous 'fire-fighter' of the Arras sector, Fritz von Lossberg, he eventually turned against his royal rulers. In the last months of the war, when Germany was racked by revolution, the aristocrat threw in his command of the Army of Lorraine and, after contacting the mutinous seamen at Kiel, he established a soviet.

For Gough, the aftermath of Bullecourt was hectic. On 19 May, two days after the ruins fell to the British, Haig ordered Gough and Malcolm to move their HQ north to La Lovie Château in preparation for the Ypres offensive. As this move for Gough had been mooted for some time, it was inconceivable that Haig would hold an enquiry into Bullecourt and risk censuring the very commander to whom he had entrusted part of his Flanders operation. Besides, previous enquiries such as 'The Dardanelles Commission', whose report had only been published two months before Bullecourt, had produced much Anglo-Australian 'mud slinging' involving the journalist Keith Murdoch. He was also an eye-witness to Bullecourt alongside Charles Bean, and was raring to have another crack at the British conduct of the war. This sort of publicity, especially if it included adverse comments on the new wonder weapon, the tank, would be unwelcome. Glaring investigations into Anglo-Australian operations might also pose a threat to recruitment drives in Australia.

Despite Edmund Allenby's loyalty to GHQ, Haig wasted little time after Arras in removing the Third Army Chief.[17] Allenby was then sent to Palestine where he was remarkably successful.

Gough, who was given a very loose rein by Haig at Bullecourt, was also allowed the same latitude at Passchendaele later in the year.[18] Early in 1918, Neill Malcolm left Gough to take up his own divisional command and was succeeded as Chief of Staff by Brigadier-General Jocelyn Percy. However, two months later, Gough's career was in ruins.

When the German Spring offensive was launched on 21 March 1918, Gough's Fifth Army stood on a front of forty-two miles. It fell back before the onslaught in the style of the German 'elastic defence', but there were no counter-attack troops in place and the men had to retreat over open ground. The Fifth Army losses were extremely heavy, but Gough handled the crisis as best he could. With most of the territory gained by the British in over three years of war wiped out within days, there was uproar in England. Lloyd George needed a scapegoat and Hubert Gough was a suitable candidate. He was ordered back to England with his staff within a week.

The mood was so dark at home that his old friend Haig no longer felt it expedient to protect him, and Sir Henry Wilson, now Chief of the Imperial General Staff, was quite happy for that old 'Curragh' score to be settled with Gough. For his part Gough was very bitter – 'These vile and rotten politicians surrounded with their intrigues,' he wrote to Paul Maze.[19] Nevertheless, he stayed in oblivion and his left-wing sympathies in the 1920s excluded him from any residual military posts.

The publication in 1933 of Bean's Volume IV of the Official History of Australia in the War goaded Gough to come out fighting again. Whatever his private thoughts, Bean publicly laid the blame for Bullecourt on the tanks together with the British High Command. Gough of course was furious with this criticism, retorting:

> Bean's judgement on my personal characteristics are childish, worthy of the anti-room or even the canteen, with a strong dash of personal animosity.[20]

And while condemnation of Gough's conduct at Bullecourt and Passchendaele was never retracted, he did eventually receive redemption for his handling of the 1918 Retreat from a most unlikely source – Lloyd George himself. The Liberal politician admitted in 1936 that he had been unfair to Gough and publicly vindicated him. [21]

Even after the Second World War, Gough continued corresponding with his old friend, Paul Maze, but his relationship with Neill Malcolm soured in later years.[22] By 1960, Gough was the last of the Great War Commanders left alive and he spent his remaining, arthritis-ridden years, in a flat in Knightsbridge. His past never left him, for opposite his drawing-room window was a large hoarding advertising whisky – 'Don't be vague. Ask for Haig!' [23]

One man who read Gough's obituary in 1963 was his old adversary, Charles Bean. Although now a frail man, he had been blessed with the most extraordinary mental stamina which had enabled him to complete six superbly detailed volumes of the Official History by 1942.[24] He had also been the inspiration and guiding hand in the creation of The Australian War Memorial, dedicated not only to remembrance but also as a centre for future study and research.

Bean's 1917 volume, of which the Bullecourt operations occupy a third, is an eye-witness account of the war with a deliberate emphasis on the actions and feelings of individual soldiers. Bean admitted that relying on eye-witness accounts had its problems. They were sometimes hopelessly inaccurate, and the narrator gave too much prominence to his own particular piece of action. But then many official communiqués and often war diaries bore little relation to fact, the most notable examples being those of the Heavy Branch and Anzac Heavy Artillery.

Bean's 1917 volume was also a Corps history and, as in most unit histories, the brief is to immortalise the unit. In his attempt to lionise the Australian fighting man he also had to find someone to blame for the appalling losses and it was invariably the British High Command. Too often he realised the constraints on this command and only conceded them privately – 'I've been purple with rage about Haig', he wrote to Gellibrand, 'and then found that he was tied to an engagement to the French.'[25] Frequently he was on target, but at times he chose to ignore stark evidence provided by his mentor John Gellibrand, that there were other reasons closer to home. Many of these weaknesses would be ironed out by 1918, when the AIF under Sir John Monash would mature into a truly professional force, and victories such as Hamel would restore Australian confidence in the tanks. Also by then, the green British battalions who had been so badly mauled at Bullecourt, would have matured beyond measure.

Today, small cemeteries dot the countryside around Bullecourt and Riencourt. For the most part they contain the fallen from the battles of 1918, as most of those who were killed at 1st and 2nd Bullecourt have no known grave. Such was the ferocity of the battles that there was nothing recognisable left of many men, while others were simply bundled by the Germans into unmarked pits. Owing to the work of the Red Cross, confirmation of POWs' whereabouts was surprisingly good, though information rarely filtered back to battalion records.

But for the relatives of the thousands of men 'missing in action', the pain went on. Buoyed by the glimmer of hope in gentle letters from company subalterns, relatives often went to agonising lengths to confirm their worst fears. Charles Swears, armed with a military pass, a photograph and the knowledge that his son Hugh always carried a pearl-handled Colt revolver, went searching for him in France. He never found him and Hugh's only memorial together with tens of thousands of others is the Faubourg-D'Amiens Monument to the Missing, at Arras. Like many monuments, it is huge and impassive but heeding the advice of the 'patron' in Sebastian Faulks' *The Girl at the Lion D'Or* brings it to life:

When next you pass the memorial, stop and look at the list of names. Try to imagine that they're not just letters chipped into rock but that each one has a face, a laugh, a look.[26]

After the war, only eight of the original twenty-eight farming families returned to rebuild Bullecourt. A new church and school were built on the same site. The surrounding countryside was cultivated again; the catacombs and fortifications filled in and the Siegfried Line slowly but surely ploughed back into the landscape.

Today trees cover the railway embankment, the 'hottest' spot in the battlefield, which is still littered with shell fragments and wire 'corkscrews'. In the Anzac re-entrant, the central road and sunken roads where the troops jumped off from are still used as farm tracks. The fields leading up to the old Siegfried Line, where so many Anzacs were slaughtered, constantly yield not only debris of the battle but 'missing' Australians. As recently as November 1994, Sergeant Jack White's 'unknown grave' was disturbed by a plough. After full ceremony and the attendance of his daughter Myrtle from Australia, Sergeant White was buried near his comrades in Quéant Road cemetery.

Bullecourt today is one of the brighter villages in this part of Picardy. The former Mayor, Jean Letaille and schoolmaster, Claude Durand, have done much to preserve the memory of those who fought here. There is an excellent museum, created by Jean Letaille and, in the centre of the village in front of the new church, on the spot where Maurice Peel was shot, there are memorials to the 7th, 58th and 62nd British divisions together with a bronze Australian Slouch Hat. Beyond the village to the east, there are more reminders in Australia Avenue. Here, where some of the most ferocious fighting took place in OG2, a stone cross commemorates the fallen Australians, including Major Percy Black. Dominating the skyline and looking towards the old German lines, stands the bronze statue of Peter Corlett's 'Digger' and Ross Bastiaan's battle plaque. It is difficult to imagine that these fields harbour so many 'evil memories'.

Few if any lessons were learnt from Bullecourt that could redeem it. Nonetheless, the story of its two battles highlights the extraordinary bravery of both the Australians and the British – a bravery that was not just confined to combatants. Both commanders and men struggled with the constraints of the 1917 battlefield and whilst careful planning could always reduce casualties, time usually conspired against it. When finally the boys 'hopped the bags', they went into chaos. And they went in alone. In the words of one who witnessed countless Great War battles:

War is a chancy game at best and a frightful, messy, blundering business unless a Napoleon runs it – and God save us from Napoleons.
Charles Bean.[27]

NOTES

1   White to Gellibrand, 8 June 1917. AWM 92 3DRL 6405 Item 2.
2   AWM 92 3DRL 1473 Item 66.
3   AWM 92 3DRL 1473 Item 48.
4   In 1918 Gellibrand was promoted Major-General to command the AIF 3rd Division in its battles from Hamel to the Siegfried Line. For an analysis of his relationship with the Australian Official Historian see 'Bean & Gellibrand: some implications of their friendship', Peter Sadler, JAWM 23 (1993) 36.
5   For the wider issues in the recording of Anzac history, 'History and Betrayal: the Anzac controversy', *History Today*, no. 43 (Jan. 1993); Robin Gerster, *Big-Noting: The Heroic Theme in Australian War Writing*.
6   D.M. Horner, *The Commanders – Australian military leadership in the Twentieth Century*, p. 43.
7   Braithwaite to Falls, 3 July 1937, CAB45/116, PRO.
8   Bean to Gellibrand 19 May 1929, AWM92 3DRL 6405 Item 4.
9   Brooke Mockett to AF, Fanshawe Papers, PFC. Hew Fanshawe later became Military Governor of Baghdad and KCB.
10 Milner-White Papers, Kings College Cambridge.
11 Major-General Shoubridge is buried in the graveyard at RMA Sandhurst.
12 The Heavy Branch battalion and brigade files in the PRO are full of reports on the tank lessons to be learned from Bullecourt.
13 Blackwood to Watson, 8/9/20, Blackwood Papers, NLS. In recent years the book has become a 'tank classic'.
14 Prior and Wilson, *Passchendaele: The Untold Story*. A revision of the role of Gough in the planning for the Third Ypres offensive.
15 Fifth Army Summary of Operations w/e 18 May 1917, WO 95/519, PRO.
16 *Das Militärisch und Politisch Wichtigste vom Weltkriege*, Belser, Stuttgart
17 III/2/15, Edmonds Papers, KCL.
18 Bean privately conceded to Gellibrand that Gough was not responsible for continuing the agony at Passchendaele. He blamed Haig, Harrington and Plumer. AWM 92 3DRL 6405 Item 4; Prior & Wilson, *Command on the Western Front* and *Passchendaele: The Untold Story*.
19 Gough to Maze, 21 April 1918, Maze Papers, KCL.
20 Gough to Edmonds 19 Aug. 1933, II/2 Edmonds Papers, KCL. For an examination of both Bean's and Edmonds' treatment of Gough in the Official Histories, see T.H.E. Travers, From Surafend to Gough' , *Journal of the AWM* no. 27 (Oct. 1995) and E.M. Andrews, *The Anzac Illusion*, p.96-102.
21 Gough File 1935-54, LH1/323/1-20, Liddell Hart Papers, KCL.
22 Gough to Maze, 17 Dec. 1951, Maze Papers, KCL.
23 William Moore, *See How They Ran*.
24 Bean's attention to detail earned him the jibe,'Bean actually counts the bullets'.
25 Bean to Gellibrand 19 May 1929, AWM 92 3DRL 6405 Item 4; 'The Writing of the Australian Official History of the Great War – Sources, Methods and some Conclusions', *Royal Australian Hist. Soc. Journal & Proceedings* Vol. 24 Part 2 (1938).
26 Sebastian Faulks, *The Girl at the Lion D'Or*. Vintage, 1990.
27 Bean to Gellibrand AWM 92 3DRL 6405 Item 4.

Appendix I

Extract from:
ORDER OF BATTLE, BRITISH DIVISIONS.
FLANKING OPERATIONS ROUND BULLECOURT
APRIL – MAY 1917[1]

FIFTH ARMY: General Sir Hubert Gough

V CORPS: Lieutenant-General Sir Edward Fanshawe

7th DIVISION: Major-General T. H. Shoubridge

    20th Brigade: Brigadier-General H. C. R. Green
        8/Devons, 9/Devons
        2/Border, 2/Gordons

    22nd Brigade: Brigadier-General J. McC. Steele
        2/Royal Warwicks, 1/RWF
        20/Manchesters, 2/HAC

    91st Brigade: Brigadier-General H. R. Cumming
        (12 May Col. W. W. Norman – acting)
        2/Queen's, 1/South Staffs
        21/Manchesters, 22/Manchesters

58th (2nd/1st LONDON) DIVISION: Major-General H. D. Fanshawe

    173rd (3rd/1st London) Brigade:
        Brigadier-General B. C. Freyberg VC
        2/1st, 2/2nd, 2/3rd, 2/4th London Bns.

[1]Officially designated as: 11 April – First Attack on Bullecourt
                       15 April – German Attack on Lagnicourt
                       3-17 May – Battle of Bullecourt

174th (2nd / 2nd London) Brigade:
   Brigadier-General C. G. Higgins
      2/5th City of London (London Rifle Brigade)
      2/6th City of London (Rifles)
      2/7th City of London
      2/8th City of London (Post Office Rifles)

175th (2nd / 3rd London) Brigade:
   Brigadier-General H. C. Jackson
      2/9th County of London (Queen Victoria Rifles)
      2/10th County of London (Hackney)
      2/11th County of London (Finsbury Rifles)
      2/12th County of London (The Rangers)

62nd (WEST RIDING) DIVISION: Major-General W. P. Braithwaite

   185th Brigade: Brigadier-General V. W. de Falbe
      2/5th, 2/6th, 2/7th, 2/8th West Yorks

   186th Brigade: Brigadier-General F. F. Hill
      2/4th, 2/5th, 2/6th, 2/7th Duke of Wellington's

   187th Brigade: Brigadier-General R. O'B. Taylor
      2/4th, 2/5th KOYLI
      2/4th, 2/5th York & Lancs

I ANZAC CORPS: Lieutenant-General Sir William Birdwood

Chief-of-Staff: Major-General C. B. White

1st AUSTRALIAN DIVISION: Major-General H. B. Walker

   1st (NSW) Brigade: Brigadier-General W. B. Lesslie
   (Lt. Col. I. Mackay – acting) 1st, 2nd, 3rd, 4th Bns.

   2nd (Victoria) Brigade: Colonel (temp. Brig.-Gen.) J. Heane
   5th, 6th, 7th, 8th, Bns.

   3rd Brigade: Brigadier-General H. G. Bennett
   (Lt. Col. L. M. Müller – acting)

9th (Q'land), 10th (S. Aus), 11th (W. Aus),
12th (S. & W. Aus., Tas.) Bns.

2nd AUSTRALIAN DIVISION: Major-General N. Smyth, VC

5th (NSW) Brigade: Brigadier-General R. Smith
17th, 18th, 19th, 20th Bns.

6th (Victoria) Brigade: Brigadier-General J. Gellibrand
21st, 22nd, 23rd, 24th Bns.

7th Brigade: Brigadier-General E. A. Wisdom
25th (Q'land), 26th (Q'land, Tas.),
27th (S. Aus), 28th (W. Aus) Bns.

4th AUSTRALIAN DIVISION: Major-General W. Holmes

4th Brigade: Brigadier-General C. H. Brand
13th (NSW), 14th (Vic), 15th (Q'land, Tas.),
16th (S. & W. Aus) Bns.

12th Brigade: Brigadier-General J. C. Robertson
45th (NSW), 46th (Vic),
47th (Q'land, Tas.), 48th (S. & W. Aus) Bns.

13th Brigade: Brigadier-General T. W. Glasgow
49th (Q'land), 50th (S. Aus)
51st (W. Aus), 52nd (S. & W. Aus., Tas.) Bns.

5th AUSTRALIAN DIVISION: Major-General J. J. T. Hobbs

8th Brigade: Brigadier-General E. Tivey
29th (Vic), 30th (NSW)
31st (Q'land, Vic), 32nd (S. & W. Aus) Bns.

14th (NSW) Brigade: Brigadier-General C. J. Hobkirk
53rd, 54th, 55th, 56th Bns.

15th (Victoria) Brigade: Brigadier-General H. E. Elliott
57th, 58th, 59th, 60th Bns.

Appendix II

Extract from:
ORDER OF BATTLE, GERMAN DIVISIONS
BULLECOURT OPERATIONS
APRIL – MAY 1917

XIV RESERVE CORPS: General von Moser

27th (Royal Württemberg) DIVISION: Major-General von Maur
53rd Brigade: 120rd, 123th, 124th Grenadier Regiments

Attached to XIV Reserve Corps

3rd GUARD DIVISION: Lieutenant-General von Lindequist
6th Guard Brigade: Guard Fusiliers, Lehr Regt., 9th Grenadiers

2nd GUARD RESERVE DIVISION: Major-General von Petersdorff
38th Reserve Brigade: 15th, 77th, 91st Reserve Regiments

38th DIVISION: Lieutenant-General Schultheis
83rd Brigade: 94th, 95th, 96th Regiments

4th ERSATZ DIVISION: General-der-Kavallerie von Werder
13th Ersatz Brigade: 360th, 361st, 362nd Regiments

207th DIVISION: Major-General Schroeter
89th Reserve Brigade: 98th, 209th, 213th Reserve Regiments

Select Bibliography

I UNPUBLISHED SOURCES

1 *Public Record Office*:
          CAB 42/7
          CAB 44/428
          CAB 45/116. 45/132 45/135 45/138 45/140 45/183.
          CAB 45/200
          CAB 103/57 103/113.
          WO 95 War Diaries of Armies, Corps, Divisions,
              Battalions etc. relating to British & Australian units.
          WO 32/11393
          WO 106/43
          WO 153/597 153/961 153/971 153/1127
          WO 154/72
          WO 157/209 157/565
          WO 158/23 158/200 158/248 158/249 158/344 158/831
          WO 161/24

2 *Australian War Memorial*
          C. E. W. Bean – Notebooks and Diaries
          Correspondence on Official History -
          Bean/ Edmonds / major participants. Leane Papers
          Holmes Papers
          Gellibrand Papers
          Hobbs Papers
          Durrant Papers
          Elliott Papers
          Documents, letters and diaries of members of AIF

3 *Australian National Library*
          White Papers
          Commonwealth Parliamentary Debate Minutes

4 *Private Papers*
        Fanshawe Papers (Peter Fanshawe)
        Gellibrand Diaries (Jane d'Arcy)
        Swears Papers (Anne Davison)
        Brudenell White Papers (Lady Derham)
        Napier Papers (Margaret Whittingdale)

5 *Imperial War Museum*
        French MSS
        Birdwood MSS
        Wilson MSS
        Barrow MSS
        Butler MSS
        Canon E. Crosse MSS
        Documents, letters and diaries of British soldiers who
            fought at Bullecourt
        Taped memoirs of Sir Edward Spears

6 *Royal Artillery Inst.*
        Anstey Papers

7 *Liddle Collection, Leeds*
        Papers of Sir Douglas Branson
            Lt. W. W. A. Phillips
            Private J. F. R. Moddrel
            Private H. Hobbs.

8 *National Library of Scotland*
        Haig Papers
        Haldane Papers
        Blackwood Papers

9 *Liddell Hart Archives, King's College, London*
        Beddington Papers
        Charteris Papers
        Sir Sidney Clive Papers
        Edmonds Papers
        Sir Alexander Godley Papers
        Kiggell Papers
        Liddell Hart Papers
        Spears Papers
        Walter Wilson Papers

10 *King's College Library, London*
      'Officer Men Relations – Morale & Discipline in the
        British Army 1902-1922', *Thesis by G. D. Sheffield*

11 *Tank Museum, Bovington*
      Records 'D' Battalion Heavy Branch MGC

12 *King's College, Cambridge*
      Milner-White Papers

13 *Regimental Archives*
      Gordon Highlanders Museum, Aberdeen
      Devonshire Regt. Museum, Exeter
      Queen's (Royal West Surrey) Regt., Clandon
      Heavy Branch MGC, Bovington Tank Museum

II PRINTED SOURCES

1 *Official Histories*
      Military Operations, France and Belgium 1916, 1917,
        1918.
      Appendices volumes to above.
      Order of Battle of Divisions, Part 1 & 2B
      Official History of Australia in the War.
      Vols.III, IV, V.
      Die Osterlacht bie Arras 1917, Reichsarchiv.
      Statistics of the Military Effort of the British Empire,
        The War Office 1922.

2 *Conference Papers*
      Andrews, Dr. Eric: *C.E.W. Bean & Bullecourt – Walking
        the Battlefield and New Findings* (AWM History
        Conference, Nov 1991)
      Thomson, Dr. Alistair: *Living with a Legend –
        Anzac Memories and Australian National Identity*
        (Leeds International Conference, 1994)

3 *Journals*
      Army Quarterly, 1920-1986.
      Journals of the R.U.S.I.
      Reveille

Revue Internationale d'Histoire Militaire
Royal Tank Corps Journal
Red Cross Lists 1917
History Today
The Times
Militär Wochenblatt
Journal of Contemporary History Australian Defence
    Force Journal
Journal of the AWM
R.E. Journal
Journal of the Royal Artillery
The Journal of Strategic Studies
War and Society
Royal Australian Historical Soc. Journal

4 *Unit Histories*

German;
Handbook of the German Army in the War, Jan. 1917.
Die Ulmer Grenadiere an der Westfront.
Das Württemberg Kaiser-Reg. Nos., 120, 124 -
Württemberg Heer Im Weltkrieg, 27th. Div.
Histories of Two Hundred and Fifty-One Divisions of
    the German Army which participated in the War
    1914-1918, War Dept. Doc. 905, United States
    War Office.
The German Forces in the Field, Oct 1917.

Australian;
Battalion Histories of 3rd, 4th, 9th, 10th, 11th, 13th, 14th,
    15th, 16th, 17th, 19th, 20th, 21st, 22nd, 23rd, 24th.,
    46th, 48th, 53rd, 54th.

British;
The Seventh Division 1914-1918,
C. T. Atkinson.
The 62nd. (West Riding) Division, Vol I,
E. Wyrell.
History of the 2/6 West Yorkshire Regt.,
E. C. Gregory.
The Devonshire Regt., C. T. Atkinson.
The Honourable Artillery Company in the Great War,
    G. Gould Walker.
Manchester Pals, M. Stedman.

5 *Printed Books*

Andrews, Eric, *The Anzac Illusion: Anglo-Australian Relations during World War I* (CUP, Cambridge 1993)

Baker-Carr, Brig. C. D., *From Chauffeur to Brigadier* (Ernest Benn, London 1930)

Barnett, Correlli, *The Swordbearers – Studies in Supreme Command in the First World War* (Eyre & Spottiswoode, London 1963)

Baynes, John, *Morale: A Study of Men and Courage* (Cassell, London 1967)

Beaumont, Joan (ed), *Australia's War, 1914-18* (Sydney 1995)

Bean, C. E. W., *Anzac to Amiens* (Canberra 1946)

—— *Two Men I Knew* (Angus & Robertson, Sydney 1957)

Beckett, Dr. Ian, *Johnnie Gough, V.C.* (Tom Donovan, London 1989)

—— *A Nation in Arms: A Social Study of the British in the First World War* co-ed. with Keith Simpson (MUP, Manchester 1985)

—— *The Army and the Curragh Incident, 1914* (ed) (Bodley Head for the A.R.S., London 1986)

Bidwell, Shelford, *Fire-Power: British Army Weapons and Theories of War 1904-45.* – & Dominick Graham (Allen & Unwin, London 1982)

—— *Gunners at War: A Tactical Study of the Royal Artillery in the Twentieth Century* (Arms & Armour Press, London 1972)

Birdwood, Field Marshal Lord, *Khaki and Gown* (Ward Lock, London 1941)

—— *In my Time* (Skeffington, London 1945)

Blake, Robert (ed), *The Private Papers of Douglas Haig 1914-1918* (Eyre & Spottiswoode, London 1952)

Bond, Brian *The Victorian Army and the Staff College 1854-1914* (Eyre Methuen, London 1972)

—— *The First World War and British Military History (ed.)* (Clarendon Press, Oxford 1991)

Buchan, John, *These for Remembrance* (Privately printed, London 1919)

Callwell, Maj.-Gen. Sir Charles, *Field-Marshal Sir Henry Wilson – His Life & Diaries* (Cassell, London 1927)

Cecil, Dr. Hugh, *The Flower of Battle* (Secker & Warburg, London 1995)

Chandler, David, (ed) & Beckett, Dr. Ian (ae) *The Oxford Illustrated History of the British Army* (OUP, Oxford 1994)

Charlton, Peter, *Pozières: Australians on the Somme* (Leo Cooper/Secker & Warburg, Sydney 1986)

Charteris, Hon. Evan, *H.Q. Tanks* (Privately printed)

Crutwell, C. R. M. F., *A History of the Great War 1914-1918* (OUP, Oxford 1936)

—— *The Role of British Stategy in the Great War* (CUP, Cambridge 1936)

Cumming, Brig. Hannay, *A Brigadier in France* (Cape, London 1922)

Dixon, Norman F, *On the Psychology of Military Incompetence* (Cape, London 1976)

Drury, Ian, *German Stormtrooper 1914-18* (Osprey, London 1995)

Dunn, Capt. J.C, *The War the Infantry Knew 1914-1919: A Chronicle of Service in France and Belgium* (P.S. King, London 1938)

Dutil, Capt L, *Les Chars d'Assaut – Le Creation et le Role pendant La Guerre 1915-1918* (Nancy, 1919)

Egerton, George, *Political Memoir: Essays on the Politics of Memory* (Frank Cass, London 1994)

Esher, Oliver, Viscount, (ed), *Viscount Esher. Journals and Letters Vol.IV* (Ivor Nicholson & Watson, London 1938)

Farndale, Gen. Sir Martin, *History of the Royal Regiment of Artillery 1914-18* (RAI, Woolwich 1986)

Farrar-Hockley, Gen. Sir Anthony, *Goughie: The Life of General Sir Hubert Gough* (Hart-Davis, MacGibbon, London 1975)

—— *The Somme* (Batsford, London 1954)

Firkins, Peter, *The Australians in Nine Wars: Waikato to Long Tan* (Robert Hale, London 1972)

Fletcher, David, *Landships: British Tanks in the First World War* (HMSO, London 1984)

—— *Tanks and Trenches* (ed.) (Grange Books, London 1994)

Fuller, Maj. Gen. J.F.C., *Memoirs of an Unconventional Soldier* (Nicholson & Watson, London 1936)

—— *Tanks in the Great War* (John Murray, London 1920)

Fussell, Paul, *The Great War and Modern Memory* (OUP, Oxford 1975)

Gammage, Bill, *The Broken Years* (ANUP, Canberra 1974)

Gerster, Robin, *Big Noting: The Heroic Theme in Australian War Writing.* (MUP, Carlton, 1987)

Glubb, Sir John, *Into Battle* (Cassell, London 1962)

Goodspeed, D. J., *Ludendorff* (Hart-Davis, London 1966)

Gough, Gen. Sir Hubert, *The Fifth Army* (Hodder & Stoughton, London 1931)

—— *Soldiering On* (Arthur Barker, London 1954)

Graham, Dominic & Shelford Bidwell, *Coalition, Politicians & Generals – Some Aspects of Command in Two World Wars* (Brassey's, London 1993)

Grange, Baroness de la, *Open House in Flanders* (John Murray, London 1929)

Grey, Jeffrey, *A Military History of Australia* (CUP, Cambridge 1990)

Griffith, Paddy, *Battle Tactics of the Western Front – The British Army's Art of Attack 1916-18* (YUP, London 1994)

—— *British Fighting Methods in the Great War* (Frank Cass, London 1996)

Haigh, Richard, *Life in a Tank* (Boston 1918)

Harris, J. P., *Men, Ideas and Tanks: British Military Thought and Armoured Forces 1903-1939* (MUP, Manchester 1995)

—— *Armoured Warfare* (Batsford, London 1990)

Hashagen, Ernst, *The Log of a U-Boat Commander* (Putnam, London 1931).

Herbillon, Colonel Herbillon, *Du General en Chef au Gouvernement, Vol. II* (Paris, 1930)

Holmes, Richard, *The Little Field-Marshal: Sir John French* (Cape, London 1981)

Horne, Alistair, *The Price of Glory* (Penguin, London 1962)

Horner, D. M. (ed), *The Commanders – Australian Military Leadership in the 20th Century* (Allen & Unwin, Sydney 1984)

Innes, John R., *Flash Spotters and Sound Rangers: How They Lived and Fought in the Great War* (Allen & Unwin, London 1935)

Johnson, Hubert C, *Breakthrough: Tactics, Technology, and the Search for Victory on the Western Front in World War I* (California 1994)

Jones, H. A, *The War in the Air, Vol.III* (OUP, Oxford 1931)

Jünger, Ernst, *The Storm of Steel* (Chatto & Windus, London 1929)

Keegan, John, *The Face of Battle* (Cape, London 1976)

Kilduff, Peter, (trans) *The Red Baron* (Bailey Bros., Folkestone 1974)

Kitchen, Martin, *A Military History of Germany* (Weidenfeld & Nicolson, London 1972)

Leed, Eric, J., *No Man's Land: Combat and Identity in World War I* (Cambridge 1979)

Liddell Hart, Sir Basil, *A History of the World War* (Faber & Faber, London 1930)

—— *The Tanks Vols. I 1914-1939* (Cassell, London 1959)

Ludendorff, Gen. Erich, *My War Memories 1914-1918* (London 1919)

Lupfer, Timothy, *The Dynamics of Doctrine – Changes in German Tactical Doctrine during the First World War* (Leavenworth Papers # 4, C.S.I. Leavenworth, Kansas 1981)

Luvaas, Jay, *The Education of an Army – British Military Thought, 1815-1940* (Cassell, London 1965)

Malins, Geoffrey, *How I Filmed the War* (IWM Reprint, originally published 1919)

Maurice, Maj.-Gen. Sir Frederick, *British Strategy – A Study of the Application of the Principles of War* (Constable, London 1929)

Maze, Paul, *A Frenchman in Khaki* (Heinemann, London 1934)

McCarthy, Dudley, *Gallipoli to the Somme: The story of C. E. W. Bean* (Leo Cooper/Secker & Warburg, London 1983)

Mitchell, Frank, *Tank Warfare: the Story of the Tanks in the Great War* (Thomas Nelson, London 1933)

Miquel, Pierre, *Le Chemin des Dames* (Librairie Academique, Perrin 1997)

Monash, Lt.-Gen. Sir John *The Australian Victories in France in 1918* (Angus & Robertson, Sydney 1920)

Moore, William, *See How They Ran (March 1918)* (London 1970)

Moser, Gen. Otto von, *Feldzugs-aufzeichnungen* (Stuttgart 1933)

Nicholls, Jonathan, *Cheerful Sacrifice* (Leo Cooper, London 1990)

Oldham, Peter, *Pill Boxes on the Western Front* (Leo Cooper, London 1995)

Oliver, F.S. *The Anvil of War – Letters between F.S. Oliver & his Brother* (Stephen Gwynn ed.) (London 1936)

Pidgeon, Trevor, *The Tanks at Flers* (Fairmile, Cobham 1995)

Prior, Robin & Trevor Wilson, *Passchendaele – The Untold Story* (Yale UP, London 1996)

—— *Command on the Western Front: The Military Career of Sir Henry Rawlinson, 1914-18* (Blackwell, Oxford 1992)

Putkowski, Julian & Julian Sykes, *Shot at Dawn* (Leo Cooper, London 1989)

Repington, Col. C., *The First World War, Vol.I & II.* (Constable, London 1920)

Robertson, John, *Anzac and Empire: The Tragedy and Glory of Gallipoli* (Leo Cooper, London 1990)

Robson, L. L., *The First A.I.F. – A Study of its Recruitment 1914-1918* (MUP, Melbourne 1970)

Rule, E. J., *Jacka's Mob* (Sydney 1933)

Rupprecht, Crown Prince, *Mein Kriegstagebuch* (Deuts. Nat. Verlag, Munich 1929)

Samuels, Martin, *Command or Control? Command, Training and Tactics in the British and German Armies 1888-1918* (Frank Cass, London 1995)

Spears, Sir Edward, *Prelude to Victory* (Cape, London 1939)

Stern, Sir Albert, *Tanks – The Logbook of a Pioneer* (Hodder & Stoughton, London 1919)

Terraine, John, *Douglas Haig: The Educated Soldier* (Hutchinson, London 1963)

—— *The Road to Passchendaele: The Flanders Offensive of 1917: a Study in Inevitability* (Leo Cooper, London 1977)

Travers, Tim, *The Killing Ground: The British Army, the Western Front and the Emergence of Modern Warfare, 1900-18* (Unwin Hyman, London 1987)

—— *How The War Was Won – Command & Technology in the British Army on the Western Front 1917-18* (Routledge, London: 1992)

Trythall, Anthony, *'Boney' Fuller: The Intellectual General 1878-1966* (Cassell, London 1977)

Watson, W. H. L., *A Company of Tanks* (Blackwood, Edinburgh 1920)

Watt, Richard, *Dare Call It Treason* (Chatto & Windus, London 1964)

Wavell, Gen. Sir Archibald, *Allenby* (Harrap, London 1940)

Wellman, Lt. Gen. R. *Mit der 18 Reserve Division in Frankreich* (Bemgruber & Henning, Hamburg 1930)

Williams, John, *Mutiny 1917* (Heinemann, London 1963)

Williams-Ellis, Clough, *The Tank Corps* (George Doran, New York 1919)

Wilson, Trevor, *The Myriad Faces of War* (Oxford 1986)

Winter, Dennis, *Haig's Command – A Reassessment* (Penguin, London 1991)

—— *Death's Men: Soldiers of the Great War* (Penguin, London 1978)

Winter, J.M, *The Great War and the British People* (Macmillan, London 1985)

Various contributors, *The Oxford Companion to Australian Military History* (OUP, Melbourne 1995)

—— *Australian Dictionary of Biography 1891-1939*

Index

(Rank shown held at time of the Battle of Bullecourt)